# Wildlife

## OF FLORIDA'S SPRINGS

T0015252

# Wildlife
## OF FLORIDA'S SPRINGS

An Illustrated Field Guide
to Over 150 Species

Sandra Poucher

Pineapple Press

Palm Beach, Florida

## Pineapple Press

An imprint of Globe Pequot, the trade division of
The Rowman & Littlefield Publishing Group, Inc.
4501 Forbes Blvd., Ste. 200
Lanham, MD 20706
www.rowman.com

Distributed by NATIONAL BOOK NETWORK

Copyright © 2022 by Sandra Poucher
Illustrations by Sandra Poucher

*All rights reserved.* No part of this book may be reproduced in any form or by
any electronic or mechanical means, including information storage and retrieval
systems, without written permission from the publisher, except by a reviewer
who may quote passages in a review.

British Library Cataloguing in Publication Information Available

**Library of Congress Cataloging-in-Publication Data**

Names: Poucher, Sandra, author.
Title: Wildlife of Florida's springs : an illustrated field guide to over
   150 species / Sandra Poucher.
Description: Lanham : Pineapple Press, [2022] | Includes bibliographical
   references and index. | Summary: "Florida is home to no fewer than 700
   freshwater springs, more than any place in the world! From the famed
   manatee to the obscure freshwater jellyfish, the springs provide
   sustenance to an abundance of wild, marine and insect life. This
   beautiful guide features over 150 species, over 130 original
   illustrations, and includes listings of commonly and not-so-commonly
   encountered "critters" living in and near Florida's springs"– Provided
   by publisher.
Identifiers: LCCN 2021048036 (print) | LCCN 2021048037 (ebook) | ISBN
   9781683343134 (paperback) | ISBN 9781683343141 (epub)
Subjects: LCSH: Spring ecology–Florida. | Freshwater
   biodiversity–Florida. | Springs–Florida.
Classification: LCC QH105.F6 P69 2022 (print) | LCC QH105.F6 (ebook) |
   DDC 508.09759–dc23/eng/20211101
LC record available at https://lccn.loc.gov/2021048036
LC ebook record available at https://lccn.loc.gov/2021048037

∞™ The paper used in this publication meets the minimum requirements of
American National Standard for Information Sciences–Permanence of Paper
for Printed Library Materials, ANSI/NISO Z39.48-1992

For Ethan

# Contents

# List of Illustrations

Redbreast Sunfish
Warmouth
Bluegill
Dollar Sunfish
Redear Sunfish
Stumpknocker
Suwannee Bass
Florida Largemouth Bass
Black Crappie
*Tilapia
Striped Bass
Sunshine Bass
Swamp Darter
Freshwater Flounder
Channel Catfish
Southern Cricket Frog
Bullfrog
Green Treefrog
Bronze Frog
Pig Frog
River Frog
Southern Leopard Frog
Two-toed Amphiuma
Peninsula Newt
Narrow-striped Dwarf Siren
Northern Dwarf Siren
Greater Siren
Alligator
Eastern Indigo Snake
Rainbow Snake
Plain-bellied Watersnake
Banded Watersnake
Brown Watersnake
Gray Rat Snake
Eastern Ribbonsnake
Florida Cottonmouth
Chicken Turtle
Barbour's Map Turtle
Suwannee Cooter
Florida Redbellied Cooter
*Red-eared Slider

Yellow-bellied Slider
Snapping Turtle
Alligator Snapping Turtle
Striped Mud Turtle
Florida Mud Turtle
Eastern Mud Turtle
Loggerhead Musk Turtle
Eastern Musk Turtle
Florida Softshell Turtle
Common Otter
Raccoon
American Beaver
*Capybara
*Rhesus Macaque
Round-tailed Muskrat
Eastern Woodrat
Cotton Mouse
Florida Manatee
Annulate Millipede
Marianna Cave Sheetweaver
Elephant Spurred Sheetweaver
Daddy Longlegs, Bishopella
Daddy Longlegs, Leiobunum
Rosy Wolfsnail
American Cockroach
Ringlegged Earwig
Camel Cricket
American Eel
Redeye Chub
Blackbanded Darter
Atlantic Croaker
White Catfish
Yellow Bullhead
Brown Bullhead
Tadpole Madtom
Flathead Catfish
*Orinoco Sailfin Armored Catfish
Three-lined Salamander
Florida Slimy Salamander
Big Brown Bat
Southeastern Myotis

# Acknowledgments

It has been said more than once that it takes a community to raise a child. The same goes for the creation of a project such as this. I am deeply indebted to those helpful and patient scholars who kept me on track and gently (or bluntly, as the need arose) guided my curiosity. Richard Franz was invaluable in pointing me in the right direction. He, Paul Moler, and Robert H. Robins pointed out criticisms of the text and illustrations, made excellent suggestions for consideration, and provided articles regarding a plethora of known and new species, making this a more concise and accurate guide. Thank you all for your help and for encouraging me to keep writing.

John R. Holsinger wrote concerning amphipod species in Florida (Dr. Holsinger passed away in November 2018). Thomas Sawicki, thank you for the help with new species of cavernicoles, such as newly described aquatic cave amphipods.

Many thanks to Buford Pruitt, Jr., for his help on life forms both within and outside of the cave environment and for his continuing support of my writing aspirations. Thank you for your years of patience and kind participation. Brett Hemphill told me about interesting life forms in submerged coastal caves. Brett, your enthusiasm and ongoing adventures in cave exploration are endlessly fascinating. Kudos to the Karst Underwater Research cave exploration team for continuing to push the limits of our understanding. Bruce Morgan, I am continually delighted with your travel adventures and your genuine support of intellectual independence. Thank you all so much for contributing to this project.

Much gratitude to Tom Greenhalgh and Garrett Evans of the Florida Geological Survey for providing karst and springshed maps for the introduction and for studying and sharing data about the foundation that supports this wonderful peninsular landscape we call home.

Thanks to Gerald "Stinger" Guala, director of both ITIS and BISON at the U.S. Geological Survey for the Integrated Taxonomic Information System (ITIS) online databases. Both ITIS and BISON are excellent resources for identifying the locations of Florida wildlife. I spent many hours perusing the entries of these databases.

Many thanks to Amy Lyons, Lauren Younker, Megan Murray, and everyone at Rowman & Littlefield and Pineapple Press for making the publishing process as smooth as possible. I appreciate your sharp eyes, humor and patience while working with me on this project.

Michael Poucher, my husband and my love, I cherish your stories about the animals your family encountered on the Rainbow River and the stories of your exploration and survey dives in and around caves. Ashley Pool and April Hoyt, my daughters, thank you as well. Your patience and generosity of spirit (and fun!) are inspiring. Michelle Double, Jennifer Pinkley, Julie Quaid, Jessica Riley, and Lynn Wiggins, my friends, I appreciate your suggestions. I am so thankful for your smiling faces, long phone calls (and Zoom gatherings), and much-welcomed interruptions of friendship after hours of staring at a computer screen or sketch pad.

Many, many thanks for curious troglodytes* everywhere. I love reading your trip reports, scientific papers, map data, and humorous stories. I applaud your triumphs in achieving training certificates, collecting sampling and survey data, completing project goals, and just seeing you enjoying the beauty of the aquatic landscape. I never tire of your photographs and videos of the intricacies, challenges and sheer wonder of your subterranean visits.

(*troglodytes: human cave dwellers, from trogle meaning hole and dyein meaning go in or dive in)

# Preface

I read *The Secret Life of Walter Mitty* by James Thurber when I was a teenager and vowed then to never be like him. However, upon "awakening" ten years later, it was obvious that I had indeed become just another Walter Mitty. So, I sat me down and made out a list of things I wanted to accomplish in life, and writing a book was one of the first of them, but ironically it was many decades before that finally happened.

I met Sandra Poucher during those decades and watched from the sidelines as she finished preparing Sheck Exley's (deceased) book, *The Taming of the Slough*. She then cooperated with Rick Copeland to compile her second book, *Speleological and Karst Glossary of Florida and the Caribbean*, and I was surprised and honored when she asked me to review its draft versions. Then she asked me to edit her third book, *A Field Guide to the Critters of Florida's Springs*, a solo accomplishment. Clearly, Sandy is no Walter Mitty, or more appropriately, no Marjorie Morningstar, and she was a critical inspiration for me to finally write my own first book.

Picture this: After preparing dinner and then eating and cleaning up after it, her family retires to the living room to do school homework or practice guitar chords while she sits back down at the dining room table and works on her next book. Now, that's ambition! That's gumption! Clearly, I had no honorable choice but to agree to edit the first edition and now this second edition of her book.

I wondered why Sandy chose me as the book's editor. She replied that my qualifications were that I was a Florida native and lifelong resident of the state, wildlife biologist, science-oriented fifty-year veteran of dry caving and cave-diving explorations, extremely familiar with Florida spring caves and springheads, author of numerous feature and conservation articles in the National Speleological Society's *NSS Newsletter*, and part-time English-language editor of technical manuscripts for foreign academicians whose second (or third) language is English.

Sandy is herself a competent and experienced caver and cave diver. She has spent many weekends over the past three decades exploring Florida's underwater caves, spring basins, and spring runs. She is a former member of a cave diving team, Karst Underwater Research, that I consider the world's cutting edge of cave diving today. Her love and general knowledge of these subterranean underwater "caverns measureless to man" are readily apparent in this book, but her specific knowledge of the denizens of these crystal waters is where she really shines through. I especially like reading the tidbits she provides about what is otherwise "dry" taxonomy, interesting life history notes, and sense of humor. Indeed, even though I am an experienced field biologist and caver, I learned much from this book and believe that you will, too.

Buford Pruitt, Jr.
September 2019

# Introduction

## What Animal Is That?

I love sitting with my family on the worn wooden dock overlooking the Rainbow River, near Dunnellon, Florida. Sunlight sparkles from ripples made by canoe paddles. A small alligator rests under the overhanging branches of sweetgum on a banked floating island of grasses and debris, while a softshell turtle's elongated nose breaks the surface for a breath of air. Inner tubes carry a variety of visitors casually making their way downstream.

A few years ago, a group of tourists floating by caught our attention. They were waving to us and gesturing at something on the other side of the river. We looked across the crowd of people floating, swimming, and kayaking by, to see two otters feeding along the edge of the water. The otters dove and resurfaced with the crunching sounds of a tasty crustacean or mollusk meal. "Otter!" I yelled in explanation to the people several times, but they still seemed perplexed as they continued drifting downstream with the current. Thinking fast, I added loudly "Water cat!" The tourists recognized those two words, smiling and nodding their heads enthusiastically as they floated further away. While happy to be able to give them an answer they at least vaguely recognized, I was exasperated, because we get questions about our wildlife on the river, but we rarely have time to give more than a quick common name. "Water cat," while colorfully descriptive, felt dishonest.

Florida is filled with opportunities for outdoor enthusiasts. Activities like canoeing and kayaking, paddleboarding, cycling, hiking, swimming, and cave diving attract visitors from all over the world. Being out-of-doors in the sunshine state exposes us to an incredibly diverse array of fauna and flora adapted to Florida's tropical and subtropical landscapes. Springs and water-filled sinkholes can be found throughout Florida, feeding freshwater lakes and rivers, hidden as gems in forests, and submerged off the coast in brackish and marine waters. These springs and their karst substructure also support a variety of eco-systems and a great diversity of life. I had a hard time finding a book that covered all of the terrestrial, aquatic, and semi-aquatic animals that we encounter, not to mention the subter-ranean life, so I felt that I was on the right track in creating this guide. I chose not to include birds because there are already many excellent birding references and field guides. It is exciting to have this opportunity to share information about the fascinating, beautiful, and sometimes surprising springshed biology of the Sunshine State. I hope you enjoy learning more about Florida's wildlife!

## Water

Florida has a lot of springs, at least seven hundred. Thirty-three of these are first magnitude springs, pumping out one hundred cubic feet or more of water per second, the equivalent of 64.6 million gallons per day (Mgal/d)! For scale, a bathtub holds about 40 gallons, so imagine 1.6 million bathtubs being filled *daily*. There are also innumerable smaller seeps and springs throughout the state. Florida has the largest concentration of springs on our planet.

Water seeps up through tiny fissures in limestone to create the sand-boiling bubblers we see on the bottom of the Rainbow River. It gushes out in massive, churning discharges from magnificent, totally submerged cavern vents such as at Manatee Springs or Weeki Wachee. Florida has tidally influenced coastal springs, where salt water flows in during high tide and fresh water flows out during low tide, such as at the Kings Bay Springs group in Crystal River. There are springs in the middle of the state, such as the world-famous Silver Springs, in North Florida, such as Jackson Blue, and in the ocean, like Crystal Beach Spring off Pinellas County. Warm Mineral Springs, on Florida's west coast in Sarasota County, is Florida's southernmost major spring. Springs and the karst that support them are a force and a presence in the lives of Floridians.

Springs are beautiful, natural, and serene places. People come from all over the world to interact, to immerse themselves, or to simply gaze at the water. We drink the water and eat the fish (and sometimes crayfish or even frogs) that live in the springs and rivers. We share these waters with our forebearers. Arrowheads, pottery, and primitive tools, evidence of indigenous communities, show us that people have been enjoying Florida's springs for more than ten thousand years.

Springs are the result of water flowing through limestone from higher pressure in the aquifer to lower pressure at the surface. The pressure is related to the volume of the water underground and the thickness and density of the land above it. The word *aquifer* means water-bearing. An aquifer is a natural underground reservoir of water. While the Floridan aquifer is spoken of as a single large resource, there are many layers and levels to the aquifer system. A springshed refers to the area of land that contributes underground water to a spring (a watershed, on the other hand, contains the water moving across the surface of the land). Each springshed, spring, and opening into the aquifer has unique characteristics.

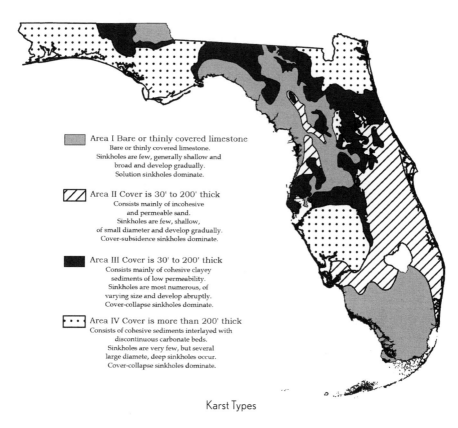

Area I Bare or thinly covered limestone
Bare or thinly covered limestone.
Sinkholes are few, generally shallow and
broad and develop gradually.
Solution sinkholes dominate.

Area II Cover is 30' to 200' thick
Consists mainly of incohesive
and permeable sand.
Sinkholes are few, shallow,
of small diameter and develop gradually.
Cover-subsidence sinkholes dominate.

Area III Cover is 30' to 200' thick
Consists mainly of cohesive clayey
sediments of low permeability.
Sinkholes are most numerous, of
varying size and develop abruptly.
Cover-collapse sinkholes dominate.

Area IV Cover is more than 200' thick
Consists of cohesive sediments interlayed with
discontinuous carbonate beds.
Sinkholes are very few, but several
large diamete, deep sinkholes occur.
Cover-collapse sinkholes dominate.

Karst Types

## The Floridan Aquifer System

The deepest, oldest, and most productive aquifer is the Lower Floridan Aquifer, which averages 1,000 feet (300 meters) below the surface, but in places extends as deep as approximately 2,000 feet (approximately 600 meters). This aquifer reaches across the southeastern United States, from South Carolina southward to beyond the Florida Keys. Because of their extreme depth, the deeper waters of the Lower Floridan Aquifer are not well understood.

The Upper Floridan Aquifer is the shallower part of the overall Floridan Aquifer. The Upper Floridan aquifer system provides drinking water to people living in Florida, Alabama, and Georgia. Most of the water Floridians drink and swim in extends from the surface to approximately 100–300 feet (approximately 30–90 meters) below ground. This water comes from the surficial aquifer, which lays just above the confined parts of the largely unconfined Floridan Aquifer. The water in the upper system recharges more quickly because it is shallower and not confined by layers of bedrock. Because of its accessibility, water from the surficial aquifer is well-studied.

The southwestern portion of the state has several aquifers that lie below the surficial aquifer and above the Floridan Aquifer, referred to collectively as the Intermediate Aquifer System. These relatively shallow aquifers are confined by layers of sand, sandstone, and porous limestone. Aquifers in the southern half of the state are shallow and do not have major springs and spring runs like those in the northern half.

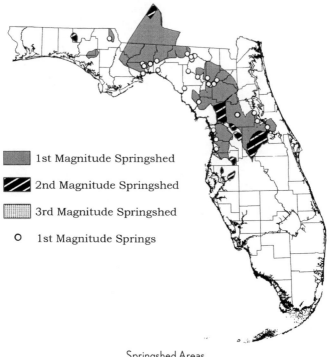

1st Magnitude Springshed

2nd Magnitude Springshed

3rd Magnitude Springshed

O    1st Magnitude Springs

Springshed Areas

## Hydrology Plus Geology Equals Hydrogeology!

The state of Florida was completely or mostly under water several times in the geologic past. Over millions of years, as marine organisms died, their shells and skeletons of calcium carbonate fell to the ocean floor. These calcareous structures incorporated into sediments that accumulated into the bedrock layers forming the foundation of Florida. Over time, other forces lifted and lowered the state to its present height, creating the peninsula we are familiar with today. We find ancient seashells in rocks all over Florida. We can see old shorelines and ancient sand dunes. Traveling on State Road 488 from Dunnellon toward Crystal River, drivers follow a series of what looks like great steps leading down toward the Gulf of Mexico. On the east side of the state, thanks to the efforts of Abraham Lincoln Lewis and MaVynee Oshun Betsch, we can hike remnant dunes of the Atlantic Coastal Ridge, deposited during the late Pleistocene (approximately 126,000 to 11,700 years ago) at American Beach on Amelia Island.

Florida's bedrock is mostly composed of limestone varying in thickness and porosity. The limestone is made of calcium carbonate (calcite) and calcium magnesium carbonate (dolomite). In some places, the bedrock is thousands of feet thick and dense, in others thin, brittle, and porous. Clay, sand, and sandstone layers create barriers separating various layers of rock and aquifers. Florida's landscape, riddled with fissures, sinkholes, and caves of dissolving bedrock, is usually referred to as karst.

The Floridan aquifer is primarily recharged by rain. Carbon dioxide in the atmosphere dissolves into raindrops, forming carbonic acid, making raindrops weakly acidic. As rain hits the ground and trickles through the soil, it picks up additional organic acids from decaying leaves and other detritus. The acids react with calcium carbonate in the limestone, slowly dissolving the rock, over time creating tunnels and voids. This water, with any accumulated minerals and other surface materials, collects in the aquifer.

Dissolved minerals in spring waters can come from rainwater entering the aquifer, eroding limestone, tidal inputs, and surface activities. Many factors affect the chemical and mineral content of spring water, such as the type of rock the water travels through, how fast the water is traveling, and the size and physical features of underground voids. We characterize springs by flow, temperature, water chemistry, and physical features. The interactions between minerals and water determines the chemical quality of the water.

Animals that can travel between salt and freshwater, such as striped bass, flounder, manatees, and *Melanoides* snails, are said to be euryhaline. The word euryhaline comes from Greek *eurus*, meaning wide or broad and *hals* or *halos*, meaning salt or sea. This feature allows the animals to move through different levels of salinity. Too much salt leads to dehydration as the body tries to get rid of the excess salt. This is why we can't drink sea water. Animals living in the marine environment use a variety of physical and behavioral processes to keep their internal environment less salty than their external environment. When marine organisms move into fresh water, they face the opposite challenge of maintaining an internal environment that is saltier than their external environment. Some marine organisms are able to inhabit spring runs because calcium and carbonate ions in the water function, as salts do in the marine environment, to help balance the movement of water and salts into and out of their bodies.

This balance of minerals in the water also affects diadromous fish species. The word diadromous describes fish who live part of their lives in freshwater and part of their lives in saltwater. Diadromous species are described as either anadromous or catadromous. Anadromous fish, such as sturgeon, live as adults in the sea but return to freshwater to spawn. Catadromous fish are adults in freshwater but return to the sea to spawn. American eels are catadromous. There are others, such as amphidromous species, like the Ohio River shrimp. Amphidromous fish travel between fresh and saltwater but not specifically for spawning purposes.

## Taxonomy

Taxonomy is the science of classifying organisms. The word taxonomy is loosely derived from Greek *taxi*, meaning arrangement and *nomos*, meaning law or custom. Taxonomy involves both the common name of an animal (the popular everyday name, such as "mullet") and the scientific name (the genus and species specifically assigned to that animal, striped mullet being *Mugil cephalus*).

Nomenclature refers to the naming system used to organize life forms by taxa, or group. Binomial nomenclature is the two-part genus and species (also called the scientific name), such as *Homo sapiens* for humans. *Homo* is the genus, *sapiens* is the specific (or species) name. The name of the person who first described the organism and the year of publication are also included. *Homo sapiens* Linnaeus, 1758 means that in the year 1758, Carl Linnaeus published a description of the human species. Every living thing on earth has a scientific name (unless it hasn't been discovered, described, and published yet!)

Carl (Carolus) Linnaeus (1707–1778) is known as the father of taxonomy. He developed the idea that each organism has distinctions and can be grouped, and he established a naming system, a hierarchy of groups, for these distinctions. Ever since then, each species of animal, plant, or any other form of life is named, described, and presented in a publication using this naming convention.

All animals are classified in one of the three domains (Archaea, Bacteria, or Eukaryota) in a hierarchy extending through the familiar kingdom, phylum, class, order, family, genus, and species we all learned in grade school. Sometimes there are supplementary taxa, breakdowns of each level into more levels, super- and sub- and infra-, as needed. I include the class, order, and family of each species to show relationships between organisms with different genus names.

To make things more fun in taxonomy, there are also the subspecies, designated by a trinomial (a third name added to the binomial genus-species name). The subspecies name usually indicates a population that is distinct, geographically or morphologically, but still similar enough to breed with the rest of the species, such as *Acipenser oxyrinchus desotoi*, or to emphasize that the organism is the type (officially described) for the species, such as *Acipenser oxyrinchus oxyrinchus*.

Adding to the fun are superorders, suborders, superfamilies, tribes, and so on to distinguish one from another. For example, the red-eared slider, *Trachemys scripta elegans* (Wied-Neuwied, 1839), belongs to: Kingdom Animalia, Subkingdom Bilateria, Infrakingdom Deuterostomia, Phylum Chordata, Subphylum Vertebrata, Infraphylum Gnathostomata, Superclass Tetrapoda, Class Reptilia, Order Testudines, Suborder Cryptodira, Superfamily Testudinoidea, Family Emydidae, Subfamily Deirochelyinae, and Genus *Trachemys*. Whew!

Each level of taxonomy was designated by someone who described the taxon and what made it unique from all other taxa. These biologists and taxonomists took time and effort to describe and differentiate their finding from any others, and then publicized these findings to share their work with others.

However, biologists sometimes disagree about the naming of things. Genus and species change in response to new information, words get misspelled, naming conventions fall out of favor. Occasionally, the same name was used for more than one creature (this situation can result in what are called homonyms). More frequently, the same animal was given different names simultaneously by people separated by distance and language, resulting in binomial synonyms. In taxonomic nomenclature, a writer will typically include the last name of the author or authors who described the original organism and the year it was described. Foreign names are written in Latin, without diacritical marks such as the accented é. A name and year in parentheses indicate that the species is now placed in a different genus than the one it was originally assigned.

Historically, taxonomic nomenclature was derived from Greek or Latin. While modern Greek is slightly different from ancient Greek, it is a living language, still being spoken. Latin is called a dead language because it is no longer spoken or commonly used. For the most part, Latin and Greek words are static, their meanings do not change. Because of this, scientists speaking Mandarin, French, or English can all refer to the same species. Currently, though, names are derived from a variety of sources: different languages, people's names, and places. Because I like to understand the history of things, I've tried to hunt down the origins of the scientific names and explain what they mean or where and who they came from. I also explain common names if they are distinct or really interesting. For example, why is one fish called a croaker and another a hog choker?

It is absolutely fascinating to read about early taxonomists: diplomats, doctors, and farmers in the eighteenth and nineteenth centuries who collected specimens for their "curiosity cabinets." It was popular to find something never described before. People of all walks of life used magnifying glasses to determine differences in their collections, creating huge books of names, descriptions, and beautifully detailed hand-drawn illustrations. They wrote about their findings and were credited through the publication of papers in proceedings at conferences or other scientific media. Many serious researchers were incredibly thorough. Brewster's *Edinburgh Encyclopaedia* (Brewster, 1830) includes eighteen large volumes of descriptions, names, and illustrations. I used Volume 9, consisting of 755 delightful pages of tiny print (I needed only pages 57–172). It is truly rewarding to see the first mention of a newly described organism and the careful drawings and comments about where the species was collected. Many of these detailed and fascinating historical descriptions can be found online.

Today, classification is far more precise. Not many diplomats and doctors have the electron microscopes needed to find and examine the very tiny details of microcrustaceans, for instance, or the facilities for differentiating between genetic varieties of snapping turtles. New findings are continually being published, explained, and peer reviewed. With a little help from dictionaries and glossaries, anyone can enjoy these contemporary articles and publications.

Taxonomy evolves as new information is discovered. The slightest differences in anatomy can indicate a new species (morphology is the study of the forms of things), and discoveries in molecular genetics have changed the way many animals, plants, and even fungi and bacteria are classified. The eastern mosquitofish (*Gambusia holbrooki*) and the western mosquitofish (*Gambusia affinis*) were originally referred to as one species, *Gambusia affinis.* These little mosquito-eating fish look similar. They were introduced into waterbodies throughout the country, completely muddying past attempts at their classification. The main way to tell the two apart is by gonopodial differences. The gonopod is an anal fin on the male fish adapted to deliver sperm to the female fish. *Gambusia holbrooki* has denticles, small toothlike projections, on its gonopods, whereas *G. affinis* does not. There are thousands of papers about these small fish, many written to clarify the species description.

Explaining genetic indicators is far beyond the scope of this book. Many excellent websites and research papers define the terminology and describe the methods used in genomic typing. It is a fascinating and growing field of study.

There are excellent online references for taxonomy. Two good examples of this are the Integrated Taxonomic Information System (ITIS) at https://www.itis.gov/ and the Nature-Serve Explorer at http://explorer.natureserve.org/servlet/NatureServe?init=Species.

Speleobiology (or biospeleology) is the study of creatures living in caves. Speleo comes from the Latin word *speleum* and the Greek word *spelaion*, meaning cave. There are many exciting books, trip reports, cave studies, caving videos and documentaries, and audio programs of cavers and cave divers discussing their discoveries and adventures. New subterranean organisms are being found and described, making caves (even underwater caves) seem far livelier than anyone previously thought.

## Species Status

There are several lists of species' endangerment status. A species' status gives us an idea of whether the species still exists and is surviving, as well as the likelihood of its future survival.

The U.S. Fish and Wildlife Service (USFWS) lists animal and plant species as endangered or threatened. More locally, the Florida Fish and Wildlife Conservation Commission (FWC) works to conserve fish and wildlife resources in the state and lists species as federally endangered or threatened, endangered, or threatened within the state, or as a state species of special concern. Officers of both the USFWS and the FWC can enforce the law to protect designated species.

The Florida Natural Areas Inventory (FNAI) collects information and lists species as critically imperiled or imperiled. Critically imperiled means extreme rarity, encountered in five or fewer occurrences or fewer than one thousand individuals. Imperiled means rare, six to twenty occurrences or fewer than three thousand individuals. All of Florida's cave crayfish fall under either imperiled or critically imperiled status. FNAI collects and compiles data from all public and private conservation agencies and the data is updated four times a year.

NatureServe Conservation Status is a compilation of data collected by governmental agencies such as the USFWS and the National Marine Fisheries Service to assess the conservation status of species and habitats. The data is summarized in rank for global, national, or subnational (state or provincial) level on a scale from critically imperiled to secure.

The USFWS, FWC, FNAI, and NatureServe rankings are similar but determined by different criteria. For further information on listed species, please refer to the appropriate organization or website. Listings change as new information is collected, so please consult online resources for the most current species status listings. If there is no listing, the critter is not considered in danger of extinction, or its status has not been evaluated by one of these agencies or organizations.

All cave life in the state is protected under Florida Statute 810.13, which states that it is "unlawful to remove, kill, harm, or otherwise disturb any naturally occurring organism within a cave, except for safety or health reasons." The provisions of this subsection do not prohibit minimal disturbance or removal of organisms for scientific inquiry. Cave life is defined as "any life form which is indigenous to a cave or to a cave ecosystem."

# Stygoxenes and Trogloxenes

*Stygo* is from Latin *Stygius* and Greek *Stygios* and refers to the river Styx, leading to the underworld. *Xenes* refers to the word *xenos*, meaning guest. Stygoxenes are the underwater inhabitants of spring basins and spring runs.

*Troglo* from Greek *troglos* meaning cave and -*xenes* refers to the word *xenos*, meaning guest. Trogloxenes are the terrestrial critters that live in the vicinity of cave openings and springs.

In the basin and spring run ecosystems there is sunlight for sight, plenty of oxygen, and many opportunities to eat.

The land around Florida's freshwater spring basins and runs are inhabited by many creatures that prefer to roam around open, sunlit areas or to rest just within the shade of a favorite hiding spot. And submerged within the basins can be found stygoxenes, or aquatic cave visitors. Passing most of their time in open water, these creatures are known to hang out in under hangs and caverns, and occasionally travel into caves in search of food or to escape predators. Some even get washed into caves during reverse flood or tidal events.

| | |
|---|---|
| Florida Shiny Spike | White Tubercled Crayfish |
| Suwannee Moccasinshell | Ohio River Shrimp |
| Oval Pigtoe | Eastern Grass Shrimp |
| *Asian Clam | Blue Crab |
| *Channeled Apple Snail | Water Flea |
| *Island Apple Snail | Copepod |
| *Giant Apple Snail | Seed Shrimp |
| Florida Apple Snail | Whirligig |
| Coffee Springs Siltsnail | Mayfly |
| *Red-rim Melania | Water Strider |
| *Fawn Melania | Mosquitoes |
| *Quilted Melania | Dragonfly |
| Ticks | Damselfly |
| Golden Silk Orbweaver | Stonefly |
| Fishing Spider | Caddisfly |

Gulf Sturgeon
Atlantic Sturgeon
Southern Stingray
Bowfin
Alligator Gar
Florida Gar
Longnose Gar
Inland Silverside
Atlantic Needlefish
American Shad
Gizzard Shad
Lake Chubsucker
Spotted Sucker
Golden Shiner
Eastern Shiners
Flagfin Shiners
Eastern Mosquitofish
Least Killifish
Redfin Pickerel
Chain Pickerel
Dusky Pipefish
Gulf Pipefish
Striped Mullet
Pirate Perch
Flier
Redbreast Sunfish
Warmouth
Bluegill
Dollar Sunfish
Redear Sunfish
Stumpknocker
Suwannee Bass
Florida Largemouth Bass
Black Crappie
*Tilapia
Striped Bass
Sunshine Bass
Darters
Freshwater Flounder
Channel Catfish
Southern Cricket Frog
Green Treefrog

Bullfrog
Green Frog
Pig Frog
River Frog
Southern Leopard Frog
Two-toed Amphiuma
Peninsula Newt
Narrow-striped Dwarf Siren
Northern Dwarf Siren
Greater Siren
American Alligator
Eastern Indigo Snake
Rainbow Snake
Plain-bellied Watersnake
Southern Watersnakes
Brown Watersnake
Gray Rat Snake
Eastern Ribbonsnake
Florida Cottonmouth
Chicken Turtles
Barbour's Map Turtle
Cooter Turtles
Florida Redbellied Cooter
*Red-eared Slider
Yellow-bellied Slider
Snapping Turtle
Alligator Snapping Turtle
Striped Mud Turtle
Florida Mud Turtle
Eastern Mud Turtle
Loggerhead Musk Turtle
Eastern Musk Turtle
Florida Softshell Turtle
Common Otter
Raccoon
American Beaver
*Capybara
*Rhesus Macaque
Round-tailed Muskrat
Eastern Woodrat
Cotton Mouse
Florida Manatee

# Bivalve Mollusks, Class Bivalvia

The word mollusk comes from Latin *mollusca*, the plural of *mollis*, meaning soft. We spell it "mollusk" in North America, but the rest of the world prefers "mollusc." Bivalve mollusks can live in freshwater or saltwater. Bivalve refers to the mollusk having two symmetrical shells flattened sideways. The shells are connected by a hinge ligament. The outside of the shell is a thin protein-based layer called the periostracum. The middle is a thick calcium carbonate ($CaCO_3$) in an organic matrix, creating the structure. The pearly, iridescent inside of the shell (called the nacre or mother-of-pearl) is made of aragonite (a form of calcium carbonate crystalized in seawater). Mollusks secrete proteins and minerals at the ventral (bottom) end of the mantle to make the shell. The shell grows outward from the outside edge. Because the shell grows as the mollusk grows, concentric rings are a rough indicator of growth.

The inside of this protective, hinged shell is where the bivalve mollusk lives. The mollusk is an invertebrate having a soft body called the visceral mass. Anterior and posterior adductor muscles allow the mollusk to close the shell, and a muscular foot allows the animal to move. Mollusks have a mantle that secretes the shell, labial palps that move food particles from the gills to the mouth, and two sets of multipurpose gills. The gills filter water, allowing the mussel to breathe and eat. In females, the gills also incubate glochidia (mussel larvae) until they are ready to be released. Mollusks also have a mouth, a stomach, a kidney and a three-chambered heart.

Mussels prefer to live in flowing water. They pump and filter water, breathing and eating what they need and storing anything else. Because mussels store unused contaminants in their bodies, they are very sensitive to water quality. Mussels may be used to alleviate the effects of eutrophication in polluted waters. Eutrophication occurs when nutrients such as nitrogen cause algae to bloom, and the algae reduces the oxygen in the water. While mussels can remove contaminants such as pesticide runoff or heavy metals from the water (and this is why you shouldn't eat bivalves from polluted waters), some chemicals such as ammonia or copper can kill them, and excessive silt can interfere with the bivalves' ability to filter feed and breathe.

Florida's freshwater mollusks are not considered edible (these are not tasty) but are used as bait by some fishermen. Seven species are protected by the U.S. Fish and Wildlife Service, collecting these can carry substantial penalties. There are state limits on the number and method of collecting freshwater bivalves. If you plan to try eating Florida's freshwater bivalves, be sure to get your fishing license, read the latest legal limits, learn how to identify which of the sixty species you can collect, and figure out how to make them palatable.

# Florida Shiny Spike, *Elliptio jayensis* (Lea, 1838)
## (Class Bivalvia, Order Unionoida, Family Unionidae)

Also known as the flat spike. This mussel has thirty-eight synonyms, such as *Elliptio buckleyi*.

**Etymology:** *Elliptio* comes from the ellipsoidal shape of the shell when viewed from the side (lateral view) and *jayensis* after John Clarkson Jay (1808–1891), a famous malacologist (someone who studies mussels).

**Size:** Up to 3 inches (7.62 centimeters) long.

**Description:** Resembles closely other bivalve species. Oval shells with slight ridges. Shell is olive to brown with darker rays on young individuals. The shell darkens with age, seeming almost black in mature individuals.

**Range:** Found throughout Florida in waterways with sand and mud bottoms and with a moderate current.

**Food sources:** Filters plankton and detritus.

**Characteristics:** So similar to other *Elliptio* that it is difficult to verify which mussel is truly this mussel. Apparently very common.

# Suwannee Moccasinshell, *Medionidus walkeri* (Wright, 1897)

## (Class Bivalvia, Order Unionoida, Family Unionidae)

**Etymology:** *Medionidus* from the Latin *medio*, meaning middle, and *nidus* for nest. *Walkeri* for conchologist Bryant Walker (1856–1936).

**Size:** Up to 2 inches (5.08 centimeters) long.

**Description:** Resembles closely other bivalve species. Oval shells with slight ridges. Shell is olive to brown with darker rays on young individuals. The shell darkens with age, seeming almost black in mature individuals.

**Range:** Found only within the Suwannee River Basin, in the lower Santa Fe and middle Suwannee.

**Food sources:** Filters plankton and detritus.

**Characteristics:** Extremely long lifespans. Mussels can live for more than one hundred years. After the male releases sperm into the water, which the female siphons, the fertilized eggs transform into larvae called glochidia, which are expelled. As glochidia, Suwannee moccasinshell larvae spend time parasitically attached to darters before transforming into juvenile mussels, which then detach from the fish and settle on the floor of the river, springs basins, and sometimes caverns.

**Note:** Listed by the FWC FT (Federally designated Threatened). FNAI ranking G1/N1 (Critically Imperiled) due to significant range decline. Because this mussel depends on the darter for part of its reproductive cycle, any threat to darters can affect the mussel population.

# Oval Pigtoe, *Pleurobema pyriforme* (Lea, 1857)
## (Class Bivalvia, Order Unionoida, Family Unionidae)

**Etymology:** *Pleuro* Greek for ribbed or side; *bema* is Greek for a step or raised place. *Pyriforme* from Latin means pear-shaped.

**Size:** Small, grows to 2.4 inches (6.1 centimeters).

**Description:** Shiny flattened oval (suboviform) yellowish to reddish brown shell with papery edges darker brown and black concentric growth bands. Iridescent bluish to pinkish interior.

**Range:** Econfina Creek and the Chipola, Ochlocknee, and Suwannee River systems (including the Santa Fe River).

**Food sources:** Filters plankton and detritus.

**Characteristics:** Commonly found in the cavern zone although has been observed by author farther into the cave, and in cave zones between sinkhole openings. The eastern mosquitofish (*Gambusia holbrooki*) and sailfin shiners (*Pteronotropis sp.*) are the primary host fish for the glochidia, the larval stage of the oval pigtoe.

**Note:** Listed by the FWC as FE (Federally designated Endangered). FNAI ranking G2/S1S2 (Globally: Imperiled/Statewide: Critically Imperiled to Imperiled).

# *Asian Clam, *Corbicula fluminea* (Muller, 1774)
## (Class Bivalvia, Order Veneroida, Family Corbiculidae)

Also known as Asiatic clam, pygmy clam, and golden clam.

**Etymology:** *Corbicula* is Latin for little basket, *fluminea* comes from *flumineus*, Latin for a river.

**Size:** Grows to 1.5 inches (3.81 centimeters) in length.

**Description:** Light brown shell with distinct dark brown to black concentric bands.

**Range:** Native range is temperate to tropical Asia west through northern Africa, and south as far as central and eastern Australia. Discovered in 1924 in British Columbia. By the 1960s had colonized Florida.

**Food sources:** Filters organic matter and is able to pedal-feed using the foot to transport food to the digestive tract.

**Characteristics:** Nonnative species. Hermaphroditic, meaning each individual possesses physiology of both sexes and the ability to self-fertilize. Sperm is released into the water and caught by another clam, then brooded in the clam's gills. Reproduction and larval release occur twice annually. The Asian clam can reproduce quickly. The rapid proliferation and high densities of this clam contribute to the clogging of human structures (such as intake pipes for industrial uses and drinking water systems) and alter dynamics of aquatic environments by displacing native populations. The Asian clam prefers warm, clean, flowing freshwater but is believed to withstand more brackish and polluted waters than most native species.

**Note:** These clams are only found in fresh water.

# Snails, Class Gastropoda

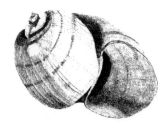

## *Channeled Apple Snail, *Pomacea canaliculata* (Lamarck, 1828)

### (Class Gastropoda, Order Architaenioglossa, Family Ampullariidae)

Also called the golden apple snail.

**Etymology:** *Pomacea* from *pomum,* Latin for apple, and *canaliculata* from Latin meaning having a channel or groove.

A nonnative apple snail from Argentina. The channeled apple snail is identified by the distinct valley, or channel, between the curve of the shell and whorls. Has gills and a lung, allowing them to breathe out of water. Dioecious, meaning it needs both a male and a female to reproduce. Very successful reproduction rate ensures the spread of this snail. Mainly herbivores, will also eat detritus. Also lay bright pink eggs in large clusters.

## Island Apple Snail, *Pomacea spp.*

**\*Island Apple Snail, *Pomacea insularum* (d'Orbigny, 1839)**
**\*Giant Apple Snail, *Pomacea maculata* Perry, 1810**

### (Class Gastropoda, Order Architaenioglossa, Family Ampullariidae)

**Etymology:** *Pomacea* from *pomum* from the Latin for apple, and *insularum* from Latin, meaning of or related to an island. *Maculata* is Latin for stained or spotted.

The most common nonnative apple snail is the island apple snail. Originally thought to be the channeled apple snail, *Pomacea canaliculata* (Lamarck, 1828). There are several species of nonnative island apple snails in Florida. The different species look very similar. Vary in color from light yellow to almost black and can have lines or stripes. Can grow to be large, with shells up to 3 inches (7.62 centimeters) across. Most likely released in southern Florida in the early 1980s from the aquarium trade, this snail rapidly expanded throughout the state and is now found across the southern United States and Hawaii. Dioecious. Island apple snail eggs tend to be more pink or reddish in color, smaller, and more densely clustered.

## Florida Apple Snail, *Pomacea paludosa* (Say, 1829)
### (Class Gastropoda, Order Architaenioglossa, Family Ampullariidae)

**Etymology:** *Pomacea* from *pomum* from the Latin for apple, and *paludosa* from the Latin for in a swamp or bog.

**Size:** Typically, 0.5–1 inch (1.27–2.54 centimeters), but can reach 3 inches (7.62 centimeters) in diameter.

**Description:** The shell is circular and in a variety of colors, from beige-white to shades of yellow to dark browns, but mostly dark olive green to black, sometimes with darker bands. The snail's soft body is dark brown to black with a fawn-colored bottom. The Florida apple snail can be differentiated from other apple snails by the almost 90-degree angle between the top part of the shell and the opening edge of the shell (although this varies slightly). Apple snails are very difficult to differentiate based on shell and color.

**Range:** Southern Georgia and Florida.

**Food sources:** Omnivorous. While primarily vegetarian, preferring soft vegetative material, it is known to eat decaying animals and eggs.

**Characteristics:** The largest freshwater snail native to North America. Possesses both a lung and gills, allowing it to survive out of the water, although it prefers to be underwater. Also has a siphon, which allows it to breathe air while submerged.

Unlike other snails, the Florida apple snail is not a hermaphrodite. It needs a male and a female to reproduce (dioecious). Pearly white to light pink egg clusters are a familiar sight just above the waterline along Florida's springs and rivers. The eggs of the Florida apple snail can be found attached to docks, riverine concrete structures, and vegetation. Egg masses of the Florida apple snail are larger but in smaller clusters than those of other apple snails. Eggs look white or light pink compared to the eggs of nonnative apple snails, which will appear greenish or pinkish.

**Note:** Apple snails are the principal prey of limpkins and snail kites (birds found along Florida's waterways) and are critical to their survival. They are also eaten by alligators and Florida softshell turtles.

# Coffee Spring Siltsnail, *Floridobia mica* (Thompson, 1968)
## (Class Gastropoda, Order Neotaenioglossa, Family Hydrobiidae)

Also known as the Ichetucknee siltsnail, the Ichetucknee Springs siltsnail and the sand grain snail.

**Etymology:** *Floridobia* comes from the state of Florida and the Greek word *bios* meaning life. The word is in the feminine, as is the standard for naming diminutive creatures. *Mica* from either Latin *mica* meaning a crumb or bit, or from *micare* meaning to glitter or flash.

**Size:** Grows to 0.08–0.09 inch (0.2–0.23 centimeter) in diameter.

**Description:** Tiny. Conical, brown body with a translucent shell.

**Range:** Found only in Coffee Spring within Ichetucknee Springs State Park in Suwannee County. The Ichetucknee River is a subsidiary feeding the Suwannee River.

**Food sources:** Algae.

**Characteristics:** Believed to live only one year. Females are larger than males. Not hermaphroditic, this siltsnail is dioecious, needing a male and a female to reproduce. Florida's hydrobiid snails are a diverse family. Most are extremely restricted in range and dependent on the food found in that one particular location. Because these snails are so tiny, identifying them can be very difficult. Their inclusion in this guide is to raise awareness of their presence.

**Note:** Not currently listed by the FWC. FNAI ranking G1/S1 (Globally: Critically Imperiled/ Statewide: Critically Imperiled because of extreme rarity or extreme vulnerability). There are thirteen species of these tiny snails in Florida; eleven exist in only one spring. They feed on algae, and it is important to understand that even the tiniest living creatures deserve our consideration. Protecting these tiny snails goes a long way in preserving Florida's beautiful springs and spring-fed rivers. All of the following are ranked FNAI ranking G1/S1 (Globally: Critically Imperiled/Statewide: Critically Imperiled because of extreme rarity or extreme vulnerability).

Other spring snails (siltsnails) in Florida:

### Alexander Siltsnail, *Floridobia alexander* (F. G. Thompson, 2000)

Endemic to Alexander Spring in the Ocala National Forest, Lake County, and in the creek downstream.

### Crystal Siltsnail, *Floridobia helicogyra* (F. G. Thompson, 1968)

Endemic to Hunter Spring, on Kings Bay in Crystal River on the Gulf Coast.

### Flatwood Siltsnail (also known as the Glen Branch Siltsnail), *Floridobia leptospira* (F. G. Thompson, 2000)

Endemic to Silver Glen Springs, found in a seep and headwaters of a branch leading into Alexander Creek. FNAI ranking G1G2/S1S2 (Globally: Critically Imperiled to Rare/Statewide: Critically Imperiled to Rare).

### Enterprise Siltsnail, *Floridobia monroensis* (Dall, 1885)

Endemic to Benson's Mineral Spring, near Lake Monroe in Enterprise, Volusia County.

### Pygmy Siltsnail, *Floridobia parva* (F. G. Thompson, 1968)

Endemic to Blue Springs in Volusia County.

### Rock Springs Siltsnail, *Floridobia petrifons* (F. G. Thompson, 1968)

Endemic to Rock Springs, north of Apopka.

### Ponderous Spring Siltsnail, *Floridobia ponderosa* (F. G. Thompson, 1968)

Endemic to the run at Sanlando Spring in Seminole County. This spring is in the middle of a gated community.

**Green Cove Springsnail,** *Floridobia porterae* **(F. G. Thompson, 2000)**

Endemic to Green Cove Spring in Clay County.

**Seminole Spring Siltsnail,** *Floridobia vanhyningi* **(Vanatta, 1934)**

Endemic to Seminole Spring, south of the Ocala National Forest.

**Wekiwa Siltsnail,** *Floridobia wekiwae* **(F. G. Thompson, 1968)**

Endemic to Wekiva Springs, only 16 miles from Orlando.

**Alligator Siltsnail,** *Notogillia wetherbyi* **(Dall, 1885)**

Endemic to Alexander Springs, in the Ocala National Forest, Lake County.

# *Red-rim Melania, Melanoides tuberculatus* (Muller, 1774)

## (Class Gastropoda, Order Neotaenioglossa, Family Thiaridae)

Also known as *Melanoides tuberculata.*

**Etymology:** *Melanoides* comes from the Greek *melas* for black and *oides* meaning similar. *Tuberculatus* from the Greek word for tubercles and *melania* from the Greek word for dark or black.

**Size:** Grows to 1.18–1.42 inches (3.0–3.61 centimeters) long.

**Description:** Slender, conical, whorled shells with fine spiral striations. Light brown with red tints and a dark red spiral band.

**Range:** Native to North Africa and Southern Asia but spread in tropical and subtropical areas worldwide. *Melanoides tuberculatus* is found primarily in slow, turbid water.

**Food sources:** Microalgae and detritus.

**Characteristics:** Lives an average of two years. Reproduces by parthenogenesis (embryos develop without needing sperm) but can reproduce sexually.

*Melanoides* is a euryhaline species, meaning it can live in a wide range of salinity.

## *Fawn Melania, Melanoides turriculus* (Lea, 1850)
### (Class Gastropoda, Order Neotaenioglossa, Family Thiaridae)

**Etymology:** *Melanoides* comes from the Greek *melas* for black and *oides*, meaning similar. *Turricula* means turreted.

**Size:** Grows to 1.18–1.57 inches (3–4 centimeters) long.

**Description:** Slender, conical, whorled shells with fine spiral striations. Light brown to greenish-brown on red-tinted shell.

**Range:** Native to the Philippines but spread in tropical and subtropical areas worldwide. In Florida it is found in freshwater tributaries near Tampa Bay, the lower St. John's and the Withlacoochee. *Melanoides turriculus* prefers oligotrophic springs and streams.

**Food sources:** Microalgae and detritus.

## *Quilted Melania, Tarebia granifera* (Lamark, 1822)
### (Class Gastropoda, Order Neotaenioglossa, Family Thiaridae)

**Etymology:** *Granifera* comes from the Latin *granifer* meaning grain-carrying. The common name "quilted" refers to the shell pattern.

**Size:** The ones we see in caverns average 0.8–1.2 inches (2.03–3.05 centimeters) in height.

**Description:** Slender, conic, whorled shell with prominent nodes or tubercles forming crenulations. Shell comes in shades of brown with many slight variations in height and ornamentation. A variety in color and detail of this snail leads even experts to disagree on which species, and how many spiral snail species, exist in Florida.

**Range:** Nonnative. From India and Southeast Asia but spread to tropical and subtropical areas throughout the world. Abundant in benthic strata (buried in sand, silt, or gravel) of freshwater springs and streams, also known to adapt to slightly brackish water. Observed in the cavern zone at Peacock III, a siphon at Peacock Springs State Park, and within the cave at Friedman Sink in Manatee Springs State Park to depths of 20 feet (6 meters).

**Food sources:** Grazes on algae and detritus.

**Characteristics:** In an odd quirk of development, the brood pouch of *Tarebia granifera* is above the esophagus.

*T. granifera* is important because it can be a host for the oriental lung fluke, *Paragonimus westermanni*. When a crab or crayfish eats an infected snail, they become the secondary host. Then, when a human eats inadequately cooked infected crab or crayfish, the lung fluke larvae infect the human host. The larvae grow within the human body, typically in the lungs. The infection is called *Paragonimiasis*.

**Characteristics:** *Tarebia* so successfully reproduce that it is believed their sheer numbers overwhelm native snails. The quilted melania is the most common mollusk encountered on the Rainbow River.

# Tick, Class Euchelicerata

## (Order Ixodida, Family Ixodidae)

**Etymology:** Acari comes from Latin acarus the plural of the word for mite. Ixodidae is said to refer to something being sticky. The word may derive from *ixōdēs*, the Greek word for birdlime, a sticky substance prepared from holly or mistletoe (*ixos* in Greek) spread on branches to capture birds.

Ixodidae are the family of the hard bodied ticks. A tick is basically a large mite. This small arachnid has a flattened body in colors from black to reddish or light brown, sometimes with ornate designs in lighter shades. Nymph and adult ticks have eight legs and range in size from less than 0.08 inch (0.2 centimeter) up to 0.6 inch (1.52 centimeters) when engorged with a host's blood. Male and female ticks express sexual dimorphism, males and females looking slightly different from one another. Ticks often have a dorsal shield or scutum, a shell on their back of contrasting colors or patterns. The female will have a smaller scutum, allowing her body to enlarge (engorge) when she feeds. Females grow much larger when engorged with blood. Once engorged, the abdomen swells and becomes a lighter tan or grey color.

Ticks have four stages in their life cycle: egg, larva, nymph, adult. The larval stage is referred to as a seed tick due to their truly tiny size, 0.2–0.6 inch (0.51–1.52 centimeters). A larval tick has six legs. Seed ticks are extremely active and are known to swarm.

Ticks are found worldwide, particularly in warm, humid climates. A parasitic hematophage, ticks feed externally on the blood of birds and other animals. Some species of ticks have a different host animal for each stage of life, others can survive using only one host.

Ticks have been around for a long time, since the Cretaceous Period. There are more than 700 species of ticks, more than 80 of those live in the United States. There are two families: the Ixodidae having hard bodies and the Argasidae having soft bodies. A tick is an arachnid with the abdomen, head and thorax fused together. The "head" of a tick, the gnathosoma, is retractable and consists of mouthparts called capitula, protrusible serrated chelicerae, and an immoveable, hypostome with backward-curving teeth, adapted for penetrating skin and sucking blood.

Ticks expel excess water back into their hosts, making ticks excellent vectors for diseases, such as Lyme disease, Rocky Mountain spotted fever, STARI (Southern Tick-Associated Rash Illness), ehrlichiosis and many others that can manifest as skin rashes, flu-like illnesses, and worse. An allergy to red meat called Alpha-gal syndrome (AGS) (specifically, an allergy to galactose-$\alpha$-1,3-galactose ($\alpha$-Gal), a type of sugar found in most mammals) can be triggered by the bite of certain tick species.

Ticks go questing! When questing, ticks can be found on the ends of grasses and leaves, waving their legs to catch passing animals. Ticks love grassy fields, meadows and other open areas, as well as tall grasses along trails and paths. The key to avoiding ticks is to stay away from tall, grassy areas and palmettos.

**Note:** One beautiful, hot autumn day, I decided to serve as surface support while my husband Mike and his dive buddy Jerry explored a sinkhole on a farmer's property in north Florida. Toting tanks is hard work, and after the divers disappeared into the underwater underground, I decided to relax and read a book. I chose a lovely, grassy overlook where I would easily see the bubbles of the returning explorers. I quickly set up my canvas camp chair, had a seat and opened my book, awaiting their return. It wasn't long before I felt something whispery-light along my lower legs. I had hiking boots and socks and wondered whether a farmer's cat was visiting me. I glanced down, immediately horrified to watch the solid black wave of seed ticks swarming up both legs toward my knees! I leapt up, abandoning the chair and the book, and raced for the car and a big can of bug spray that I never, ever use. I bathed my legs in bug spray that day. I got most off, but I found seed ticks in interesting and embarrassing places for a couple of days afterward.

## Lone Star Tick, *Amblyomma americanum* (Linnaeus, 1758)

**Etymology:** Greek *amblus* for dull or faint and *omma* meaning eye. *Americanum* refers to the species being found in America.

**Range:** Southeastern United States but expanding.

**Note:** Shown in the illustration above. Most common tick in Florida. 0.13 inch (0.33 centimeter) up to 0.44 inch (1.12 centimeters) when engorged. Ornate—the male has spots, and the female has a distinctive white spot at the base of the scutum. Like the Gulf Coast tick, this tick has noticeably long mouthparts (called palps). This tick has eyes.

## Gulf Coast Tick, *Amblyomma maculatum* Koch, 1844

**Etymology:** Greek *amblus* for dull or faint and *omma* meaning eye. *Maculatum* comes from *macula* meaning a spot or variegated.

**Range:** Along the Gulf of Mexico and southern Atlantic Coast.

**Note:** Grow to 0.24 inch (0.61 centimeter). Ornate—brown and orange tints with a metallic sheen. Female has a white circle edging the scutum. Male has light or silvery lines down scutum. Like the Lone Star tick, this tick has noticeably long mouthparts (called palps). Has eyes.

## American Dog Tick, *Dermacentor variabilis* (Say, 1821)

Also known as the eastern wood tick.

**Etymology:** *Dermacentor* comes from Latin *derma* for skin and Greek *kentór* for one who pricks or pokes (a goader). *Variabilis* is Latin for variable or changeable.

**Range:** Eastern half of the United States and along the Pacific Coast of California.

**Note:** 0.2 inch (0.51 centimeter). When fed swell to 0.6 inch (1.52 centimeters) long. Dark brown. Female has a white circle on the scutum. The male has white streaks along the scutum.

**Brown Dog Tick, *Rhipicephalus sanguineus* (Latreille, 1806)**

Also known as kennel tick and pan-tropical dog tick.

**Etymology:** *Rhiphis* is Greek meaning fan and *cephalus* refers to the head. *Sanguineus* in Latin refers to the tick being bloodthirsty.

**Range:** Entire United States.

**Note:** 0.13 inch (0.33 centimeter). When fed swell to 0.5 inch (1.27 centimeters) long. The dog tick is a plain, brown-colored tick with a distinctive hexagonal basis capituli (a six-sided head base). This tick can complete its entire life cycle outside or inside, where it can infest kennels and homes.

**Deer Tick, *Ixodes scapularis* Say, 1821**

Also known as blacklegged tick.

**Etymology:** *Ixodes* refers to the tick sticking to things. *Scapularis* is Latin meaning having to do with the shoulder. Common name deer tick after white tailed deer (*Odocoileus virginianus*), the main host of the tick during its reproductive cycle.

**Range:** Eastern United States.

**Note:** 0.12 inch (0.3 centimeter). Darker brown to black coloration. The body of the female is an orange or red body behind the scutum. Lacks eyes. Each stage in development needs a different host. Theses ticks thrive in areas with a large deer population. The deer tick is the vector for Lyme disease bacterium *Borrelia burgdorferi*. Older papers refer to *Ixodes dammini*, these were found to be the same species.

# Spiders, Class Arachnida

## Golden Silk Orbweaver, *Trichonephila clavipes* (Linnaeus, 1767)
### (Class Arachnida, Order Araneae, Family Nephilidae)

Synonymous with *Nephila clavipes* (Linnaeus, 1767).

Also known as golden orbweaver, golden silk spider, banana spider, calico spider.

**Etymology:** *Trikhos* is Greek for hair. *Nephilia* is from the Greek word *nema* meaning thread, and *philos* meaning loving. *Clavipes* from Latin *clava* for club or knotted staff and *pes* for foot (club-footed).

**Size:** Females average 1.24–2 inches (3.15–5.08 centimeters) in length but can reach 3 inches (7.62 centimeters). Males are much smaller, growing only to around 0.22 inch (0.56 centimeter).

**Description:** The female is a large spider with distinctive yellow and black markings. The male is the tiny indistinct spider typically found above the female on the same web.

**Range:** Throughout Florida.

**Food sources:** Small insects.

**Characteristics:** This large spider creates huge, strikingly strong webs across wide-open spaces such as walking trails. While intimidating, the spider is harmless and prefers to retreat to hiding until it can rebuild or repair the web.

# Fishing Spider, *Dolomedes* Latreille, 1804
## (Class Arachnida, Order Araneae, Family Pisauridae)

Also known as dock spiders.

**Etymology:** *Dolomedes* is from Greek *dolometis* and means wily or treacherous.

**Size:** Females typically grow 0.67–1.02 inches (1.7–2.59 centimeters), and males grow 0.35–0.51 inch (0.89–1.3 centimeters). With a wide leg span, these spiders look much bigger.

**Description:** Large, hairy, gray to brown spider. Has eight eyes in two rows of four. Different species of *Dolomedes* have distinct markings, such as spots on *Dolomedes triton*.

**Range:** Coastal New England south along and throughout the Atlantic Coastal Plain to Florida and west as far as the Dakotas and Texas.

**Food source:** Primarily insect larvae, but also tadpoles, frogs, and small fish.

**Characteristics:** Hunts by sight primarily during the day. Can be seen touching the water lightly with its front legs to tempt prey. Senses prey through concentric circles that break the still surface when insects become trapped by the surface tension at the air-water interface. The fishing spider is also able to dive under the water to catch prey. The fishing spider is covered by hydrophobic hairs allowing it to walk across the surface of water or dive into water without drowning. Tiny air bubbles on the spider's body allow the spider to breathe while underwater.

They can remain underwater for nearly a half hour. While they prefer to be near water, *Dolomedes* are sometimes found hunting in forested areas.

These spiders can and will bite, so leave them alone.

# Crustaceans, Class Malacostraca

## White Tubercled Crayfish, *Procambarus spiculifer* (Le Conte, 1856)

### (Class Malacostraca, Order Decapoda, Family Cambaridae)

Also known as the Florida springs crayfish.

**Etymology:** *Procambarus* comes from the Latin *pro* for before and *cambarus*, derived from the Greek word *kammaros* for lobster, Latinized as *cammarus* or *gammarus*. *Spiculifer* from the Latin *spicula*, a point, and *-fer* for having.

**Size:** Averages 4–6 inches (10.16–15.24 centimeters) in length.

**Description:** Comes in a variety of coloration, usually in shades of red and black with distinctive white bumps, or tubercles. First three leg pairs with pinchers (claws), with first pair being very large.

**Range:** Found in the rivers, streams, springs, and spring runs of north Florida, southern Georgia, and southern Alabama.

**Food sources:** Omnivorous.

**Characteristics:** The white tubercled crayfish is the most abundant crayfish in springs and one of the most colorful crayfish in North America. Most often encountered at night when it emerges from crevices in the limestone walls of the springs to scavenge on decaying organic material. While many crayfish can survive drought conditions by burrowing into the moist ground and remaining until water returns (aestivation), the white tubercled crayfish occurs only in permanent water and does not burrow.

# Ohio River Shrimp, *Macrobrachium ohione* (Smith, 1874)

## (Class Malacostraca, Order Decapoda, Family Palaemonidae)

Also known as Ohio shrimp.

**Etymology:** *Macrobrachium* from Greek *makros* meaning long and *brachium* meaning arm. *Ohione* is from the location of the holotype (the specimen described came from the Ohio River).

**Size:** Can grow to 4 inches (10.16 centimeters).

**Description:** Gray to greenish brown with light spots or mottling. Females grow larger than males. The first two pairs of legs are clawed, the second pair of legs has larger claws than the first. The rostrum (the protective top of the head extending over the eyestalks and antennae) is curved and has up to thirteen spiny serrations along the top.

**Range:** While originally described from Ohio, the present range is the Atlantic drainage from North Carolina to the northeastern coast of north Florida.

**Food sources:** Macroinvertebrates, plankton, algae, and detritus.

**Characteristics:** Lives in deep freshwater rivers and streams but requires access to brackish water for spawning. Amphidromous (adults may spawn in freshwater or saltwater, the juveniles swim upstream to live in freshwater after developing in saltwater).

**Note:** Used as bait for fishing and as food for dinner.

# Eastern Grass Shrimp, *Palaemonetes paludosus* (Gibbes, 1850)

## (Class Malacostraca, Order Decapoda, Family Palaemonidae)

Also known as grass shrimp, ghost shrimp, freshwater prawn, and Florida glass shrimp.

**Etymology:** The genus derives from the Greek *paleo* meaning ancient, *mon* for one and *etes* for dwell, dweller or one that dwells; *paludosus* is Latin meaning living in swamps, marshes, or bogs.

**Size:** Averages 1 inch (2.54 centimeters) long.

**Description:** Almost translucent. Some have light tan or brown vertical lines or mottling. First two leg pairs have pinchers (or claws) and are comparable in length. Females may have a green saddle on the back or may even be carrying eggs underneath the abdomen. Females also have a more pronounced ridge between the back and the beginning of the abdomen.

**Range:** Found in vegetation and algae growing in spring basins and spring runs.

**Food sources:** Microscopic plankton.

**Characteristics:** Sensitive to drought, freshwater shrimp do not have the coping capabilities of macroinvertebrates such as many crayfish.

Friendly but cautious, this shrimp will remind you of their marine cousins the cleaner shrimp, by examining and cleaning your hands during surface decompression.

# Blue Crab, *Callinectes sapidus* Rathbun, 1896
## (Class Malacostraca, Order Decapoda, Family Portunidae)

**Etymology:** From Greek *kallos*, meaning beauty, and *nektes*, meaning swimmer. *Sapidus* is Latin meaning savory or tasty.

**Size:** The shell can grow to 10 inches (25.4 centimeters) long and 20 inches (50.8 centimeters) wide.

**Description:** Has a hard, broad exoskeleton with marginal teeth and large lateral spines. Has five pairs of legs, with last pair for swimming, and a pair of claws (called chelipeds). The shell can be a range of hues from greenish to darker olive-brown to gray. Underside is lighter, shades of whitish-beige. Common name is for the distinctive blue coloration along the front and chelipeds. The females have bright red claws.

**Range:** Western Atlantic and inland Florida along tributaries of the St. Johns River.

**Food sources:** Will eat almost anything, such as mollusks, vegetation, and other crabs. Will also scavenge fresh carrion.

**Characteristics:** Begins life in the ocean in a series of larval stages, starting as zoea, having seven stages over thirty to fifty days. Each of the larval stages is a slightly larger version of the earlier stage. Calcium in seawater contributes to the hardness of the shell after molts. The next stage as a megalops (six to twenty days) is with more of a crab-like body but retaining the extended abdomen. The megalops moves into estuaries and molts into a crab shape. Female blue crabs prefer the higher salinity of the ocean, while males can often be found in the springs and spring runs. Male crabs seek out females just before the female molts. When the female molts, the male is able to deliver sperm to the female. The male holds the female underneath him and protects the female as her new shell hardens. The females fertilize their eggs with the sperm. The eggs are placed on tiny hairs on the female's abdomen. Female crabs with eggs are known as berry crabs or sponge crabs because of the appearance of the mass of eggs attached to her underside. Blue crabs can live to be two to three years old.

**Notes:** There is a population of blue crabs living in Salt Springs in the Ocala National Forest. While considered nocturnal, these crabs can be observed among the rocks around the spring vent during the day. Blue crab tastes delicious, and the crabs are popularly trapped for food.

# Microcrustaceans

## (Kingdom Animalia, Phylum Arthropoda, Subphylum Crustacea)

The word *crustacean* comes from the Latin meaning a crust or shell. They include barnacles, crabs, shrimp, lobsters, crayfish, isopods, and amphipods. *Micro* comes from the Greek word *mikros* and means extremely small. Microcrustaceans are tiny versions of crustaceans and include copepods, ostracods, and cladocerans. Sometimes what we notice in the water column are juvenile crustaceans, sometimes other species altogether.

Each of these creatures is an extremely important contributor to life in the aquatic environment worldwide because they make up the base of many food chains. The presence of these tiny critters indicates a healthy water ecosystem.

While you may have good enough eyesight to notice truly tiny creatures frolicking in the water column, a microscope is necessary to be absolutely sure which creatures you are observing.

## Water Flea, Class Branchiopoda
### (Class Branchiopoda, Order Diplostraca, Suborder Cladocera)

Also known as Daphnia.

**Etymology:** From Greek words *klados* meaning branch or shoot and *keras* meaning horn.

**Size:** Smaller than 0.1 inch (0.25 centimeter) in length.

**Description:** Cladocera are tiny crustaceans. The body is protected by a shell shaped like an oval folded in half. Has one black compound eye.

**Range:** Worldwide. Primarily freshwater.

**Food sources:** Almost all are herbivorous filter feeders. *Daphnia* (the genus of the most commonly known water flea) feeds on bacteria, tiny pieces of detritus, and small algae, and are in turn food for almost everyone else. Insect larvae, other crustaceans, and small fish depend on cladocerans as a food source.

**Characteristics:** When swimming, they use their antennae as paddles or their legs to move in a jerky rowing or hopping motion, giving them the common name water fleas. Because they are transparent, except for their eye, the internal organs are easy to see, making cladocera a favorite subject for microscopic study. They give birth to live young. Cladocera are capable of parthenogenesis, when an unfertilized egg can develop into an embryo.

# Copepod, Class Maxillopoda
## (Class Maxillopoda, Subclass Copepoda)

**Etymology:** From the Greek words *kope* meaning oar and *podos* meaning feet.

**Size:** Rarely exceeds 0.04 inch (0.1 centimeter) long in fresh water.

**Description:** Copepods are a segmented aquatic crustacean related to crabs and shrimp having one simple eye and five pairs of broad, paddle-like legs.

**Range:** Copepods are abundant in marine, brackish, and freshwater habitats from shallow polar ice to deep-sea vents. Any place where water exists, you will find copepods.

**Food sources:** Bacteria, diatoms, and phytoplankton (tiny plants) in algae and sea grasses.

**Characteristics:** They scoot around the water column in jerky movements. Copepods also inhabit detritus on saturated forest floors. Divers in anchialine cave environments, freshwater caves on islands, have discovered some of the most primitive forms of copepods.

There are many orders of copepods, and their classification is changing as we learn more about this abundant species.

Copepods in some parts of the world are themselves hosts for various parasites that can ultimately infect humans. On the other hand, another copepod parasite attacks larval mosquitoes and may provide an effective means of biological control.

# Seed Shrimp, Class Ostracoda

Also called ostracods, mussel shrimp, and seed shrimp.

**Etymology:** From the Greek word *ostrakon*, meaning shell.

**Size:** Grows up to 0.04 inch (0.1 centimeter) long.

**Description:** Very small, laterally compressed bivalved microcrustaceans with smooth, weak, kidney-bean-shaped, calcified carapace. Appears translucent, with shades of pale white, pink, and beige. Appears in large numbers.

**Range:** Found on aquatic plants and the benthos (bottom) in nearly all aquatic environments including springs, subterranean caves, and temporary ponds. Some ostracods live on host species, such as crayfish.

**Food Sources:** Filter feeder preferring diatoms, bacteria, and detritus.

**Characteristics:** Ostracods are ancient. Fossil ostracods are known from the Late Cambrian period (approximately 545 to 490 million years ago), and fossil shells dating back even further. Ostracods are also a food source in the benthic environment. While both ostracods and cladocera have similar folded-oval shells, ostracods have some pigmentation to their shells, whereas cladocera are transparent. Lack a heart and gills but have a single eye capable of detecting shapes and motion when the shell is open and light when the shell is closed. Cave-dwelling ostracods are usually blind.

# Insects, Class Insecta

## Whirligig, Family Gyrinidae
### (Class Insecta, Order Coleoptera)

**Etymology:** *Gyrinus* refers to the Greek word *gyrinos* for tadpole, which comes from the Greek word *gyros* for round.

**Size:** 0.1–1.4 inches (0.25–3.56 centimeters) in length.

**Description:** A small, black beetle often seen in large numbers moving around on the surface of the water by rowing with flat oar-like legs. Seems to be moving in rapid circles and infinity patterns. Oval, streamlined body allows it to move around quickly.

**Food sources:** Small insects that become trapped in the surface tension of the water.

**Characteristics:** Whirligig eyes are divided in half, allowing it to see both above and below the water simultaneously.

Flies around at night, searching for new water bodies.

# Mayfly, Order Ephemeroptera
## (Class Insecta)

The order Empheroptera includes three suborders and more than twenty families of mayflies!

**Etymology:** Order name from Greek *ephemeros*, meaning to last only one day, and *pterón*, meaning wing.

Also known as fishflies, shadflies. In the northeastern United States known as Canadian soldiers.

**Size:** Body 0.5–1 inch (1.27–2.54 centimeters) in length (not counting threadlike tail projections), wingspan up to 2 inches (5.08 centimeters).

**Description:** Shorter body in relation to head and wings. Body color light tan, brown, gray, or yellow with a variety of markings. Able to fold wings together above the body like the damselfly. Long, delicate legs. Long tail projections differentiate the mayfly from dragonflies and damselflies.

**Range:** Worldwide near water, except subterranean.

**Food source:** Naiads are omnivorous. Adults do not eat.

**Characteristics:** Adults have a very short lifespan, from minutes to only a few days. Lay eggs at or on the water surface. Naiads remain aquatic, living up to two years before developing rudimentary wings and leaving the water as what is called a sub-imago (also called a dun, a version of an adult), then molting into an imago (or spinner, the sexually mature adult stage). Naiads look nothing like the adults, with tiny wing buds, bigger legs and three hairy tail projections. They can be differentiated from stonefly naiads by the three tail projections, external gills on first seven body segments and one claw on the last segment of each leg. Naiads can only survive in clean water. The presence of mayflies indicates good water quality.

Metamorphoses from aquatic nymph (naiad, larva) into terrestrial adult. In springtime along rivers, it swarms in the trees along the riverbanks.

Mayflies appear oblivious of humans and can accidentally end up in your eyes, nostrils, or even your mouth. Be careful where you steer your kayak!

**Note:** Several mayflies are ranked by FNAI as Critically Imperiled, Imperiled, Rare, Apparently Secure, or Demonstrably Secure. None are listed by the USFWS or FWC.

# Water Strider, Family Gerridae
## (Class Insecta, Order Hemiptera)

Also called Jesus bugs, pond skaters, pond skippers, water skaters, water skippers.

**Size:** 0.3–0.47 inch (0.76–1.2 centimeters) in length.

**Description:** Dark brown or black body sometimes with lighter horizontal stripes on either side. Very long legs.

**Range:** Worldwide. There is a marine version as well.

**Food sources:** Small insects that become trapped in the surface tension of the water.

**Characteristics:** Equipped with very long legs with special hairs that trap air, allowing it to "walk" on water, this bug is light enough not to break the surface tension. It skates along the surface of calm and slowly moving water. Will travel over land in search of water bodies if home water dries up. Adult water striders have three sets of legs.

# Mosquitoes, Order Diptera
## (Class Insecta, Family Culicidae)

Also known as nighthawk and skeeter.

**Etymology:** There are more than thirty genera, or genus names, for mosquitoes. Eighty species are reported to live in Florida. The common name derives from Spanish *mosca* (and Latin *musca*), meaning a fly with the diminutive suffix *ito*, indicating "little."

**Size:** Typically, less than 0.5 inch long (1.27 centimeters).

**Description:** Small, thin flying insect with long, delicate-looking legs. Typically brown or black, some with white bands.

**Range:** Throughout Florida.

**Food sources:** Adult mosquitos feed on plant nectar. The female mosquito requires blood only for the protein to produce eggs.

**Characteristics:** Mosquitoes prefer warm, dark, damp areas with still water. Known to live in damp leaf litter as well as anything holding water.

Mosquitoes can make visiting Florida miserable. There are a variety of methods for avoiding mosquitoes, from wearing mosquito netting to staying inside when mosquitoes are believed to be most active (dawn and dusk, incidentally also often the coolest parts of the day!) Known vectors (carriers) of diseases that afflict humans. Only the female feeds on human blood.

### *Yellow Fever Mosquito, *Aedes aegypti* (Linnaeus, 1762)

Found throughout Florida, except the panhandle. Vector primarily of dengue virus, also malaria, chikungunya, and Zika virus. Nonnative.

### *Asian Tiger Mosquito, *Aedes albopictus* (Skuse, 1895)

Shown in illustration. Found throughout Florida. While this mosquito can be a vector of dengue, eastern equine encephalitis (EEE), chikungunya, and other viruses, it is not considered as aggressive as *Aedes aegypti*. Nonnative.

Both *Aedes aegypti* and *A. albopictus* are developing a tolerance for insecticides. The recommendation is now to be sure to empty containers of standing water, limiting their opportunities for breeding.

### Southern House Mosquito, *Culex quinquefasciatus* Say, 1823

Found throughout Florida. Small 0.16–0.17 inch (3.96–4.25 millimeters), plain brown mosquito. Vector of dog heartworm, St. Louis encephalitis, and West Nile viruses.

### Gallinipper, *Psorophora ciliata* (Fabricius, 1794)

Also known as the shaggy legged gallinipper.

Found throughout Florida. Prefers floodwater areas. Large, dark brown body with yellow bands and feathery legs. This species is not a known vector of disease. The larvae of this huge mosquito feed on the larvae of other mosquitos.

# Dragonfly, Order Odonata
## (Class Insecta, Suborder Anisoptera)

Six of the eight families of dragonflies live in Florida.

**Etymology:** The order name Odonata comes from Greek and loosely means tooth, referring to the dragonfly's mandibles. The suborder name Anisoptera is from Greek *ánisos*, meaning unequal, and *pterón*, meaning wing.

There are many genera and species in the families of dragonflies. They all have a similar body type to that of the dragonfly illustrated.

**Size:** 1–4 inches (2.54–10.16 centimeters).

**Description:** A large head and elongated abdomen in a variety of colors and markings. Compound eyes. Eyes touch or are very close to touching. Tiny antennae. Legs are near the head. Long, thin wings of various widths and markings covered in fine veins. Rear wings are wider than front wings. Differentiated from damselflies by resting with wings spread open to either side of the body. Can be very colorful, bright green, blue, yellow, red, and even pink.

**Range:** Near water bodies throughout the United States.

**Food sources:** Smaller invertebrates.

**Characteristics:** To tell the dragonflies apart involves differences in eye placement and color, face color, and body and wing color and markings.

Lays round eggs in and near water. Has an aquatic larval stage called a nymph (or naiad). Dragonfly nymphs are stout. Their gills are inside the abdomen. Odonata naiads have a variety of body shapes but are distinguished by their shovel-like lower jaw, which they extend to grab prey. The nymphs will molt as many as fifteen times before leaving the water. Dragonflies live only two months or less after metamorphosis.

Ancient insect. Fossils of dragonflies date back to the Carboniferous period (approximately 359 to 299 million years ago).

If you are very still and hold one finger in the air out from your body, a dragonfly may land and rest for a while.

They eat mosquitos!

# Damselfly, Order Odonata
## (Class Insecta, Suborder Zygoptera)

Three of the twelve families of damselflies live in Florida. Family in illustration: Coenagrionidae.

There are many genera and species in the twelve families of damselflies. They all have a similar body type to that of the damselfly illustrated.

Also known as mayflies (a separate insect), bog dancers, and sprites.

**Etymology:** Order name Odonata comes from Greek and loosely means tooth, referring to the damselfly's mandibles. Suborder name Zygoptera from Greek *zugós* meaning even and *pterá* meaning wings.

**Size:** 1.8 inches (4.57 centimeters).

**Description:** Smaller and more slender than dragonflies and has more solid coloration than dragonflies, typically blue or black. Males typically more intensely colored than females. Compound eyes. Eyes are set apart on the head. Very short antennae. Legs are near the head. Long, thin wings of various but equal widths and markings, covered in fine veins. Differentiated from dragonflies by resting with wings folded together over the body.

**Range:** Near water bodies throughout the United States.

**Food sources:** Smaller invertebrates.

**Characteristics:** Lays cylindrical eggs in and near water. The damselfly nymph begins life as a slender aquatic naiad. Damselfly nymphs have gills protruding from their rear. Like the dragonfly, damselfly naiads have a wide variety of body shapes but can be distinguished by their shovel-like lower jaw, which they extend to grab prey. Nymphs prey on aquatic invertebrates smaller than themselves. They may go through as many as fifteen molts before emerging as an adult damselfly. In the adult stage nymphs leave the water, molt, unfold, dry out, and take to the air.

Damselflies are not afraid of humans and will land on fingers, toes, heads, clothing.

They eat mosquitoes!

# Stonefly, Order Plecoptera
## (Class Insecta)

There are two suborders, Antarctoperlaria (in the southern hemisphere) and Arctoperlaria (in the northern hemisphere). In the suborder Arctoperlaria, there are two infraorders,

Euholognatha (having a long basal tarsal segment and including several families) and Systellognatha (having a reduced basal tarsal segment and including several families). Fossil-dating indicates the separation of the suborders to the Jurassic period (approximately 146 to 200 million years ago) during the breakup of the supercontinent Pangea. Stoneflies are intolerant of salt water, the orders developed independently on the separated landmasses. The diversity of the families developed immediately following, during the Cretaceous period (approximately 146 to 65 million years ago).

**Etymology:** Order name Plecoptera from Greek *plektos*, meaning twisted or plaited, and *pteron* or *pterux*, meaning wing.

**Size:** Adults grow to 0.35–1.57 inches (0.89–4 centimeters) long.

**Description:** Long, narrow, gray, black, or brown bodies, and highly veined wings that fold flat over the body at rest. Wings unfold out from the body. Eyes on either side of head. Very long antennae.

**Range:** Most common in north Florida. Found near all aquatic environments, except subterranean.

**Food sources:** Naiads feed on algae. Adult stoneflies do not eat.

**Characteristics:** Stoneflies are one of the most common aquatic insects in northeast Florida and the panhandle. They prefer cooler temperatures. Lay eggs in water. Adult stoneflies are found resting on debris in or near flowing water. Stonefly naiads can be differentiated from mayfly naiads by the two tail projections (cerci), lack of gills on abdominal body segments and having two claws on the last segment of each leg. Naiads can be found under stones and logs in water. Prefer clear, unpolluted, running water. Indicator species, meaning their presence indicates that the water quality is good.

# Caddisfly, Order Trichoptera
## (Class Insecta)

**Etymology:** From Greek *trichos*, meaning hair, and *ptera*, meaning wing.

**Size:** Can be from 0.10–1.58 inches (0.25–4 centimeters).

**Description:** Adults are moth-like insects with hairy wings that they hold over their bodies like a tent. Come in a variety of browns, grays, and even white, with a variety of shades and markings.

**Range:** Worldwide near water.

**Food sources:** Most nymphs eat detritus; some catch small prey. Adults do not eat but may drink nectar or other liquids.

**Characteristics:** Primarily nocturnal. They live as adults only a short time. Can be differentiated from moths by having paired mouthparts instead of a long proboscis.

Caddisflies go through life stages from egg, to larva, to pupa, and then adult. Caddisflies can live several years as larvae. Larvae resemble those of other aquatic insects except that they live in a protective and portable "case" created by the larva with silk from a special gland in its mouth and covered with leaves and debris. Larvae live in clear, spring-fed streams, and ponds. An indicator species, the presence of caddisfly larvae indicates that the water quality is good.

Love artificial light and will swarm bright lights at night.

**Note:** Several caddisflies are ranked by FNAI as Critically Imperiled, Imperiled, Rare, Apparently Secure, or Demonstrably Secure. None are listed by the USFWS or FWC.

# Sturgeons, Class Chondrostei

## Gulf Sturgeon, *Acipenser oxyrinchus desotoi* (Vladykov, 1955)

### (Class Chondrostei, Order Acipenseriformes, Family Acipenseridae)

**Etymology:** *Acipenser* is the Greek word for sturgeon. *Oxyrinchus* derives from Greek *oxus* for sharp and *rhunkhos* for bill (or snout). *Desotoi* honors Hernando de Soto (1495–1542), a Spanish explorer and conquistador.

**Size:** A large fish, sturgeon can grow as long as 8 feet (2.44 meters) and weigh more than 300 pounds (136 kilograms).

**Description:** Dark brown to silvery back fading to white underbelly. A hard snout with four barbels and a suction mouth on the bottom. Does not have teeth. Has a cartilaginous skeleton, like sharks and rays, and instead of scales, has five rows of scutes, hard plates that protect the head and the top of the body. The top lobe of the tail is larger than the bottom lobe. The Gulf sturgeon is a subspecies of the Atlantic sturgeon. It is difficult to tell them apart.

**Range:** Gulf of Mexico from the Mississippi to the Suwannee River. Occasionally found as far south as Tampa Bay. They are anadromous, meaning they swim up rivers in the spring to spawn and back to the ocean to feed. They spawn between February and April and return to the Gulf of Mexico between September and November.

**Food sources:** They are benthic feeders, feeding off the bottom, eating macroinvertebrates like amphipods, grass shrimp, crabs, mollusks, and other crustaceans.

**Characteristics:** A prehistoric group of fish that dates to the Triassic period (246 to 208 million years ago). Typical lifespan is twenty to twenty-five years, but they can live more than forty years. Females grow larger than males. Sturgeon spawn in flowing rivers in areas with rocky or gravel bottoms, where the broadcast eggs adhere. The nonvegetated rocky places where the sturgeon return to spawn each year are referred to as spawning reefs. The sturgeon requires large rivers for spawning. While in the rivers, sturgeon are believed to not feed.

Sturgeon leap as high as 9 feet into the air and have been known to collide with passing boaters. Sturgeon may leap to regulate their swim bladder and to communicate with other sturgeon. It is recommended boaters go more slowly during late afternoons in summer and early fall, when sturgeon are known to leap. Places where the sturgeon jump are called holding areas. Some known holding areas are on the Suwannee River below Manatee Springs, and at the confluence of the Santa Fe and the Suwannee.

**Note:** During spawning, sturgeon make creaking noises. One method biologists use to determine where the sturgeon live is to place microphones in the water and listen for them.

Sturgeon are protected, and it is illegal to kill or harm them. Listed by the FWC as FT (Federally designated Threatened). FNAI ranking G3T2T3/S2? (Globally: Rare, Taxonomic subgroup: Imperiled/Statewide: Critically Imperiled, uncertain).

## Atlantic Sturgeon, *Acipenser oxyrinchus oxyrinchus* (Mitchill, 1815)
### (Class Chondrostei, Order Acipenseriformes, Family Acipenseridae)

**Etymology:** *Acipenser* is the Greek word for sturgeon. *Oxyrinchus* derives from Greek *oxus* for sharp and *rhunkhos* for bill (or snout). The specific name is written twice to indicate that this is the type for the species.

**Size:** Grow as long as 14 feet (4.27 meters) and up to 800 pounds (362.9 kg).

**Description:** Dark brown to silvery back fading to white underbelly. A hard snout with four barbels and a suction mouth on the bottom. Does not have teeth. Has a cartilaginous skeleton, like sharks and rays, and instead of scales, five rows of scutes, hard plates that protect the head and the top of the body. The top lobe of its tail is larger than the bottom lobe.

**Range:** Rivers and coast along the Atlantic Coast from Canada to the St. Johns River.

**Food sources:** Benthic feeder, feeding on the bottom, eating macroinvertebrates like amphipods, grass shrimp, crabs, mollusks, and other crustaceans.

**Characteristics:** Sturgeon are slow growing, not reaching maturity until long after other fishes, and will not spawn at all if conditions are not just right. If they skip a spawning, they will wait another three years before spawning. Sturgeon are anadromous, adults living in the sea and returning to freshwater to spawn. Can live as long as sixty years in northern waters, but only believed to live to thirty in the southern United States.

**Note:** Sturgeon are protected, and it is illegal to kill or harm them. A recent survey discovered no Atlantic sturgeon in the St. Johns River, a historical habitat, although they are seasonally present in the estuary (at the mouth of the river).

Listed by the FWC as FE (Federally designated Endangered). FNAI ranking G3T3/S1 (Globally: Rare, Taxonomic subgroup: Rare/Statewide: Critically Imperiled).

# Cartilaginous Fish, Class Chondrichthyes

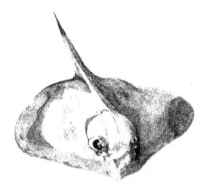

## Southern Stingray, *Dasyatis sabina* (Lesueur, 1824)
### (Class Chondrichthyes, Order Myliobatiformes, Family Dasyatidae)

Synonymous with *Hypanus sabinus*.

Also known as the freshwater ray and Atlantic stingray.

Stingrays belong to the subclass Elasmobranchs, cartilaginous fish including sharks, skates, and rays.

**Etymology:** *Dasyatis* comes from Greek *dasus*, meaning rough or dense, and *batis* refers to a fish, such as a shark, ray or skate. *Sabina* might refer to Sabin Berthelot (1794–1880), a French naturalist and ethnologist who lived in the Canary Islands and a contemporary of Lesueur.

**Size:** 12–14 inches (30.48–35.56 centimeters) wide.

**Description:** Circular to oval-shaped with a broadly pointed snout (looking like a shovel head) and a long, thick tail. Tan to brown on top, darkest along the center and fading toward the edges, with a beige to white underside.

**Range:** Western North Atlantic Ocean from Chesapeake Bay to Florida and in the Gulf of Mexico along the Florida coast, and south to Mexico. Found in the St. Johns River.

**Food sources:** Invertebrates such as snails, amphipods, crustaceans, clams, and worms.

**Characteristics:** Not aggressive but has a venomous spine on the tail used for defense if stepped-on or harassed. While most elasmobranchs can only tolerate limited ranges of salt water (stenohaline), the Atlantic stingray can live in brackish or fresh water (euryhaline). The stingray breathes by sucking water through holes behind its eyes and expelling the water through the gills on its underside. The stingray has electroreceptive sensory cells called the "Ampullae of Lorenzini," which are used to sense the electric fields generated by organisms buried in the benthos (bottom). They may also use this ability to locate other stingrays. Stingrays give birth to live young.

# Gars and Bowfin, Class Holostei

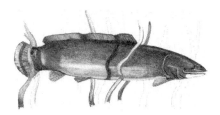

## Bowfin, *Amia calva* Linnaeus, 1766
### (Class Holostei, Order Amiiformes, Family Amiidae)

Also known as dogfish, grindle, lawyer, and mudfish.

**Etymology:** *Amia* is Greek referring to fish, and *calva* is Latin for smooth.

**Size:** Can grow to just over 3 feet (1 meter) in length and 20 pounds (9.07 kilograms).

**Description:** Dark olive to dark brown body fading to light cream on the belly. Males have a dark spot edged in yellow or orange on the caudal fin. Very long dorsal fin running from the middle of the back to the base of the tail. The tail has a single lobe. The bowfin has a large, flat, broad head with a large mouth and two barbels projecting up from its nose. Obvious rows of teeth. Lower fins are bright green during breeding season. Body is covered in soft, leathery, smooth scales. Swims by undulating entire body. Usually appears sluggish but is capable of surprisingly quick bursts of speed.

**Range:** Throughout North America. Prefers still, muddy, heavily vegetated bodies of water, although also found in the clear, flowing Rainbow River.

**Food sources:** Carnivorous, feeds on frogs, fish, crayfish, invertebrates, pretty much anything it can fit in its mouth.

**Characteristics:** Amiiformes, the bowfins, are an order of primitive ray-finned fishes. While only one species of bowfin exists today, past varieties included Leedsicthys, the largest fish that ever existed. Bowfin and gar are two freshwater fish that exist little changed since the Jurassic period (approximately 146 to 200 million years ago). The bowfin has a swim bladder that can function as a lung, allowing the fish to gulp air when levels of dissolved oxygen become low. Believed to be able to aestivate (burrow in mud) during droughts. Spawns in the spring. Male bowfins build circular nests in gravel and fibrous root mats, clearing stems and leaves. One male may breed with two or three females. The male guards the nest and fry. Fry remain in schools guarded by the male until about 4 inches (10.2 centimeters) long. An aggressive fish, the bowfin is known to attack fishermen who hook them.

# Alligator Gar, *Atractosteus spatula* (Lacepede, 1803)
## (Class Holostei, Order Lepisosteiformes, Family Lepisosteidae)

Also known as gator, greater gar, garfish, and Mississippi gar.

**Etymology:** The genus name *Atractosteus* comes from the Greek *atractus*, meaning spindle, and *osteos*, meaning bony. *Spatula* is a Latin derivative of the Greek *spathe*, referring to any tool with a broad, flat blade.

**Size:** Can exceed 6 feet (1.83 meters) in length and weigh more than 200 pounds (90.72 kg).

**Description:** Largest member of the gar family. A long, cylindrical, dark olive green or brownish body with metallic overlapping scales. Belly is white and fins have a pink tint. Short, broad snout with pointy teeth on both top and lower jaws. Alligator gar have a double row of sharp teeth on the upper jaw.

**Range:** Found in large rivers and bays in fresh and brackish water only west of the Apalachicola River.

**Food sources:** Primarily piscivorous, meaning they eat fish but also crabs and other small animals.

**Characteristics:** Gar encountered in Florida springs and spring runs are most likely the Florida gar. Alligator gar are found in the Florida panhandle.

Alligator gar live a long time. Females mature at eleven years and live as long as fifty years. Males mature at six years and can live to twenty-six years.

Like the Florida gar, the Alligator gar has a modified swim bladder that enables it to breathe from both water and air, allowing it to survive almost any water condition.

The roe of gar is toxic to humans.

**Note:** FNAI ranking G3G4/S3 (Globally: Rare to Apparently Secure/Statewide: Rare).

# Florida Gar, *Lepisosteus platyrhincus* DeKay, 1842
## (Class Holostei, Order Lepisosteiformes, Family Lepisosteidae)

Also known as gar and spotted gar.

**Etymology:** *Lepisosteus* is from the Greek *lepis*, meaning scale, and *osteon*, meaning bone. *Platyrhincus* comes from *platy*, meaning flat, and *rhincus*, meaning snout.

**Size:** No longer than 4 feet (1.22 meters) in length.

**Description:** Long and thin, with greenish to olive brown along the back fading horizontally to yellowish-white on undersides. The Florida gar has dark spots on the body, fins, and top of the head. The distance from the front of the eye to the back of the gill cover is less than two-thirds the length of the snout. Adult Florida gar are smaller than other adult gar species.

**Range:** Poorly oxygenated waters in peninsular Florida. Prefers lakes and rivers with sand or muddy bottoms and plenty of vegetation.

**Food sources:** Juveniles eat zooplankton (tiny animals, such as copepods or ostracods) and adults stalk small fish, frogs, and crustaceans.

**Characteristics:** This is the gar visitors are most likely to see in springs and spring runs. The gar has the capacity to use an air bladder to breathe air at the water's surface when aquatic oxygen levels fall.

The roe of gar is toxic to humans.

Gar and bowfin are two freshwater fish (infraclass Holostean) that exist little changed since the Jurassic period (approximately 146 to 200 million years ago).

# Longnose Gar, *Lepisosteus osseus* (Linnaeus, 1758)
## (Class Holostei, Order Lepisosteiformes, Family Lepisosteidae)

**Etymology:** *Lepisosteus* from Greek *lepis*, meaning scale, and *osteon*, meaning bone (*osseus* means bony).

**Size:** Grow longer than 6 feet (1.83 meters).

**Description:** Elongated, torpedo-shaped fish with overlapping, interlocking scales. Olive to brown on the back, fading to beige or white underneath. The color of the longnose depends on the water clarity—in clear water longnose gar are brighter and have more of a green tint. In dark water, longnose gar will be more darkly tinted. Has long, sharp, slender teeth. The snout of the longnose gar is more than twice as long as the snout on other species of gar.

**Range:** Eastern half of North America.

**Food sources:** Juveniles eat crustaceans and invertebrates. Adults prefer fish.

**Characteristics:** Prefer slow-moving fresh and brackish water. Nocturnal feeders. Longnose gar lifespan in the wild averages eleven years, although some in captivity have lived as long as thirty years.

**Notes:** Seen in the Rainbow River. The roe of gar is toxic.

# Ray-finned Fish, Class Teleostei

## Inland Silverside, *Menidia beryllina* (Cope, 1867)
### (Class Teleostei, Order Atheriniformes, Family Atherinopsodae)

Also known as the tidewater silverside, shiner, minnow.

**Etymology:** *Menidia* from the Greek word *mēnē* for moon or crescent and *-oides*, meaning resembling. *Beryllina* is from Latin meaning emerald or green-colored.

**Size:** Reach an average size of 3.94 inches (10 centimeters).

**Description:** Small, narrow, bright pale olive to golden olive fish with a metallic silver line running length of sides. Flat, silver head with large eye.

**Range:** Eastern North America. Throughout Florida.

**Food sources:** Omnivorous, primarily zooplankton.

**Characteristics:** Schooling fish. Prefer slowly moving water and sand or gravel bottoms, but spawns over vegetation in freshwater or brackish water. Lives for two years. Euryhaline, able to tolerate a range of salinity. Some populations live their entire lives in freshwater. Introduced as a baitfish and for mosquito control in various lakes and rivers.

**Note:** The term minnow is used for any number of small or young fish under 3 inches in length.

# Atlantic Needlefish, *Strongylura marina* (Walbaum, 1792)
## (Class Teleostei, Order Beloniformes, Family Belonidae)

**Etymology:** From the Greek word *strongylos*, meaning round, and *oura*, meaning tail. *Marina* comes from the Latin *marinus*, meaning of the sea.

**Size:** Grows to 2 feet (60.96 centimeters) long.

**Description:** Extremely long, slender body with one dorsal fin near the tail. Long jaws with lots of pointy teeth. Silvery to greenish-tan with a darker blueish stripe or tint along the upper body. Black behind the eye. Scales of the needlefish reflect light, making the fish nearly invisible just under the surface of the water when viewed from below.

**Range:** Marine and fresh water in the western Atlantic Ocean from Maine to South America, and along the Gulf Coast.

**Food sources:** Mainly small fish. Juvenile needlefish have a slightly longer lower jaw than upper to feed on small crustaceans such as amphipods and shrimp. Adult needlefish upper and lower jaw are the same size. Needlefish will actually leap out of the water to prey on fish from above.

**Characteristics:** Spawn in fresh water. Eggs adhere to objects in the water by tendrils on the eggs' surface. Needlfish jump and skip across the water surface when surprised. People have been impaled by the fish. Known to lunge at predators. Swim in an undulating motion, called anguilliform swimming, like an eel. Needlefish have blue or green bones due to biliverdin. The same pigment is responsible for the blue tint in some bird eggs and in human bruises. Needlefish are attracted to light and can be found at night near lighted piers.

**Notes:** Commonly seen in the Rainbow River, near Dunnellon, Florida. They blend in well and it takes a sharp eye to see them.

# American Shad, *Alosa sapidissima* (Wilson, 1811)
## (Class Teleostei, Order Clupeiformes, Family Clupeidae)

Also known as the Atlantic shad and common shad.

**Etymology:** *Alosa* from the Latin *alausa*, a fish cited by Ausonius and also the old Saxon name for shad, which was *alli*. *Sapidissima* means "most delicious." The common name shad derives from Saxon *sceadd*, which means herring.

**Size:** Reach an average size of 24 inches (60.96 centimeters).

**Description:** Metallic silvery body with blue-green tint to back. Dark brown spot on shoulder. White belly with scutes. Females grow larger than males.

**Range:** North American Atlantic Coast. Shad have been found 170 miles (274 kilometers) up the St. Johns River in the Wekiva River.

**Food sources:** Plankton, small shrimp, and other crustaceans, occasional small fish.

**Characteristics:** Anadromous, living in schools in the ocean but swimming up freshwater rivers in spring or early summer to spawn at their preferred breeding grounds. Shad from further north can spawn several times after maturing (iteroparous), while Southern shad spawn only once before dying (semelparous). Shad breed by swimming close together and releasing eggs and milt simultaneously. Young shad, reaching 0.79 to 1.18 inches (2 to 3 centimeters), begin to form schools and migrate downstream toward the ocean. Lives for six to ten years.

Not closely related to other shad, instead the American shad is believed to be descended from an early European shad population. This delicious fish is described as the fish that fed our founders. The meat and the roe of American shad are considered delicious!

# Gizzard Shad, *Dorosoma cepedianum* (Lesueur, 1818)

### (Class Teleostei, Order Clupeiformes, Family Clupeidae)

Also known as the American gizzard shad, mud shad, and skipjack.

**Etymology:** *Dorosoma* comes from Greek *doris* for lance, referring to the last ray of the dorsal fin, and *soma* meaning body. In Greek myth, Doris was the daughter of Oceanus and Tethys. *Cepedianum* is named after Bernard Germain Étienne de la Ville sur Illon, compte de Lacépède (1756–1825), a French naturalist and senator.

The common name gizzard shad comes from the fish having a gizzard-like muscular stomach (a gizzard being an organ used to help digest foods.)

**Size:** Average size 9–14 inches (22.86–35.56 centimeters). Weight to 2 pounds (0.91 kilogram).

**Description:** Short, deep, metallic silvery body with a blue tint to the back, fading to white on the belly. Small, rounded mouth and large eyes. No teeth. No scales on the head. Very distinctive, long final ray of dorsal fin.

**Range:** Atlantic and Gulf Coast drainages throughout Florida.

**Food sources:** Planktivore, algae, phytoplankton, zooplankton as well as detritivore (eating detritus found in bottom sediment).

**Characteristics:** Euryhaline, can tolerate a range of salinity, but breeds in freshwater. Cold-intolerant, preferring warmer water temperatures. Gizzard shad is a food source for many popular gamefish such as bass and catfish. Waterbirds also feed on gizzard shad. When populous, can negatively impact the food systems by eating the available planktonic food sources.

Gill rakers, more than four hundred, filter small particles into the gizzard shad's extensive digestive system.

Once plentiful in Silver Springs, it is believed the damming of the river curtailed the population.

**Note:** Similar to the threadfin shad, another rounded metallic fish having a long final dorsal ray. Threadfin shad have a more pointed mouth with a slightly jutting lower jaw.

## Lake Chubsucker, *Erimyzon sucetta*
## (Lacepede, 1803)
### (Class Teleostei, Order Cypriniformes, Family Catostomidae)

**Etymology:** Greek *eri-* is a prefix meaning very, much, or a lot. *Myzon/myza*, derived from *muzaō*, means to suck.

**Size:** Averages 10.16 inches (25.8 centimeters) in length.

**Description:** Deep-bodied and laterally compressed with a protrusible mouth and prominent lips.

Back is olive to brown, lighter in juvenile fish and turning darker in adults. Cream or white belly. Rounded dorsal fin, tail fin is bilobed (two rounded parts). Small mouth. No lateral line.

**Range:** Southeastern United States, through central states to southern Great Lakes area.

**Food sources:** Microcrustaceans, aquatic larvae and other invertebrates, algae.

**Characteristics:** Stays in calmer waters of lakes, ponds, sloughs, creeks, and rivers.

**Note:** Suckers differ in appearance from carp by the shape of their mouths. Suckers have protrusible mouths on the bottom of their heads. Carp have mouths like other fish but sometimes have barbels on either side of their mouths.

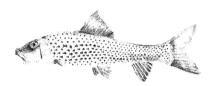

## Spotted Sucker, *Minytrema melanops*
## (Rafinesque, 1820)
### (Class Teleostei, Order Cypriniformes, Family Catostomidae)

**Etymology:** *Minytrema* from *minuthō*, Greek meaning to decrease, refers to the reduced or incomplete lateral line, and *melanops* from Greek *mela*, meaning black and *ops*, meaning eye.

**Size:** A medium-large fish, up to 24 inches (60.96 centimeters) in length.

**Description:** Deep-bodied and laterally compressed with a protrusible mouth and prominent lips. Silvery to golden to olive-hued body fading from back to belly. Fins are tinged in red. A spot on each scale gives the fish its spotted appearance.

**Range:** Throughout the eastern United States and south to Florida; panhandle rivers from Suwannee and Santa Fe westward.

**Food sources:** Omnivorous bottom-feeders, preferring invertebrates.

**Characteristics:** Stays in small schools. Prefers deeper water, hiding under vegetation during the day and becoming more active as evening approaches.

**Note:** Suckers differ in appearance from carp by the shape of their mouths. Suckers have protrusible mouths on the bottom of their heads. Carp have mouths like other fish but sometimes have barbels on either side of their mouths. The one in the illustration is in the process of stretching its mouth.

## Golden Shiner, *Notemigonus crysoleucas* (Mitchill, 1814)
### (Class Teleostei, Order Cypriniformes, Family Cyprinidae)

**Etymology:** *Notemigonus* is Greek for angled back, *noton* for back and *gonia* means angled. *Crysoleucas* from the Greek meaning gold and white, or golden-white.

**Size:** Maximum length 8 inches (20.32 centimeters), but usually smaller.

**Description:** A silvery fish with yellow or reddish fins. Has a distinctive scale-less strip on the underside between the pelvic fin and the anus.

**Range:** Medium to large bodies of slow moving or still water. Usually stays close to aquatic plants but swims more actively in open water at night. Requires good, clear water quality.

**Food sources:** Algae, small crustaceans, and insects at the water surface, small fish, and zooplankton.

**Characteristics:** A minnow related to the goldfish; golden shiners school and spawn in schools. Females are larger than males. Females lay their eggs in aquatic plants or other fish nests and abandon them.

# Eastern Shiners, *Notropis* (Rafinesque, 1818)

**Ironcolor Shiner, *Notropis chalybaeus* (Cope, 1867)**

**Taillight Shiner, *Notropis maculatus* (Hay, 1881)**

**Coastal Shiner, *Notropis petersoni* Fowler, 1942. Illustrated above.**

## (Class Teleostei, Order Cypriniformes, Family Cyprinidae)

Also referred to as minnows and shiners.

**Etymology:** *Notropis* from the Greek *noton*, the backside of an animal. Specific names: *chalybaeus* means "steely" from Latin *chalybs* for steel (*khalups* in Greek) and Greek *baios* for small or little, referring to the lateral stripe. *Maculatus* Latin meaning spotted or blotched. *Petersoni* is named for C. Bernard Peterson, who helped collect the type specimen.

**Size:** Typically, approximately 2–3 inches (5.08–7.62 centimeters) in length.

**Description:** Small, slender, cylindrical sand-colored fish having a lateral band, sometimes dark, one dorsal fin, large eyes, and a small mouth. These small fish resemble other species of the family Cyprinidae, such as the redeye chub and other shiners and minnows. Exhibit sexual dimorphism, in the taillight shiner, the male is bright red with the dark lateral band and red on the fins.

**Range:** Throughout Florida.

**Food sources:** Algae, microcrustaceans, insect larvae, zooplankton.

**Characteristics:** Short-lived, typically only one to four years, depending on the species. These small fish resemble each other very closely. Except for differences in coloration, it is very difficult to tell them apart (for example, the inside of the ironcolor shiner's mouth is black, unless she yawns, you might not be able to tell the difference between her and other shiners.)

**Note:** This genus has the largest number of species of North American fishes.

# Flagfin Shiners, *Pteronotropis* Flower, 1935

### Apalachee Shiner, *Pteronotropis grandipinnis* (Jordan, 1877)

Found in the Apalachicola River drainage.

### Metallic Shiner, *Pteronotropis metallicus* Jordan and Meek, 1884

Found near vegetation in headwaters, runs, and rivers of the Atlantic and Gulf drainages of the north half of Florida.

### Flagfin Shiner, *Pteronotropis signipinnis* (Bailey and Suttkus, 1952)

Found in spring runs from the Apalachicola River westward to the Pearl River at the western border of Mississippi.

### Bluenose Shiner, *Pteronotropis welaka* (Evermann and Kendall, 1898)

Juvenile male illustrated above. Found in deeper runs and rivers in only two locations: the middle St. Johns River drainage in eastern Florida and in the western panhandle Gulf drainages from the Apalachicola River westward to the Pearl River at the western border of Mississippi.

## (Class Teleostei, Order Cypriniformes, Family Cyprinidae)

Also referred to as minnows and shiners.

**Etymology:** *Pteronotropis* comes from *ptero*, Greek for wing. *Notropis* from the Greek *noton*, the backside of an animal, refers to species with an enlarged dorsal fin (a "back keel") on breeding males. Specific names: *grandipinnis* is Latin, *grandi*, meaning big, and *pinni*, meaning wing or fin. *Metallicus* is from Latin *metallium*, meaning metal. *Signipinnis* comes from Latin and means "banner fin." The word *welaka* is after the town of Welaka, on the St. John's River, where the bluenose shiner was discovered.

**Size:** Small, typically less than 2 inches (5.08 centimeters).

**Description:** Small, slender, cylindrical fish having a bold, dark lateral band, large eyes, and one dorsal fin. These small fish resemble other species of the family Cyprinidae, such as the redeye chub and other shiners and minnows. This species exhibits sexual dimorphism. Males will develop brighter coloring, distinctive markings on fins, enlarged dorsal fins, and growths around the mouth called breeding tubercles.

**Food sources:** Algae and zooplankton.

**Characteristics:** Schooling fish preferring sand or silt-bottomed vegetated areas of river and spring run waters, darting to the surface to feed.

**Note:** Both male and female bluenose shiners are long, slender fish distinguished by a blue nose (although some females lack this). The female has an olive-colored back, a dark lateral line running from nose to the base of the tail bordered by smaller lighter lines, and a white belly. Males develop stages of coloration, resembling the female when a juvenile and developing into a mature condition as a blue fish with larger fins. Bluenose shiner males in full breeding colors have a bright blue head, with a brilliant dark blue body flecked with gold, an enlarged dorsal fin also in blue, and the other fins touched with gold and black dashes. Males will circle and arc their bodies, displaying fins to entice females and intimidate challengers. Because of their beautiful colors, bluenose shiners are considered desirable to native fish collectors, but because of their dwindling numbers in their native range, captive breeding populations are attempting to maintain the species. While the population of most of these little shiners appears to be stable, the beautiful bluenose shiner (*P. welaka*) is considered under the FNAI ranking as G3G4/S3S4 (Globally: Rare to Apparently Secure/Statewide: Rare to Threatened), primarily due to habitat destruction.

# Eastern Mosquitofish, *Gambusia holbrooki* Girard, 1859
## (Class Teleostei, Order Cyprinodontiformes, Family Poeciliidae)

**Etymology:** *Gambusia* comes from the Cuban word *gambusino*, meaning prospector or miner, and *holbrooki* for an unknown person.

**Size:** Very small, up to 1.5 inches (3.81 centimeters) long.

**Description:** Light olive brown top, fading to a silvery yellowish on the sides and lighter to the underside. The mouth is near the top of the fish's head.

**Range:** Found statewide in shallow waters of ponds, lakes, marshes, and slow-moving streams.

**Food sources:** This surface-feeding fish eats anything it can fit in its mouth, including worms, insects, crustaceans, algae, and snails. Mosquitofish are known for their voracious appetite for mosquito larvae.

**Characteristics:** Very aggressive, attacks other fish including each other. Live birth to more than two hundred fry.

**Note:** The one in the image above is a pregnant female, appearing somewhat pot-bellied and with a distinctive spot that serves to guide the males. Host fish for the larval stage of the oval pigtoe mussel.

# Least Killifish, *Heterandria formosa* Girard, 1859
## (Class Teleostei, Order Cyprinodontiformes, Family Poeciliidae)

Also called a dwarf livebearer.

**Etymology:** From the Greek *heteros*, meaning other, and *andros*, meaning male. *Formosa* from Latin *fōrmōsus*, meaning beautifully formed, made up of the Latin word *fōrma* for form or shape and adjective suffix *-ōsus*, meaning full of.

**Size:** Very small, females average 1.18 inches (3 centimeters) and grow larger than males, which average 0.8 inch (2 centimeters).

**Description:** Golden olive upper body with a bold, black stripe along the lateral line with vertical bars fading to a white belly. Dark spot on dorsal fin. Females have a dark spot on their anal fin. Male killifish anal fins have a thin rod they use during mating to deliver sperm. The name of the modified anal fin is a gonopodium.

**Range:** Densely vegetated, slow moving, or still water. Lower Atlantic and Gulf Coastal Plain, from South Carolina south and west to extreme eastern Texas.

**Food sources:** Omnivorous, primarily aquatic invertebrates and crustaceans.

**Characteristics:** One of the smallest freshwater fish in North America. Related to guppies and mollies. Not really a killifish because killifish are oviparous (they release eggs). As a live-bearing fish, the female least killifish nurtures her eggs internally until they hatch, and releases the fry, a few at a time, into the water. Least killifish are capable of superfetation, carrying more than one brood at different levels of development.

## Redfin Pickerel, *Esox americanus* Gmelin, 1789
### (Class Teleostei, Order Esociformes, Family Esocidae)

Also known as pike and redfin pike.

**Etymology:** *Esox* from the Greek for big fish, and *americanus* refers to America.

**Size:** Grow only to 11.81 inches (30 centimeters) in length.

**Description:** Long, torpedo-shaped body with a greenish-brown stripe down the body and dark markings of irregular vertical bands, bars or columns of spots on a lighter green or bronze background. Distinctive red tint on the fins. Distinct vertical bar crosses the eye and cheek. Long snout with bottom jaw jutting slightly. Smaller than other pickerel.

**Range:** Slow-moving, vegetated streams in the eastern United States. Atlantic slope from Quebec south to Lake Okeechobee, Florida.

**Food sources:** Small crustaceans while juveniles, mainly fish as adults.

**Characteristics:** Can live up to eight years. Females grow larger than males. Breeding is late winter to early spring, and again in late summer to early winter. The females are polyandrous, meaning they choose more than one male to breed with. Fry hatch without scales. The scales begin to develop when they are 1.18 inches (3 centimeters) and are complete at 2.56 inches (6.5 centimeters). Young grass pickerel are sometimes mistaken for juvenile chain pickerel.

## Chain Pickerel, *Esox niger* Lesueur, 1818
### (Class Teleostei, Order Esociformes, Family Esocidae)

Also known as pike and southern pike.

**Etymology:** *Esox* from the Greek for big fish. *Niger* is Latin for black, referring to the dark bars.

**Size:** 30–36 inches (76.2–91.44 centimeters) in length.

**Description:** Long, torpedo-shaped body with dark markings of vertical bands, bars, or columns of spots on a lighter green or bronze background. Distinct vertical bar crosses the eye and cheek. Long snout with bottom jaw jutting slightly.

**Range:** Throughout Florida in vegetated slow-moving streams, lakes, and ponds.

**Food sources:** Primarily small fish but also small invertebrates and vertebrates.

**Characteristics:** Chain and redfin pickerel (*Esox americanus americanus* Gmelin, 1789), interbreed. The fish spawn in vegetation and abandon the young. Chain pickerel can live up to ten years.

# Dusky Pipefish, *Syngnathus floridae* (Jordan and Gilbert, 1882)
## (Class Teleostei, Order Gasterosteiformes, Family Syngnathidae)

**Etymology:** From the Greek *syn*, meaning grown together, and *gnathos*, meaning jaw. *Floridae* refers to the state of Florida.

**Size:** Can grow to 10 inches (25.4 centimeters) long.

**Description:** Long, narrow body ranging in color from white to brown with darker markings. Has trunk rings. Lacks pelvic fins. Stouter body than other *Syngnathus*. Longer snout than gulf pipefish.

**Range:** In seaweed and sediment in marine and fresh water along the entire coast of Florida.

**Food sources:** Siphon small crustaceans such as copepods and amphipods through their tubular mouths.

**Characteristics:** Both males and females mate with multiple partners (polygynandry). The female deposits her eggs in a brood pouch in the male during copulation. The male carries the eggs in the brood pouch, located under the tail.

# Gulf Pipefish, *Syngnathus scovelli* (Evermann and Kendall, 1896)

## (Class Teleostei, Order Gasterosteiformes, Family Syngnathidae)

Also called American Gulf pipefish and Scovell's pipefish.

**Etymology:** From the Greek *syn*, meaning grown together, and *gnathos*, meaning jaw. *Scovelli* in honor of Josiah T. Scovell, M.D. (1841–1915) a doctor and professor of natural science who helped collect the first specimens.

**Size:** Averages 3 inches (7.62 centimeters).

**Description:** Long, narrow body of brown or dark green with silvery white bars. Has trunk rings. Lacks pelvic fins and ribs. Shorter snout than other *Syngnathus*. Female has a banded dorsal fin.

**Range:** In seaweed and sediment in shallow marine and fresh water along the entire coast of Florida. Common in seagrass in bays and estuaries.

**Food sources:** Siphons small crustaceans such as copepods and amphipods through tubular mouths.

**Characteristics:** The male carries the eggs in a brood pouch located under the tail.

# Striped Mullet, *Mugil cephalus* (Linnaeus, 1758)

## (Class Teleostei, Order Mugiliformes, Family Mugilidae)

**Etymology:** From the Latin *mugil* for fish, and *cephalus* for mullet.

**Size:** Averages 10–20 inches (25.4–50.8 centimeters) in length.

**Description:** Grayish to silvery cylindrical fish, most often seen in schools.

**Range:** Found worldwide in coastal tropical and subtropical waters. Striped mullet are catadromous, meaning they spawn in salt water but spend most of their lives in fresh water. Juvenile striped mullet prefer estuaries and areas with lower salinity, while adults can stand higher salinity levels.

**Food sources:** Primarily bottom feeders of zooplankton, they also graze on algae, aquatic plants, and debris (planktivores). Juvenile mullet feed on microcrustaceans such as copepods.

**Characteristics:** Not specifically catadromous, spawn in saltwater but will travel into freshwater mainly in search of food. One of the best known of all saltwater visitors to the springs, mullet are easily recognized from the surface by their distinct habit of leaping into the air.

Mullet are one of the few fish species to have a gizzard, which helps them digest the larger particles in the detritus they pick up while eating along the bottom of the waterways.

**Note:** Finger mullet are young mullet and are used as baitfish.

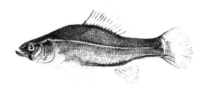

## Pirate Perch, *Aphredoderus sayanus*
## (Gilliams, 1824)

### (Class Teleostei, Order Percopsiformes, Family Aphredoderidae)

**Etymology:** From the Greek *aphod* for excrement and *dere* for throat. The anal vent in the adult pirate perch can be found directly behind the throat. *Sayanus* comes from the name of Thomas Say (1787–1834), renowned as the father of American entomology.

The common name, pirate perch, comes from noted ichthyologist Charles C. Abbott, who noticed that when kept in an aquarium, the fish ate only other fish.

**Size:** A small fish less than 5 inches (12.7 centimeters) in length.

**Description:** Typically, with a dark reddish-purple body with gray undersides, although the pirate perch can also have a green or copper tint. Pirate perch are believed to exhibit chemical crypsis (camouflage involving scent rather than visual cues). During breeding season, from October to December in Florida, males can become darker, almost black in color.

**Range:** Found in warm, muddy, slow-moving freshwater marshes, ditches, pools, and ponds across most of Florida.

**Food sources:** Aquatic insects such as mosquito larvae and water fleas, small minnows, earthworms, and small crustaceans.

**Characteristics:** Nocturnal. Distantly related to cavefish, being in the same order Percopsiformes. The only member of the family Aphredoderidae, the pirate perch is noted for the location of the anus, which is near the base of the anal fin when young, then gradually migrating forward to below the pectoral fin (at the throat) of the mature fish. The pirate perch exhibits transbranchioral spawning, meaning that the eggs move from the urogenital tract through the gill chambers, and are spat from the mouth into the nesting area, typically underwater root masses. Gill-brooding is only known among cavefish.

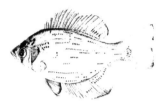

# Flier, *Centrarchus macropterus* (Lacepede, 1801)
## (Class Teleostei, Order Perciformes, Family Centrarchidae)

Also known as round sunfish, millpond flier, goggle-eye, and sand perch.

**Etymology:** *Centrarchus* from the Greek meaning anal-spined (for the long spines on the anal fin), and *macropterus* meaning big or long fin.

**Size:** Small, 5–7 inches (12.7–17.78 centimeters) in length.

**Description:** Has a round body and a small mouth. The long dorsal and anal fins are nearly the same size. Coloration varies from shades of green and tan on the back fading to cream or white on the belly, with darker spots on the scales.

**Range:** Atlantic and Gulf Coastal Plains, and throughout north and central Florida. Inhabit dark, tannic, slow-moving waters such as swamps, ponds, and canals. Like heavy vegetation. Fliers can tolerate higher acidity than some other sunfish.

**Food sources:** Prefer insects, worms, small crustaceans, fish, and occasionally phytoplankton.

**Characteristics:** Small but tasty fish known for fighting well when hooked. Males prepare the nest and guard the young. Known to hybridize with other sunfish.

# Redbreast Sunfish, *Lepomis auritus* (Linnaeus, 1758)

## (Class Teleostei, Order Perciformes, Family Centrarchidae)

Also known as redbelly, yellowbelly, bream, long ear sunfish, sun perch, and redbreast bream.

**Etymology:** *Lepomis* from the Greek meaning scaled cheek or operculum, and *auritus* from the Latin for eared in reference to the elongated opercle (ear) flap.

**Size:** Small fish growing to 12 inches (30.48 centimeters).

**Description:** Has an oval profile. Very pronounced, long, narrow, black earflap, which is actually an extension of the gill cover (the operculum). Colorful males have a bright yellow, orange, or red breast, and blue streaks on the cheek. Females are less colorful, with a less intense yellow or red breast.

**Range:** Common in central and north Florida. Found throughout the Eastern Seaboard as far north as Canada.

**Food sources:** Insects, insect larvae, small crustaceans, snails, small clams, and small fish.

**Characteristics:** Prefers sand-bottom areas of rivers and lakes around limestone outcroppings, snags, and aquatic vegetation. Constructs circular beds in water 1 to 3 feet (30 to 90 centimeters) deep, in isolation under logs or overhangs. Like other sunfishes, the redbreast sunfish breeds with other sunfish.

# Warmouth, *Lepomis gulosus*
## (Cuvier in Cuvier and Valenciennes, 1829)
### (Class Teleostei, Order Perciformes, Family Centrarchidae)

Also known as mud bass, redeyes, wood bass, and goggle-eye.

**Etymology:** *Lepomis* from the Greek meaning scaled cheek or operculum, and *gulosus* from the Latin for big-mouthed.

**Size:** Body length averages 5–8 inches (12.7–20.32 centimeters) but can reach 12 inches (30.48 centimeters).

**Description:** Oblong body resembling other sunfish. Large mouth with upper jaw extending to or past middle of the eye. Bold vertical stripes radiating out from a red-colored eye toward gill cover resemble a warrior's war stripes, giving the fish its common name. Varied mottled coloring, often striking in variation, fading to a beige or yellow belly.

**Range:** Native throughout the eastern United States.

**Food sources:** Crayfish, isopods, insect larvae, and smaller fish.

**Characteristics:** Prefers slow-moving and muddy or tannic water with vegetative cover. Slow growing, can take as long as four years to reach 6 inches (15.2 centimeters) in length. Breeds with other sunfish. Males build nests near objects such as rocks and stumps, and guard the nest until the fry disperse.

# Bluegill, *Lepomis macrochirus* (Rafinesque, 1819)
## (Class Teleostei, Order Perciformes, Family Centrarchidae)

Also known as bream.

**Etymology:** *Lepomis* from the Greek meaning scaled cheek or operculum, and *macrochirus* from the Greek for large hand, referring to the body shape and size or the size of the pectoral fin.

**Size:** Typically, 6–10 inch (15.24–25.4 centimeters) long.

**Description:** A sunfish with an oval profile. Black vertical stripes down both sides of the body. Distinguished by a dark spot at the base of the dorsal fin, vertical bars on its sides, and a small mouth. Often with a blue tint on the cheek and gill cover.

**Range:** Clear water with plenty of vegetation. Common throughout the eastern United States.

**Food sources:** Fry feed on plankton, but as they grow, bluegill switch to aquatic insects and larvae.

**Characteristics:** Curious—will approach divers. Spawn throughout the summer in large congregations. Breeding males have more intense colors, vertical bars may have a reddish hue. Older adults, growing close to 1 foot (30 centimeters) in length, develop a purple background color. Long spawning season frequently leads to overpopulation in areas with low predation. Males guard the eggs. Nest in colonies, clustering together. Sunfish interbreed with other sunfish.

## Dollar Sunfish, *Lepomis marginatus* (Holbrook, 1855)

### (Class Teleostei, Order Perciformes, Family Centrarchidae)

**Etymology:** *Lepomis* from the Greek, meaning scaled cheek or operculum, and *marginatus*, meaning edged, probably in reference to the coloring on the opercle flap.

**Size:** A small fish, usually less than 5 inches (12.7 centimeters) in length.

**Description:** Has a small mouth and a short body. Dollar sunfish display a wide variety of coloration, mostly of a greenish or orange background with light-colored specks of bright metallic, iridescent hues. The opercle flap has a blue or green metallic edge. While normally a greenish or olive on the back with light orange and brown flecks, spawning males develop iridescent blue scales. Vertical fins are translucent yellow to gray. The black opercle flap is elongate and angled upward with a light green edge.

**Range:** Throughout Florida and the southeastern United States.

**Food sources:** Include detritus, filamentous algae, and insects.

**Characteristics:** Prefers murky, slow-moving bodies of water. As observed by the author, the dollar sunfish appears to shift coloration depending on interest or perceived threat.

## Redear Sunfish, *Lepomis microlophus* (Gunther, 1859)

### (Class Teleostei, Order Perciformes, Family Centrarchidae)

Also known as chinquapin, shellcracker, sun perch, and bream.

**Etymology:** *Lepomis* from the Greek, meaning scaled cheek or operculum, and *microlophus* from the Greek for having a small nape or neck.

**Size:** Averages 5–9.5 inches (12.7–24.13 centimeters) in body length.

**Description:** Deep, compressed body with a relatively small mouth. Black opercular spot, males have a distinct red edge to the opercle flap, and females a distinct orange edge. The opercle is not as long as in the redbreast sunfish. They have large eyes, a lobed tail fin, and a long, pointed pectoral fin. Spotted olive-green to silver or light blue bodies that, depending on spawning season and hybridization, may shift in color when agitated. Males turn light gold during spawning seasons.

**Range:** Native to the eastern United States, introduced west of Texas. Prefers clear, warm water with little or no current and plenty of vegetation.

**Food sources:** Bottom feeders preferring insect larvae, invertebrates such as cladocerans (water fleas), snails, mussels, and fish. Snails are a major food source, hence the nickname shellcracker.

**Characteristics:** Prefers remaining near the sandy or shell-covered bottom of just about any slow-moving, clear body of water. Spawning activity peaks during the full moon of March and April when water temperatures are 68–75 degrees Fahrenheit (20–24 degrees Celsius). Nests in colonies near vegetation in shallow water. Males build the nests and guard the fry. Breeds with other sunfish. Fry stay together, often with the fry of other sunfish, until adulthood.

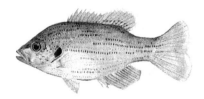

## Stumpknocker, *Lepomis punctatus* (Valenciennes in Cuvier and Valenciennes, 1831)
### (Class Teleostei, Order Perciformes, Family Centrarchidae)

Also known as spotted sunfish.

**Etymology:** *Lepomis* from the Greek meaning scaled cheek or operculum, and *punctatus* for little spots or spotted.

**Size:** Body length rarely exceeds 8 inches (20.32 centimeters).

**Description:** Small, olive-tinted sunfish covered with black to orange-tinted spots. Dark pelvic and anal fins.

**Range:** Fresh water throughout north Florida.

**Food sources:** Crayfish, insects, and snails. Feeds on insects attached to submerged limbs and trunks, hence the nickname stumpknocker.

**Characteristics:** Prefers low current with submerged vegetation and snags. Able to tolerate higher salinity than other sunfishes. Solitary nesters. Spawning males grunt and actively guard their nest. One of the most common fish found in the Rainbow River.

# Suwannee Bass, *Micropterus notius* (Bailey and Hubbs, 1949)
## (Class Teleostei, Order Perciformes, Family Centrarchidae)

**Etymology:** From the Greek *micropterus*, meaning small fin, and the Greek *notius*, for south, referring to the distribution.

**Size:** Seldom exceeds 12 inches (30.48 centimeters).

**Description:** Round body, dark olive fading to dun and lighter on the underside with dark vertical bars along the lateral lines, and a distinct dark blotch where the lateral line meets the tail fin. Males display a turquoise coloring on cheeks and breast. Relatively small mouth. Has teeth on its tongue. Separation between anterior and posterior dorsal fins.

**Range:** Limited range. Originated in the Suwannee and Ochlocknee rivers and introduced into the St. Marks and Aucilla/Wacissa river systems.

**Food sources:** Insects, small crustaceans, crayfish, and small fish.

**Characteristics:** Prefers flowing water with vegetation. Hangs out near logs and debris where there is a noticeable current.

**Note:** FNAI ranking G3/S3 (Globally: Rare/Statewide: Rare).

# Florida Largemouth Bass, *Micropterus salmoides floridanus* (Bailey and Hubbs, 1949)
## (Class Teleostei, Order Perciformes, Family Centrarchidae)

Also known as bigmouth, black bass, chub, Florida bass, and green trout.

**Etymology:** From the Greek *micropterus*, meaning small fin, and *salmo*, meaning trout. *Floridanus* refers to the state of Florida.

**Size:** Medium to large fish averaging 18 inches (45.72 centimeters) but capable of growing up to 24 inches (60.96 centimeters) and exceeding 20 pounds (9.07 kilograms).

**Description:** Bright to olive green with a lateral (horizontal) stripe down the sides; underside from light green to cream to white. Upper jaw reaches beyond the eye. Has needle-like inward-facing teeth on its lips. Dorsal fin is divided with nine anterior spines and twelve to thirteen posterior soft rays.

**Range:** Originally found only in Florida, has spread to and been stocked in other states and countries. Inhabits brackish to freshwater habitats with aquatic vegetation. Prefers depths less than 20 feet (6 meters).

**Food sources:** Food source depends on the size of the fish, ranging from zooplankton and small crustaceans to other fish, frogs, and turtles.

**Characteristics:** Nests in quiet, well-vegetated areas. Females lay thousands of eggs. Males then chase the females away and guard the nest and fry for several days after they have hatched.

**Note:** The largemouth bass is the state freshwater fish of Florida, Alabama, and Georgia (although ours are bigger).

# Black Crappie, *Pomoxis nigromaculatus* (Lesueur in Cuvier and Valenciennes, 1829)
## (Class Teleostei, Order Perciformes, Family Centrarchidae)

Also known as calico bass, speckled perch, and specks.

**Etymology:** *Pomoxis* from the Greek word for sharp, referring to the spines on the fish's gill covers, and *nigromaculatus* is Latin for black-spotted. The common name crappie derives from the French word *crapet*, which refers to sunfish.

**Size:** Up to 20 inches (50.8 centimeters) in length.

**Description:** Silvery olive to light gray back and sides with irregular black blotches. Large mouth. Large dorsal and anal fins are almost the same size. Fins have rows of spots.

**Range:** Clear, slow-moving water such as lakes and slow rivers throughout North America.

**Food sources:** Mostly insects and small crustaceans, but also small fish.

**Characteristics:** Travels in schools. Builds nests in the spring when water temperature reaches above 60 degrees Fahrenheit (16 degrees Celsius). Males guard the eggs and fry.

# *Tilapia, *Oreochromis aureus* (Steindachner, 1864)
## (Class Teleostei, Order Perciformes, Family Cichlidae)

Also known as blue tilapia, tilapia azul.

**Etymology:** *Oreos* is Greek for mountain or from the mountains, and *chromos* from the Greek for color. *Aureus* is also Greek and means golden.

The common name tilapia derives from a regional South African word for fish, *tlhapi*. The word is from the Setswana language of the Tswana tribes of Botswana and South Africa. Andrew Smith, the first Superintendent of the South African Museum in Cape Town, led the Expedition for Exploring Central Africa from 1834 to 1836. He came up with many names for the animals he encountered, but the reasons for the names was often unrecorded or lost, and the names subsequently changed to follow standard taxonomy and nomenclature.

**Size:** Body length averages 5–8 inches (12.7–20.32 centimeters) and 6 pounds (2.72 kilograms). Florida's record tilapia was more than 12 inches (30.48 centimeters) and weighed just under 10 pounds (4.54 kilograms)!

**Description:** Looks very similar to fishes in the family Centrarchidae (sunfishes). Tilapia have one set of nostrils (or nares, used for smelling only) on each side of the nose, while the Centrarchidae have two. Round, stout fish having a bluish gray body and lighter underside. Red edge to tail (caudal) fin. Males ready for breeding display a brilliant blue tint on their heads and a red edge along the dorsal fin. Females have a lighter red or orange caudal fin edge. Females ready for breeding also display a red tint along the edge of the dorsal fin.

**Range:** Throughout Florida. Native to Africa and Western Asia.

**Food sources:** Algae, phytoplankton and zooplankton, and detritus.

**Characteristics:** Schooling fish. During breeding, the male clears a sandy area and entices a female to lay her eggs. As soon as the male fertilizes the eggs, the female takes the eggs into her mouth and swims away. The male remains to guard and defend the nest and continue breeding. The fry hatch and remain with the female for around three months, hiding in her mouth when disturbed.

One really cool feature of the tilapia is the gill rakers, tiny filters located in the gills that "rake" food particles, such as phytoplankton, from the water.

Cold tolerant to between 50–86 degrees Fahrenheit (10–30 degrees Celsius) and heat tolerant to 100 degrees Farenheit (40 degrees Celsius)! Able to breed in freshwater as well as brackish water. And readily hybridizes with other tilapia. This fish is a super-competitor, displacing native fish populations by moving in, multiplying, and eating all the food. Known as a particularly delicious fish.

# Striped Bass, *Morone saxatilis* (Walbaum, 1792)
## (Class Teleostei, Order Perciformes, Family Moronidae)

Also known as striper or rockfish.

**Etymology:** *Morone* derivation unknown. *Saxatilis* is Latin for living among the rocks.

**Size:** Grows to 9–20 inches (22.86–50.8 centimeters) in length. Grow quickly and can reach 40 pounds (18.14 kilograms) or larger.

**Description:** A light-olive to silvery fish fading to white on the underside, with prominent irregular stripes running the length of the body. The striped bass is longer and sleeker than other bass and has a longer head and a small mouth. Dorsal fin is clearly separated into spiny anterior portion and soft-ray posterior portion.

**Range:** Prefers rivers with clear warm water along the Atlantic and Gulf coasts.

**Food sources:** Feeds on small fish and crustaceans.

**Characteristics:** A member of the seabass family, unlike other bass, which are sunfish. Anadromous in other parts of the country, living in brackish waters and traveling up streams to spawn. Potamodromous in Florida, migrating entirely within freshwater systems for spawning. As a euryhaline organism, striped bass can tolerate a wide range of salinity. Iteroparous, meaning they can spawn more than once (unlike fish that are semelparous, meaning they spawn only once before dying).

Striped bass can live for thirty years.

# Sunshine Bass, Morone saxatilis x Morone chrysops, Morone hybrid
## (Class Teleostei, Order Perciformes, Family Moronidae)

Also known as hybrid striped bass, wiper, whiterock bass, Cherokee bass.

**Etymology:** The use of two names indicates that this is a hybrid of the two named species. *Morone* derivation unknown. *Saxatilis* is Latin for living among the rocks. *Chrysops* comes from Greek *chrys-*, meaning golden, and *-ops*, meaning eye.

**Size:** Grows to 20 inches (50.8 centimeters) in length. Can reach 15 pounds (6.8 kilograms).

**Description:** A light silvery fish fading to white on underside, with prominent dark stripes running the length of the body. The stripes may be broken in places. The deep body of the sunshine bass is stouter than that of the striped bass, but it is difficult to tell the difference between the hybrid and the parent species. Dorsal fin is clearly separated into spiny anterior portion and soft-ray posterior portion.

**Range:** Because this is a hybrid, there is no native range.

**Food sources:** Feeds on small fish and zooplankton.

**Characteristics:** The sunshine bass was created in Florida in 1973, the fertilization of the eggs of a female white bass with the sperm of a male striped bass. The original cross, called a palmetto bass, was between the eggs of a female striped bass and the sperm of a male white bass and was created in South Carolina in 1965. Sunshine bass were developed to add to the sports fish population. Known for rapid growth, but not growing as large as striped bass. Hybrid bass are capable of breeding with the parent species. Hybrid bass grow quickly but live for only five or six years.

**Note:** You can encounter sunshine bass in large numbers in the cool basin of Silver Glen Springs in the Ocala National Forest during the summer.

# Darter, *Etheostoma* Rafinesque, 1819

**Coastal Darter, *Etheostoma colorosum* (Suttkus and Bailey, 1993)**

Gulf Coastal Plain from the Perdido River to the Choctawhatchee River in Alabama and the Florida panhandle.

**Brown Darter, *Etheostoma edwini* (Hubbs and Cannon, 1935)**

From the Perdido River in Alabama east to the St. Johns River and north in a broad area between Alabama and Georgia including northern Florida and panhandle.

**Swamp Darter, *Etheostoma fusiforme* (Girard, 1854)**

Illustrated above. Atlantic and Gulf Coastal Plains from southern Maine to Louisiana and west to eastern Oklahoma and throughout Florida.

## (Class Teleostei, Order Perciformes, Family Percidae)

**Etymology:** From Greek *etheo* for filter and *stoma* for mouth. *Colorosum* for colorful. *Edwini* after Edwin P. Creaser, who provided specimens of the brown darter for identification. *Fusiforme* is from the Latin *fusus* for spindle and *forma* for shape (spindle-shaped).

**Size:** Very small fish, 1.2–2.3 inches (3.05–5.84 centimeters) long.

**Description:** The coastal darter is the color of light sand with darker brown markings. The brown darter is light whitish-beige to yellow with darker tan and reddish-brown markings and a dark brown or black broad lateral line low along the sides. The swamp darter has darker coloring and a lighter distinctive lateral line that arches along the fish's body. Fins have rows of colorful markings.

**Food sources:** Aquatic insects and larvae.

**Characteristics:** Prefers clear, moving freshwater creeks and streams. The brown darter and the swamp darter are found in and among aquatic vegetation, whereas the coastal darter can be found in more open sandy areas. The brown darter can also be found under rocks and ledges in springs, basins, and runs.

Eggs are deposited on plants and not guarded.

Darters do not have bladders like many other fish. This allows them to remain on the bottom and hop around. When darters do swim, they maintain an upright position for very short periods of time.

**Note:** The author observes swamp darters in abundance in the basin at Eagle's Nest sink in Chassahowitzka Wildlife Management Area. These curious little fish will chase the end of a pine straw pulled along the bottom, a very entertaining diversion during decompression.

# Freshwater Flounder, *Trinectes maculatus* (Bloch and Schneider, 1801)
## (Class Teleostei, Order Pleuronectiformes, Family Achiridae)

Also known as hogchoker and sole.

**Etymology:** *Trinectes*, meaning three-swimmer for the dorsal, ventral, and caudal fins, and *maculatus*, Latin meaning spotted or blotched, for the color pattern of the top (eyed) side.

**Size:** Maximum body length of 5 inches (12.7 centimeters).

**Description:** A small, flat fish with both eyes on one side of its head. Lacks pectoral fins. Swims on its side with both eyes up. Top of body blends in with surroundings, while the bottom is light cream to white.

**Range:** Lives on sandy bottoms of streams and spring basins. Found in both salt and freshwater environments. Can burrow in the substrate.

**Food sources:** Macroinvertebrates and tubificid worms, among other small things.

**Characteristics:** Catadromous, adults live in freshwater and move to saltwater to spawn. The flounders we find in fresh water are juvenile fish. Sometimes, but rarely, it will rest on a diver's hand. When molested, the hogchoker takes a defensive position, darting at the diver's face before swimming a short distance away to rest.

**Note:** Historical sources report freshwater flounder were once so prolific they were used as food for pigs. If swallowed tail-first, the fin rays would catch in the hog's throat, causing the hog to choke.

# Channel Catfish, *Ictalurus punctatus* (Rafinesque, 1818)

## (Class Teleostei, Order Siluriformes, Family Ictaluridae)

Also known as spotted cat, blue channel cat, river catfish.

**Etymology:** From the Greek *Ictalurus, ichthys* meaning fish and *ailouros*, meaning cat, and *punctatus* Latin for little spots or spotted.

**Size:** Average 2 feet (61 centimeters) but can grow larger.

**Description:** In Florida's fresh water, channel catfish are cylindrical and lack scales. They are typically blue-gray to gray-green with scattered black spots and a white belly. Juveniles and larger channel catfish, also white across the belly, have a darker blue, almost black coloration on the back. Males become very dark during the four- to five-week spawning season and develop a thick pad on the top of their head. The channel catfish is noted for its small, narrow head. All catfish are distinguished by the presence of barbels around their mouths, four on the bottom, and two on the top of the mouth. The barbels allow the catfish to find food in the bottom sediment of lakes and rivers. The channel catfish has a rounded anal fin with twenty-four to twenty-nine rays and scattered black spots along its back and sides, whereas the blue catfish has a squared-off anal fin with thirty to thirty-five rays and typically lacks dark spots.

**Range:** Throughout mainland Florida in rivers, streams, lakes, reservoirs, and ponds with a preference for current and deep water.

**Food sources:** Include aquatic insects, insect larvae, crayfish, mollusks, crustaceans, and fish. Nocturnal feeders, channel cats use taste buds in their barbels and throughout the skin to locate prey.

**Characteristics:** Spawning occurs for four to five weeks in the spring and early summer in rivers and streams when waters warm to 70–85 degrees Fahrenheit (21–29 degrees Celsius). They also spawn in larger lakes where suitable habitat is available. Eggs are deposited in nests secluded under rocks or logs. The male selects the site, clears the nest, and attracts a female. The female channel catfish may lay from 2,000 to 21,000 eggs depending on the age and size of the fish. The eggs hatch in four to six days depending on water temperature; higher temperatures can accelerate egg development. The male then guards the eggs and young. Males protect the fry until they leave the nest in about a week.

In Florida, the channel catfish can grow to 45 pounds (20.4 kilograms), although weight generally averages 10 pounds (4.5 kilograms). Studies indicate fourteen years as the average maximum age, but some channel catfish live as long as twenty years.

# Frogs and Salamanders, Class Amphibia

## Southern Cricket Frog, *Acris gryllus* (LeConte, 1825)

### (Class Amphibia, Order Anura, Family Hylidae)

**Etymology:** *Acris* from Greek *acr*, meaning sharp, and *is*, meaning equal. *Gryllus* from the Greek word *grill* for a cricket.

**Size:** 0.6–1.3 inch (1.52–3.3 centimeters).

**Description:** Warty skin with a variety of colors and patterns. Brown, gray, or green skin mottled with darker splotches and specks. Has a distinctive stripe starting as a triangle with corners behind each eye and toward another stripe running down the back. A similar stripe runs down the back of each thigh. Pointy snout.

**Range:** Atlantic and Gulf Coastal Plain and throughout Florida.

**Food sources:** Small invertebrates.

**Characteristics:** Their call is a series of clicks. Live near water, preferring shallow, slow-moving water. Males are territorial. Females deposit eggs in clumps attached to vegetation underwater or along the bottom.

## Green Treefrog, *Hyla cinerea* (Schneider, 1799)
### (Class Amphibia, Order Anura, Family Ranidae)

**Etymology:** *Hyla* from Greek, meaning forest, and *cinerea*, meaning the color of cinders.

**Size:** 1.3–2.3 inches (3.3–5.84 centimeters).

**Description:** Smooth-skinned green frog with long legs. Wide range of green, from yellow-green to gray-green, sometimes having small specks of yellow. Underside is white to creamy beige. Has a distinct line running down either side of the body. Has large, sticky toepads.

**Range:** Southeastern United States from southern Maryland through the coastal plains, Arkansas and into Texas. Throughout Florida.

**Food sources:** Small insects and other invertebrates.

**Characteristics:** Call is a loud, quick buzz-chirp that becomes more frequent just prior to rain. Likes open areas near water and prefers to be in vegetation. Commonly found tucked into plants and structures in backyards.

## Bullfrog, *Lithobates catesbeianus* (Shaw, 1802)
### (Class Amphibia, Order Anura, Family Ranidae)

Also called the American bullfrog.

**Etymology:** *Lithobates* comes from Greek *litho*, meaning stone, and *bates*, one that walks. *Catesbeiana* comes from the name Mark Catesby (1683–1749), an English naturalist who provided specimens for identification and created detailed watercolor illustrations.

**Size:** Up to 12 inches (30.48 centimeters) long.

**Description:** Warty to smooth-skinned frog, dark green to brown on back, sometimes with mottling, creamy white on underside. Rounded nose. Differs from the pig frog by lacking a light stripe across its rear end and having the longest toe extending slightly beyond the webbing of its back foot.

**Range:** In Florida freshwater lakes, ponds, and creeks ranging as far south as Lake Okeechobee.

**Food sources:** Anything smaller than itself.

**Characteristics:** The bullfrog has a loud, deep, resonating call. Females lay eggs in clumps floating on the water's surface. Bullfrog tadpoles can get very large, around 5 inches (12.7 centimeters) long. Bullfrogs can live as long as ten years.

**Note:** The hind legs of the bullfrog are considered by some to be a delicacy. They are usually served fried.

# Green Frog, *Lithobates clamitans* (Latreille in Sonnini de Manoncourt and Latreille, 1801)
## (Class Amphibia, Order Anura, Family Ranidae)

**Etymology:** *Lithobates* comes from Greek *litho*, meaning stone, and *bates*, one that walks. *Clamitans* comes from Latin, meaning loud or noisy.

**Size:** Grow to 2–4 inches (5.08–10.16 centimeters).

**Description:** Smooth skin, bright green, and green-tinted shades of bronze, brown, and yellow, with small black spots or splotches. White underside with darker spots. The tympanum (eardrum) is large. Males have larger tympanums than females. Prominent ridges on either side of the backbone (called the dorsolateral ridges, lateral folds or lateral lines), run from behind each eye to the middle of the back.

**Range:** Wet habitats in eastern North America, from Canada south through northern Florida, and west into Texas.

**Food sources:** Tadpoles eat algae and zooplankton. Adults eat insects and other invertebrates, and the occasional small vertebrates.

**Characteristics:** The call is short and resonating, sounding like a plucked rubber-band banjo.

**Notes:** Green frogs are occasionally hunted for their legs.

### Bronze Frog, *Lithobates clamitans clamitans* (Latreille in Sonnini de Manoncourt and Latreille, 1801)

Illustrated above. The specific name is written twice to indicate that this is the type for the species. This subspecies is more bronze or brown tinted, and the markings are more muted. Found in north Florida. The bronze frog is nocturnal, while the green frog can be active either day or night.

# Pig Frog, *Lithobates grylio* (Stejneger, 1901)
## (Class Amphibia, Order Anura, Family Ranidae)

Also known as Florida bullfrog and Everglades bullfrog.

**Etymology:** *Lithobates* comes from Greek *litho*, meaning stone, and *bates*, one that walks, treads, or climbs. *Grylio* comes from Latin *gryllus* for cricket or grasshopper.

**Size:** Up to 8 inches (20.32 centimeters) long.

**Description:** Smooth skin, light green back with black specks, lightly mottled creamy white on bottom. Light stripe across hind end. Hind foot's webbing extends to the end of the longest toe.

**Range:** Throughout Florida.

**Food sources:** Anything that it can fit in its mouth but often crayfish.

**Characteristics:** The frog legs on the menu might be those of the pig frog. In the spring, the pig frog makes a loud deep call that is often mistaken for an alligator call. The call of the pig frog is often compared to that of a pig's grunt.

# River Frog, *Lithobates heckscheri* (Wright, 1924)
## (Class Amphibia, Order Anura, Family Ranidae)

Also known as Heckscher's frog and alligator frog.

**Etymology:** *Lithobates* comes from Greek *litho*, meaning stone, and *bates*, one that walks. *Heckscheri* is named for the Heckscher Foundation for the Advancement of Research, established in 1920 by August Heckscher (1848–1941) at Cornell University. A. H. Wright, who described the species in 1924, received funding from the Foundation to work in the Okefenokee Swamp.

**Size:** 3–5.3 inches (7.62–13.46 centimeters) in length

**Description:** Wrinkly skinned large frog with beige to muddy dark green or brown on back, belly dusky gray with white vermiculation (irregular, wavy markings). White spots on lower jaw.

**Range:** Throughout north and north central Florida near freshwater rivers and swamps. Also found in Mississippi, Georgia, Alabama, and South Carolina.

**Food sources:** Mostly insects and other invertebrates, occasionally small vertebrates such as other frogs.

**Characteristics:** The river frog lays its eggs as a surface film on the water. The tadpoles of river frogs grow up to 5 inches (12.7 centimeters) long, have a black edge on the top and bottom of the tail, and distinctive red eyes. The tadpoles swim together in schools. Adults play dead when threatened and secrete a toxic substance through the skin that leave an unpleasant odor on anything that touches it. Their call is a low-pitched grunt or snore.

# Southern Leopard Frog, *Lithobates sphenocephalus* (Cope, 1886)

## (Class Amphibia, Order Anura, Family Ranidae)

**Etymology:** *Lithobates* comes from Greek *litho*, meaning stone, and *bates*, one that walks, treads, or climbs. *Sphenocephalus* is Greek for wedge-headed.

**Size:** Averages 2.3–3.5 inches (5.84–8.89 centimeters) but can reach 5 inches (12.7 centimeters) long.

**Description:** Smooth, light-brown or light-green skin with dark brown spots. The prominent ridges on either side of the backbone (called the dorsolateral ridges, lateral folds or lateral lines) are light beige. Identified by a light spot in the middle of the tympanum (ear).

**Range:** Throughout Florida in grasses and vegetation next to springs, ponds, and creeks.

**Food sources:** Carnivorous, will eat anything that fits in its mouth.

**Characteristics:** Will call out and leap around 3 feet (1 meter) into the water when disturbed. Eggs are laid as a mass, typically attached to submerged vegetation. Call is a low chuckle or the sound made by running one's thumb along a balloon.

# Two-toed Amphiuma, *Amphiuma means Garden in Smith, 1821*

## (Class Amphibia, Order Caudata, Family Amphiumidae)

Also called mud eels, fish eels, ditch eels, Conger eels, and Congo eels.

**Etymology:** From the Greek *amphi*, meaning around or both sides, and *pneuma*, meaning to breathe (under the mistaken idea that salamanders can breathe both air and water). *Means* refers to an unknown person named Means.

**Size:** Adults average 1.31–2.95 feet (0.4–0.9 meter). Can grow greater than 3 feet (0.91 meter) in length.

**Description:** Dark gray to black, smooth, shiny skin with tiny front and hind legs, each with two toes. Has gill slits but no external gills.

**Range:** Throughout Florida northward along the Atlantic Coastal Plain as far as Virginia. Found in a variety of habitats, including swamps, rivers, and ditches; often prefers areas of heavy vegetation.

**Food sources:** Insects, crayfish, mollusks, and small fish.

**Characteristics:** Primarily nocturnal, the amphiuma is very secretive and rarely seen. One of three large species of aquatic salamanders found in Florida (the others are the greater siren, *S. lacertina,* and the reticulated siren, *S. reticulata*). A food source for birds, snakes, otters, and alligators.

Reproduces via eggs using internal fertilization. They lay eggs under rocks and logs in moist areas near or in water. Often lay in alligator nests. Eggs look like a string of beads in a tube.

Most interesting is the ability of these salamanders to bury into the mud, create a cocoon, and go into a dormant state, referred to as aestivation. During aestivation, the salamander lives off its fat reserves. This habit allows the amphiuma to live in either permanent or temporary water bodies.

Please note that these guys will bite if handled.

# Peninsula Newt, *Notophthalmus viridescens piaropicola* (Schwartz and Duellman, 1952)

## (Class Amphibia, Order Caudata, Family Salamandridae)

**Etymology:** *Notophthalmus* from Greek *noto* for back and *ophthalmos* for the eye. *Viridescens* comes from Latin *viridis* for green, referring to a greenish tint often found in this species. *Piaropicola* comes from Greek *Piaropus*, the former genus name for water hyacinth, and refers to the newt's preference for living among water hyacinths.

**Size:** Grows to almost 5 inches (12.7 centimeters) long.

**Description:** With or without external gills. Darker than the eastern newt and lacks the spots found on other newts. Dull brown or reddish-brown newts are those that have recently transformed from larval stage to adult. Adults are dark brown, almost black.

**Range:** Peninsular Florida south of Alachua County in aquatic environments among vegetation.

**Food sources:** Insects, worms, crustaceans, small fish, small eggs, and other small vertebrates.

**Characteristics:** Newts typically have three life stages: an aquatic larval stage (tadpole), an eft (juvenile, terrestrial) stage, and finally an aquatic adult stage. The peninsula newt skips the juvenile eft stage.

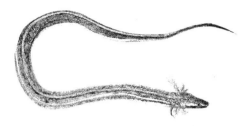

# Narrow-striped Dwarf Siren, *Pseudobranchus axanthus axanthus* Netting and Goin, 1942

## (Class Amphibia, Order Caudata, Family Sirenidae)

Also called the southern dwarf siren.

**Etymology:** *Pseudobranchus* comes from Greek *pseudes*, meaning false or deceptive, and *branchia*, meaning gills. *Axanthus* from Greek *a*, meaning without, and *xanthus*, meaning yellow.

**Size:** 4–9 inches (10.16–22.86 centimeters) in length.

**Description:** Small, slender salamander frequently mistaken for an eel. Blunt snout. Two thin front legs with three toes. No hind legs. No eyelids. Primarily dark or muddy colors with narrow, dark stripes on its back and sides. The northern dwarf siren typically has a well-defined yellow stripe down each side.

**Range:** Cypress and gum ponds and other shallow wetlands throughout peninsular Florida in and south of the St. Johns and Withlacoochee (southern) river drainages. Can be found among water hyacinths.

**Food sources:** Small invertebrates and worms.

**Characteristics:** Lays eggs in water. Like the larger salamanders (amphiumas and greater siren), the dwarf siren can aestivate by burrowing into bottom sediments when its aquatic home dries up. They remain buried until the wetland refills.

# Northern Dwarf Siren, *Pseudobranchus striatus* (LeConte, 1824)

## (Class Amphibia, Order Caudata, Family Sirenidae)

**Etymology:** *Pseudobranchus* comes from Greek *pseudes*, meaning false or deceptive, and *branchia*, meaning gills. *Striatus* is Latin, meaning striped.

**Size:** 4-9 inches (10.16–22.86 centimeters) in length.

**Description:** Small salamander frequently mistaken for an eel. Blunt snout. Two thin front legs with three toes. No hind legs. Brown, black or gray with distinct yellow or tan stripes on its back and sides. No eyelids. Belly is dark grey to black with spots.

**Range:** Adults prefer the muck and bottom vegetation in cypress and gum ponds, ditches, swamps, and marshes throughout the panhandle and northern peninsula.

**Food sources:** Very small invertebrates and worms.

**Characteristics:** Lays eggs in water. Also capable of aestivation.

# Greater Siren, *Siren lacertina* Linnaeus, 1767

## (Class Amphibia, Order Caudata, Family Sirenidae)

Also called mud eel or ditch eel.

**Etymology:** *Siren* from the Greek mythological mermaids who lured sailors to their deaths and the Latin *lacerta* for lizard.

**Size:** Typically grows to 1.5–2.5 feet (45.72–76.2 centimeters) in length; recorded maximum is 3.2 feet (97.54 centimeters).

**Description:** Dark gray-green to black, typically with gold flecks. Smooth, shiny skin. No hind legs. Small front legs with four toes on each limb. External gills. No eyelids.

**Range:** Throughout Florida northward along Atlantic Coastal Plain as far as Virginia. Found in a variety of habitats including swamps, rivers, and ditches. Seems to prefer heavily vegetated areas.

**Food sources:** Insects, crayfish, mollusks, and small fish. May be partially herbivorous.

**Characteristics:** Primarily nocturnal, the siren is very secretive and rarely seen. One of the largest salamanders in the world and one of three large species found in Florida (others are the reticulated siren and two-toed amphiuma). A food source for birds, snakes, otters, and alligators. Reproduces via eggs, although little is known of the reproductive habits. Like the two-toed amphiuma, the greater siren is also capable of aestivation, allowing it to inhabit both permanent and temporary water bodies. Said to make a loud squeak when handled and also known to make clicking sounds.

# Alligators, Snakes, and Turtles, Class Reptilia

## Alligators, Order Crocodilia

## American Alligator, *Alligator mississippiensis* (Daudin, 1802)
### (Class Reptilia, Order Crocodilia, Family Alligatoridae)

Also known as alligator, Florida alligator, gator, Louisiana alligator, and Mississippi alligator.

**Etymology:** From Latin *lagarto* for lizard, *mississippiensis* for of or from Mississippi. Order name Crocodilia is synonymous with Crocodylia.

**Size:** Males can grow to 14 feet (4.27 meters). Females grow to approximately 10 feet (3.05 meters).

**Description:** One of the largest reptiles in North America. Coloring is dark olive to black with lighter undersides. The alligator has a broad head with a flattened snout, a thick neck and a thick powerful tail. Juvenile is brightly banded, black and yellow, and gradually loses the bands as it grows.

**Range:** Throughout Florida and southeastern United States.

**Food sources:** Pretty much anything it can fit in its mouth. Larger gators can eat larger prey.

**Characteristics:** Males are larger than females. The alligator "calls" or bellows during mating season and to establish territory. The sound is like a loud bullfrog or a low, sustained rumble or roar. Males also vibrate the water to attract females. May dig dens in soft soil at the edge of the water. If a water body dries up, it is able to travel over land in search of a new home. Known to inhabit small caverns, such as the cavern at Bonnet Spring in Peacock Springs State Park, where a reputed 12-foot (3.7 meters) female alligator lived and raised her young. Female alligators will protect their young. If you find a bundle of babies, the mama is sure to be nearby watching you. Alligators are frequently found in the freshwater lakes and springs cave divers enjoy throughout Florida. "El lagarto" is a very large lizard!

**Note:** Listed by the USFWS as threatened due to similarity of appearance to other croco-dilians and by the FWC as FT(S/A) (Federally designated Threatened. Due to similarity of appearance to another listed species, listed for protection.) FNAI ranking G5/S4 (Glob-ally: Demonstrably Secure/Statewide: Apparently Secure).

## A Rather Maudlin' Cave Adventure, by Buford Pruitt, Jr.

A lady I worked with came into my office one day and said, "Buford, you're a caver. My son Ty wants to see a cave. Will you take us caving?" Of course, I agreed.

At the appointed day, time, and place, not one mom but two showed up, with not one little boy but three in tow, plus a girl. I took them to Rather Maudlin' Cave, which has a plan view like a capital letter "H." I took them into its entrance at the lower end of the left H-leg and gave them a guided tour, pointing out features like stalactites, bats, and cave crickets, and explained how the cave formed and why the stalactites and critters were there.

They then wanted to see the rest of the cave, which involved a belly crawl through the body-tube cross-tunnel. I had seen glass jars and old boards in that passage, so I told them I needed to check it out first to make sure it was safe. I crawled to and up on top of the pile of debris, in conditions tight enough that I had to squeeze against the ceiling to get there. Fortunately, the boards didn't have any nails and all the glass was unbroken, and then I noticed what looked like an old tire underneath it all.

Suddenly, I realized the "tire" had big yellow blotches on it. It dawned on me that it was actually a five-foot-long alligator asleep for the winter, now merely inches from my soft underbelly. I slowly crawled backward, hoping not to awaken the predator. Squirming back out into the taller passage, I rolled over, sat up, and calmly said to my eager audience, "Um, there's an alligator in there."

Both moms immediately began screaming and ran as fast as they could toward the entrance. The three boys saw them bailing and they, too, began yelling and running for the exit. The little girl, however, just stood there and watched them go, astonished. She then turned to me and with a grin asked, "Can I go see the alligator?"

The others returned when I told them that El Lagarto was brumating (the reptile equivalent of hibernation), and one by one, they all crawled down that pregnant passage to see the reptile. But it was a brave little girl who went first.

So, gals, don't ever let anyone convince you that boys are braver than girls. Bravery is individual.

# Snakes, Order Squamata

## Eastern Indigo Snake, *Drymarchon couperi* (Holbrook, 1842)
### (Class Reptilia, Order Squamata, Family Colubridae)

Also known as a gopher snake.

Scientific name synonymous with *Drymarchon corais couperi*.

**Etymology:** *Drymarchon* comes from the Greek word *drymos* for forest, and *archon*, meaning ruler. *Couperi* comes from a J. Hamilton Couper, who wrote to John Holbrook about the snake.

**Size:** Can grow to more than 8 feet (2.44 meters) long.

**Description:** Thick-bodied, iridescent, bluish-black snake. Can have reddish or tan chin and neck.

**Range:** Throughout Florida and southern Georgia.

**Food sources:** Other snakes, frogs, lizards, turtles, birds, small mammals, and other small animals.

**Characteristics:** Nonvenomous. One of the longest snakes native to North America. Known to live in gopher tortoise burrows, but searches for food in forested areas.

**Note:** Listed by USFWS as Threatened (and by the FWC as FT, which means Federally designated Threatened). FNAI ranking for Eastern Indigo Snake is G3/S3 (Globally: Rare/Statewide: Rare).

## Rainbow Snake, *Farancia erytrogramma erytrogramma* (Palissot de Beauvois, 1801)

### (Class Reptilia, Order Squamata, Family Colubridae)

Also known as eel moccasin.

**Etymology:** From the Greek *erythron*, meaning red, and *gramma*, meaning line. Origin of the name *Farancia* is unknown. The specific name is written twice to indicate that this is the type for the species.

**Size:** Can be large, up to around 5 feet (1.52 meters) long.

**Description:** Brightly colored snake having three narrow red lines on a glossy black body. Belly is red or pink with black spots, creating a line or lines along the belly. Larger rainbow snakes may also have bright yellow coloration along the sides and on the head. Smooth scales.

**Range:** Atlantic and Gulf Coastal Plains, ranging into central Florida, mainly in and around aquatic vegetation of swamps and habitats with flowing water. Occasionally seen out of the water when moving between water bodies.

**Food sources:** Primarily eels, leading to their common name, eel moccasin.

**Characteristics:** Beautiful, very secretive, nonvenomous, nonaggressive aquatic snake. Males are smaller than females.

# Plain-bellied Watersnake, *Nerodia erythrogaster* (Forster in Bossu, 1771)

## (Class Reptilia, Order Squamata, Family Colubridae)

Red-bellied Watersnake, *Nerodia erythrogaster erythrogaster* (Forster in Bossu, 1771)

Once believed to be a subspecies, now understood to be a color variant having a bright red underside. The specific name is written twice to indicate that this is the type for the species.

Yellow-bellied Watersnake, *Nerodia erythrogaster flavigaster* (Forster in Bossu, 1771)

Also once believed to be a subspecies, now understood to be a color variant having a more gray-tinted upper body with a yellow, yellowish-orange underside.

**Etymology:** From Greek *neros*, meaning flowing or liquid, and *dia*, meaning through. *Erythrogaster* from Greek *eruthrós*, meaning red, and *gaster*, meaning belly or stomach. *Flavigaster* from *flavus*, meaning golden or yellow, and *gaster*, meaning belly or stomach.

**Size:** Grow to 28–48 inches (71.12–121.92 centimeters) long.

**Description:** An olive to reddish to dark brown snake having a creamy white belly without markings. The scales are keeled (not glossy) and the pupil of the eye is round.

**Range:** Water bodies in the southeastern United States south into north Florida.

**Food sources:** Crustaceans, small fish, and other small vertebrates.

**Characteristics:** Aquatic snake, common in west Florida rivers. Will flatten its head and strike as a defensive posture.

**Notes:** Nonvenomous.

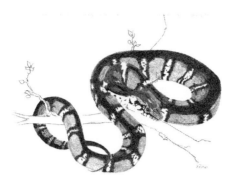

# Southern Watersnakes, *Nerodia fasciata* (Linnaeus, 1766)

**Banded Watersnake, *Nerodia fasciata fasciata* (Linnaeus, 1766)**

**Florida Watersnake, *Nerodia fasciata pictiventris* Cope, 1895**

## (Class Reptilia, Order Squamata, Family Colubridae)

**Etymology:** From Greek *neros*, meaning flowing or liquid, and *dia*, meaning through. *Fasciata* comes from Latin *fascia*, meaning band, stripe, or strip. *Pictiventris* from Latin *pictus*, meaning painted or embroidered, and *ventris*, meaning of the belly.

For *Nerodia fasciata fasciata*, the specific name is written twice to indicate that this is the type for the species.

**Size:** Grows to 2–4 feet (0.61–1.22 meters) long.

**Description:** Medium-sized snake with black, brown, or red crossbands (bands that reach around the body but not around the belly) on a tan, beige, reddish, or gray background. Belly is light with spots. Scales are keeled, having a ridge down the middle. A dark stripe extends from the eye to the jaw. Pupil of the eye is round.

**Range:** Florida panhandle.

**Food sources:** Fish, frogs, salamanders, crayfish, tadpoles.

**Characteristics:** The banded watersnake rests among the branches of trees, often overhanging water. If disturbed, the snake drops into the water and swims away. If a canoeist happens to be beneath the branch, the snake may fall into the canoe. Often confused with the cottonmouth. From above, eyes of the Florida banded watersnake are visible, while eyes of the cottonmouth are hidden. Nonvenomous but will bite to defend itself. Secretes a noxious musk when threatened.

# Brown Watersnake, *Nerodia taxispilota* (Holbrook, 1838)

## (Class Reptilia, Order Squamata, Family Colubridae)

**Etymology:** From Greek *neros*, meaning flowing or liquid, and *dia*, meaning through. *Taxispilota* from Greek *taxis*, for regular arrangement, and *spilos*, for spot or stain.

**Size:** Typical size is 2.5–5 feet (0.76–1.52 meters) long.

**Description:** Brown body with darker brown squarish blotches. Head is large and triangular. Scales are keeled, with a ridge down the middle. Often confused with the cottonmouth. From above, eyes of the brown watersnake are visible, while eyes of the cottonmouth are hidden. The pupil of the eye is round.

**Range:** Throughout Florida, north as far as southwest Virginia.

**Food sources:** Fish, small frogs, and carrion.

**Characteristics:** Nonvenomous. Males are much smaller than females. Climbs high in trees and drops out if disturbed. Often found along the shore of water bodies coiled in overhanging branches.

## Gray Rat Snake, *Pantherophis spiloides* (A. M. C. Dumeril, Bibron and A. H. A. Dumeril, 1854)

### (Class Reptilia, Order Squamata, Family Colubridae)

Also known as the central rat snake.

**Etymology:** From Greek *panther*, meaning—wait for it—panther and *ophis*, meaning serpent. *Spilos* is Greek for spot or speck, and *eidos* is Greek for form or type.

**Size:** Typically, 3–6 feet (0.91–1.83 meters) long.

**Description:** Long, slender, gray snake with dark blotches, and a lighter beige, grayish belly. Pupil of eye is round.

**Range:** Florida panhandle.

**Food sources:** Small reptiles, rodents, birds, and bird eggs.

**Characteristics:** Nonvenomous. Primarily nocturnal. Excellent tree climber.

# Eastern Ribbonsnakes, *Thamnophis saurita* (Linnaeus, 1766)

**Blue-striped Ribbonsnake, *Thamnophis saurita nitae* Rossman, 1963**

**Peninsula Ribbonsnake, *Thamnophis saurita sackenii* (Kennicott, 1859)**

## (Class Reptilia, Order Squamata, Family Colubridae)

Also called the southern ribbon snake.

**Etymology:** *Thamnophis* from Greek *thamnos*, meaning bush, and *ophis*, meaning snake. *Saurita* from Latin *sauritas*, meaning lizardlike. *Sackenii* comes from the name of Baron C. R. Osten Sacken (1828–1906) a Russian Baron and entomologist who collected the holotype. Douglas A. Rossman named this snake *nitae* in honor of his wife, Nita J. Rossman, who collected the first living example of this snake for him.

**Size:** Grows to 20–28 inches (50.8–71.12 centimeters) long.

**Description:** Slender olive to dark brown snake with a very light tan to yellowish stripe down middle of back and lighter tan to green stripes on each side. Has keeled scales. Pupil of eye is round.

**Range:** Along most of Gulf Coast into lower Keys and north as far as South Carolina. Replaced by the blue-striped ribbonsnake (*Thamnophis saurita nitae*) in the coastal lowlands from Wakulla County south to Hernando County. The blue-striped ribbonsnake has either a very faint or no dorsal stripe, a light blue stripe on each side of the body and a relatively long tail.

**Food Sources:** Small fish, frogs, and salamanders.

**Characteristics:** Nonvenomous. Semiaquatic during the day. Active at night during hot weather. Found near springs, rivers, lakes, and other wet areas. Gives birth to live young.

# Florida Cottonmouth, *Agkistrodon piscivorus conanti* Gloyd, 1969

## (Class Reptilia, Order Squamata, Family Viperidae)

Also known as water moccasin. Scientific name synonymous with *Agkistrodon conanti* (Gloyd, 1969).

**Etymology:** *Agkistrodon* is from the Greek and refers to the hooked teeth or fangs, *piscis* is Latin for fish, *voro* is Latin for to eat, and *conanti* refers to herpetologist Roger Conant (1909–2003).

**Size:** Can grow to 6 feet (1.83 meters) long.

**Description:** Olive brown to black with darker bands or patterns on body or appearing solid black. Juveniles have more intense coloring than adults. Scales are strongly keeled, meaning they have a distinctive ridge down the middle. The Florida cottonmouth has more intense facial patterns than other cottonmouths. The pupil of the eye is a vertical slit (like a cat's eyes).

**Range:** Wetlands in the southeastern United States.

**Food sources:** Carnivorous, small animals, birds, and eggs.

**Characteristics:** Venomous. Extremely dangerous. Prefers to flee but will defend itself. Gives birth to live babies instead of laying eggs. When viewed from above, the eyes of the cottonmouth cannot be seen, whereas the eyes of nonvenomous snakes mistaken for the cottonmouth can be seen. The cottonmouth also floats almost entirely on top of the water, whereas nonvenomous snakes tend to have more of their head and neck above the water. Cottonmouths are known for their habit of exposing the white (cottony) insides of their mouths in a defensive posture. Some nonvenomous watersnakes will imitate this posture but with the mouth closed. Best to just leave them all alone.

## Is That a Moccasin? by Bruce Morgan

Florida springs are so beautiful that visitors often imagine themselves to have discovered a veritable Eden, but what of the serpent(s) said to dwell therein? Should you be afraid? The danger is real, but a bit of knowledge will help you to identify the potentially deadly moccasin.

Many field guides identify snake species by technical characteristics, such as the number of scale rows beneath the tail, or the presence of heat sensory pits near the nostrils, but if you are that close, you are too close!

For many people throughout the South, every ugly brown snake found near the water is considered to be a moccasin, also known as the cottonmouth; but such is rarely the case, for the majority of serpents seen near the water are merely harmless water snakes.

Fear fires the imagination, so the tales told of encounters with imaginary moccasins grow taller with every telling. "We were enjoying our picnic when suddenly the moccasin attacked, so we ran for our lives!" The problem with this story is that moccasins never attack anyone. They will defend themselves if someone steps too close, but under no circumstances will they crawl forward to attack some hapless picnicker. If you are three feet away, then you are perfectly safe. Any snake seen crawling toward someone is simply scared and trying to escape!

My favorite "moccasin" stories involve fishermen who venture near overhanging branches along a lake or river and describe snakes flying out of trees, which often land in the boat. These are rarely, if ever, moccasins, for moccasins normally stay on the ground. The fishermen are seeing harmless water snakes, which often bask on branches overhanging the water and drop off when disturbed. The best part of the story is when the snake lands in the boat and Bubba blasts a hole in the bottom with his shotgun in an attempt to escape the deadly "attack" and thus sinks his boat. Ha!

Despite countless tales to the contrary, snakes in the United States never attack anyone. The only exception is the harmless blacksnake, the males of which will sometimes chase intruders during mating season. I know this to be true, for I have spent my entire life searching for serpents both here and abroad, have found many thousands, including famously deadly species, but not a single one has ever attempted to attack me!

So, how to tell the difference between a harmless water snake and a potentially deadly moccasin?

Color and pattern don't mean a thing, for many snakes are variable in their appearance. Both moccasins and water snakes are generally some shades of dark brown and may or may not display transverse reddish or yellowish bands. Don't count on it, for I have seen many moccasins that were entirely black, or more rarely those which were dull greenish yellow or even red. Young moccasins are more brightly colored than adults and often resemble their close cousin the copperhead.

Pay no attention to the old wives' tale about venomous snakes having triangular heads. When scared, many species of harmless snakes flatten their heads into a triangular shape in an attempt to fool you into thinking they are dangerous. Likewise, water snakes often puff up and/or flatten their bodies to look as fat as a real moccasin, but it is all bluff.

Real moccasins are much chunkier and more robust than other snakes. Because of their girth they appear to be larger than they are. Three and a half feet is the average size of an adult, but large males over four feet long may be as thick as your arm; so, if you see an extraordinarily short, fat snake leave it alone!

"But why do you have such a big head and such long teeth Mr. Moccasin?" "The better to bite you with my dear!" Moccasins have big, thick, chiseled heads shaped more like a fist than a flattened triangle. The lips are often whitish, and a dark mask runs across the eyes, but don't count on that. Again, you are too close! Moccasins have big heads because they have enormous fangs and large capacity glands full of potentially deadly venom. They didn't get their terrible reputation for no reason, but if you stay a few feet away you will be safe.

Just to make sure you understand, an angry moccasin will often open up its mouth to display its fangs, thus the name "cottonmouth," for the white of the interior of the mouth is in vivid contrast to the dark exterior. Harmless water snakes never do this.

Habitat preference is not a good indication of species, for moccasins are often found far from water. Like the proverbial 800-pound Gorilla, a snake as formidable as a moccasin can sleep wherever it pleases!

The best way to safely distinguish a water snake from a moccasin is by behavior. Water snakes will flee at the first sign of danger, whereas a moccasin will often stand its ground, especially if it is coiled up and resting. Unlike most other snakes, pit vipers such as rattlesnakes, copperheads, and moccasins often coil in a perfect circle with the head in the center. Other snakes coil too, but rarely in a perfect circle.

Many people believe they can chase away snakes by making a disturbance, but that doesn't work with moccasins. They are too slow moving to easily escape, so they rely upon camouflage. A resting moccasin will usually not move unless directly confronted. If so, it may open its mouth, rattle its tail, and stand its ground. Even if you get within striking range, you may escape unscathed, for I have accidently stepped near moccasins on many occasions but have never been bitten.

If a moccasin is resting on open ground and sees you coming straight toward it from a distance, it may go into an active threat display, which sometimes includes violently thrashing, then crawling diagonally away from the threat. Though some herpetologists may not believe it, I have seen several angry moccasins actually throw their bodies off the ground in an effort to get my attention. This is the sort of behavior that leads people to believe they are being attacked!

So, the bottom line is: Stay away from any short fat snake with a big head distinct from the neck, especially if it is coiled in a circle! Snakes, like all life forms, have a right to exist. They are an important component of our Florida springs ecosystems; so, either enjoy them from a distance, or better still, just leave them alone!

# Turtles and Tortoises, Order Testudines

## Chicken Turtles, *Deirochelys reticularia* (Latreille in Sonnini and Latreille, 1801)

**Florida Chicken Turtle,** *Deirochelys reticularia chrysea* **Schwartz, 1956**

**Eastern Chicken Turtle,** *Deirochelys reticularia* **(Latreille in Sonnini and Latreille, 1801)**

### (Class Reptilia, Order Testudines, Family Emydidae)

**Etymology:** *Deirochelys* comes from Greek words *deire*, meaning neck, and *chelys*, meaning tortoise. *Reticularia* comes from Latin *reticulatus*, meaning net-like.

**Size:** Grows up to 10 inches (25.4 centimeters) long.

**Description:** Unusually long, striped neck. Shell has a pattern of light beige webbing. Rear of shell is wider than the front. Broad yellow band on its front legs and yellow striped pattern on rump are easily seen when the turtle draws into its shell. Also has yellow stripes on the back legs and tail.

**Range:** Semi-aquatic. Prefers calm water throughout peninsular Florida and across the south and eastern United States.

**Food sources:** Crayfish is a favorite food. Also eats other aquatic invertebrates.

**Characteristics:** Hibernates in northern range. Will bite if molested. Females are larger than males. Males have longer front claws and thicker tails than females.

**Note:** Named the chicken turtle either due to the fine hatch-lines across its shell resembling feathers or because its meat is reported to taste remarkably like chicken.

# Barbour's Map Turtle, *Graptemys barbouri* Carr and Marchand, 1942
## (Class Reptilia, Order Testudines, Family Emydidae)

**Etymology:** *Graptemys*, from Greek *grapho*, meaning writing, and *emys*, meaning turtle. The specific name *barbouri* is named after Thomas Barbour (1884-1946), an American herpetologist and Director of the Museum of Comparative Zoology at Harvard and author of "That Vanishing Eden."

**Size:** Males reach only 4-6 inches (10.16-15.24 centimeters), whereas females reach 11-12 inches (27.94-30.48 centimeters) in length.

**Description:** Carapace on adults is usually greenish-gray, although sometimes covered in algae. The shell is distinctive for having two to four spikes along the top that become worn down with age. The plastron is yellow with darker seams. The turtle's body is dark with yellowish markings, neck has yellow lines, and chin has a yellow mark.

**Range:** Gulf Coastal Plain in the Apalachicola and Choctawhatchee River systems in the Florida panhandle.

**Food Sources:** Mollusks and insects.

**Characteristics:** Seems to prefer flowing streams with plenty of fallen trees for basking to floodplains or still water areas.

**Note:** Listed by the FWC as ST (State-designated Threatened). FNAI ranking G2/S2 (Globally: Imperiled/Statewide: Imperiled).

# Cooter Turtles, *Pseudemys* Gray, 1856
## (Class Reptilia, Order Testudines, Family Emydidae)

Also known as cooter, Florida cooter, Florida pond cooter, Florida river cooter, river cooter.

**Etymology:** From the Greek *pseudos*, meaning false, and *emys*, meaning turtle.

**Size:** Up to 17 inches (43.18 centimeters) long.

**Description:** A large, aquatic turtle typically having a muddy dark brown shell with very attractive yellow or beige patterns, occasionally obscured by algae growing on shell. Head is black with yellow stripes. Posterior of carapace is slightly flared. Profile is flatter than other aquatic turtles. Broken pattern on the rump differentiates the peninsula cooter from the yellow "striped pants" of the yellowbellied slider and the chicken turtle. Three distinct spots run along the side of the bridge between the carapace and plastron. There are more spots in front of and behind the three large bridge spots. Plastron is solid yellow.

**Range:** North Florida up through Virginia.

**Food sources:** Herbivorous, feeds on plants and algae.

**Characteristics:** Usually seen basking on logs and rocks in and around freshwater rivers and springs.

**Note:** The common name cooter comes from the African Congo word *kuta*, for turtle.

### Suwannee Cooter, *Pseudemys concinna* (Le Conte, 1830)

**Etymology:** From the Greek *pseudos*, meaning false and *emys*, meaning turtle. *Concinna* comes from Latin for beautifully arranged or pleasant.

**Size:** Shell grows to 17 inches (43.18 centimeters).

**Description:** Large turtle. Dark, almost black, olive-green to brown upper shell. Some yellow lines appear on the large middle scales on the shell as the letter C backward. Yellow stripes on head and neck. Shown in illustration.

FNAI ranking G5T3/S3 (Globally: Demonstrably Secure but subspecies is Rare/Statewide: Rare).

**Florida Redbellied Cooter,** *Pseudemys nelsoni* **Carr, 1938**

**Etymology:** From the Greek *pseudos*, meaning false, and *emys*, meaning turtle. *Nelsoni* comes from the name of American zoologist George Nelson (1876–1962), who collected the type specimen.

**Size:** Up to 15 inches (38.1 centimeters) long.

**Description:** Under-shell is usually distinctively orange to red.

**Range:** Freshwater springs, ponds, and marshes throughout peninsular Florida. Plastron solid yellowish in adults, juveniles may have spots or patterns.

**Food sources:** Herbivorous.

**Characteristics:** Spends lots of time basking. Male redbellied turtles have long claws on their front feet. During courting, the male swims backward in front of the female and caresses the sides of her head with their claws. This turtle sometimes lays its eggs in alligator nests. Females grow larger than males.

**Note:** NatureServe status G5 (Globally Secure) and N5 (Nationally Secure).

There is a separate population in the Florida panhandle, referred to as the *Pseudemys nelsoni* Population 1. FNAI ranking G5T2Q/S2 (Globally: Demonstrably Secure but this population is Imperiled and needs further study/Statewide: Imperiled).

# *Red-eared Slider, *Trachemys scripta elegans* (Wied-Neuwied, 1839)

## (Class Reptilia, Order Testudines, Family Emydidae)

**Etymology:** *Trachemys* from Greek *trachys*, meaning rocky or rough, and *emys*, meaning turtle. *Scripta* comes from Latin, meaning writing. *Elegans* from Latin meaning elegant or fine.

**Size:** Can grow to 8 inches (20.32 centimeters).

**Description:** It is named for bright red patches behind the eye. Oval, flattened carapace. Plastron yellow with two or more black spots at the front or rear.

**Range:** Still or slow-flowing bodies of water with soft bottoms and plenty of vegetation. Red-eared sliders not native to Florida. These turtles are native to the midwestern United States but found worldwide due to the pet trade.

**Food sources:** Omnivorous but grows more herbivorous with age. Likes aquatic insects, crustaceans, small fish, vegetative matter, algae, and carrion. Because aquatic turtles do not have saliva, they must eat their food in the water.

**Characteristics:** Once very popular as pets. Buying and selling these turtles is illegal in Florida. Enjoys basking, which dries out algae and bacteria that grow on the shell. Males grow long front nails when courting and caress the female's face during a courting dance.

## Yellow-Bellied Slider, *Trachemys scripta scripta* (Thunberg in Schoepff, 1792)
### (Class Reptilia, Order Testudines, Family Emydidae)

**Etymology:** *Trachemys* from Greek *trachys*, meaning rocky or rough, and *emys*, meaning turtle. *Scripta* comes from Latin, meaning writing. The specific name is written twice to indicate that this is the type for the species.

**Size:** Grow to 8–13 inches (20.32–33.02 centimeters) long.

**Description:** It has a yellow bar or patch behind each eye. Shell has yellow bars on each side, and a bright yellow plastron. When turtle draws into its shell, a bright yellow striped pattern on its rump resembles striped pants.

**Range:** Lakes, ponds, streams, and rivers from northern Florida to Virginia.

**Food sources:** Omnivorous, preferring plants and carrion. Females are more herbivorous.

**Characteristics:** Females grow up to 13 inches (33 centimeters) long, larger than males, which reach only up to 8 inches (20.3 centimeters) long.

## Snapping Turtle, *Chelydra serpentina* (Linnaeus, 1758)
### (Class Reptilia, Order Testudines, Family Chelydridae)

Also called the common snapping turtle and the eastern snapping turtle.

**Etymology:** *Chelydra* is Greek referring to the aquatic nature of these turtles; *serpentina* is Latin and refers to a creeping animal or sprung from a serpent.

**Size:** Up to 19 inches (48.26 centimeters) long.

**Description:** Muddy, dark brown color. Hooked beak. Jaw is lighter colored, and there are barbels on the chin. Very long neck can reach back half as far as the length of its shell. Three ridges of spines run the length of the tail. Lacks the prominent ridges along the back of its shell found on the alligator snapping turtle.

**Range:** Ponds and lakes throughout Florida.

**Food sources:** Carnivorous, carrion.

**Characteristics:** Stays in water unless moving from one place to another. This turtle cannot completely withdraw into its shell and will defend itself by biting.

# Alligator Snapping Turtle, *Macrochelys* Gray, 1856
## (Class Reptilia, Order Testudines, Family Chelydridae)

**Size:** Can get very large, up to 29 inches (73.66 centimeters) and over 200 pounds (90.72 kilograms).

**Description:** Muddy dark brown color occasionally covered in algae growth. Very long, large, thick neck. Hooked beak. Jaw is lighter colored. Fleshy growths around eyes. Three prominent, knobby ridges along the length of its shell.

**Range:** Florida panhandle and in large river drainages east to the Suwannee and Santa Fe rivers.

**Food sources:** Fish, mussels, smaller turtles. Also forages for vegetation and occasionally scavenges.

**Characteristics:** Largest freshwater turtle in North America. Not aggressive in the water but will defend itself by biting. Hunts using a vermiform appendage on the bottom of its tongue that it wiggles to attract fish. Biologists were able to determine the distinct species by differences in morphology (shapes of parts of the turtle) and using molecular data.

Apalachicola Alligator Snapping Turtle, *Macrochelys apalachicolae* (Thomas, Granatosky, Bourque, Krysko, Moler, Gamble, Suarez, Leone, Enge, and Roman, 2014)

**Etymology:** *Macro* is Greek for large, and *chelys* means turtle; *apalachicolae* refers to the Apalachicola River.

*Macrochelys apalachicolae* species status is not ranked.

**Suwannee Alligator Snapping Turtle, *Macrochelys suwanniensis* (Thomas, Granatosky, Bourque, Krysko, Moler, Gamble, Suarez, Leone, Enge, and Roman, 2014)**

**Etymology:** *Macro* is Greek for large, and *chelys* means turtle; *suwanniensis* refers to the Suwannee River.

*Macrochelys suwanniensis* is listed by the FWC as ST (State-designated Threatened). A Florida Species of Special Concern. FNAI ranking G2/S2 (Globally: Imperiled/Statewide: Imperiled).

**Alligator Snapping Turtle, *Macrochelys temminckii* (Troost in Harlan, 1835)**

**Etymology:** *Macro* is Greek for large, and *chelys* refers to the aquatic nature of these turtles. *Temminckii* after Coenraad Jacob Temminck (1778-1858), a Dutch zoologist.

*Macrochelys temminckii* FNAI ranking G3G4/S3 (Globally: Rare to Apparently Secure/Statewide: Rare).

## Striped Mud Turtle, *Kinosternon baurii* (Garman, 1891)

### (Class Reptilia, Order Testudines, Family Kinosternidae)

**Etymology:** From the Greek *kineo* for move and *sternon* for chest (for their ability to move their lower shell), and *baurii* after George Baur (1859-1898), a herpetologist and professor of osteology and paleontology.

**Size:** Grows to 3-4 inches (7.62-10.16 centimeters) in length.

**Description:** Small, dark, drab turtle with an oval shell. Most have three light stripes running the length of the carapace. Carapace is usually dark, and plastron is usually yellow. A light stripe runs between the nose and the eye, and the skin is usually dark and mottled. Males have longer, thicker tails than females.

**Range:** Throughout Florida east of the Apalachicola Basin and north along the Atlantic Coastal Plain to Virginia. Prefers shallow, slow, or still water such as cypress swamps with a soft benthos of sand or mud and plenty of vegetation.

**Food sources:** Carnivorous, preferring insects, small fish, occasionally algae. Digs around in muck searching for food.

**Characteristics:** In the past two subspecies were recognized, *Kinosternon baurii baurii* in the Lower Keys and *K. b. palmarum* Stejneger, 1925, in the remainder of the range. However, the distinguishing characters proved not to be distinctive, and the striped mud turtle remains *Kinosternon baurii*.

# Florida Mud Turtle, *Kinosternon steindachneri* Siebenrock, 1906
## (Class Reptilia, Order Testudines, Family Kinosternidae)

**Etymology:** From the Greek *kineo* for move and *sternon* for chest (for their ability to move their lower shell). *Steindachneri* refers to Franz Steindachner (1834–1919) an Austrian zoologist.

**Size:** Up to 5 inches (12.7 centimeters) long.

**Description:** Dark olive to dark brown oval shell without any markings. A stripe runs from the nose across the eye and down the neck. Pectoral scutes are triangular. Usually smaller than the Eastern mud turtle, *Kinosternon subrubrum subrubrum* (Bonnaterre, 1789).

**Range:** Peninsular Florida.

**Food sources:** Omnivorous.

**Characteristics:** Semi-aquatic. It is capable of aestivation, burrowing a few inches into the mud when its aquatic habitat dries up or during the winter. The Florida mud turtle also emits a yellowish musk when disturbed.

## Eastern Mud Turtle, *Kinosternon subrubrum subrubrum* (Bonnaterre, 1789)

### (Class Reptilia, Order Testudines, Family Kinosternidae)

Also called the southeastern mud turtle.

**Etymology:** From the Greek *kineo* for move and *sternon* for chest (for their ability to move their lower shell). *Subrubrum* comes from Latin *sub* meaning under and *rubrum* meaning red. The specific name is written twice to indicate that this is the type for the species.

**Size:** Grows to 5 inches (12.7 centimeters).

**Description:** Dark oval shell without markings

**Range:** In small shallow bodies of fresh or brackish water with lots of vegetation throughout the eastern United States. In Florida, found only west of the Suwannee River.

## Loggerhead Musk Turtle, *Sternotherus minor* (Agassiz, 1857)

### (Class Reptilia, Order Testudines, Family Kinosternidae)

Also called a mud turtle.

**Etymology:** From the Greek *sterno* for chest and *thairos* for hinged, and the Latin *minor* for little or small.

**Size:** Grows to 4–5.5 inches (10.16–13.97 centimeters).

**Description:** Brown carapace with dark seams. In juveniles, the carapace is highly domed, or keeled. May have spots or streaks. Dark spots on head and barbels on chin.

**Range:** South Alabama and Georgia, and throughout north to central Florida.

**Food sources:** Aquatic invertebrates, snails, and clams.

**Characteristics:** Primarily aquatic. The large head is an adaptation that allows the loggerhead musk to feed on mollusks.

Males have a spine-tipped tail that extends beyond the margin of the carapace, whereas the female's tail barely reaches the edge of the carapace. Like the stinkpot, or common musk turtle, the loggerhead may also emit a musk odor if disturbed.

**Note:** The name loggerhead refers to the slowness and clumsiness of this small aquatic turtle.

## Eastern Musk Turtle, *Sternotherus odoratus* (Latreille in Sonnini and Latreille, 1801)
### (Class Reptilia, Order Testudines, Family Kinosternidae)

Also called common musk turtle, musk turtle, or stinkpot.

**Etymology:** From the Greek *sterno* for chest and *thairos* for hinged. The Latin word *odoratus* means having an odor.

**Size:** Grows to 4 inches (10.16 centimeters).

**Description:** Small, dark turtle with two distinct lightly colored stripes running down its head. Very long neck, a pointy snout with a sharp beak and barbels on the chin. High-domed, or keeled, carapace.

**Range:** Still or slow-moving water throughout the eastern United States.

**Food sources:** Omnivorous. Fish, aquatic invertebrates, carrion, and vegetation are among its many foods.

**Characteristics:** Primarily nocturnal. Will secrete a smelly odor from musk glands if disturbed.

# Florida Softshell Turtle, *Apalone ferox* (Schneider, 1783)

## (Class Reptilia, Order Testudines, Family Trionychidae)

Also known as Florida softshell.

**Etymology:** *Apalone* comes from the Greek word *apalos* for soft or tender, and *ferox* from Latin ferocious or defiant.

**Size:** Can grow to 25 inches (63.5 centimeters). Florida's largest freshwater turtle, with a maximum reported size of 96 pounds (43.54 kilograms).

**Description:** Large, flat turtle with skin covering its shell. Dark brown to olive green carapace with a lighter underside. Very long neck and a long nose for breathing air while remaining submerged. Juveniles are more colorful, with spots on the carapace, and yellow to red stripes on the head and edge of the shell, and a dark, purplish underside.

**Range:** Prefers calm water bodies with abundant vegetation. South Carolina to Alabama, but most commonly found in Florida.

**Food sources:** Carnivorous. Mostly fish, snails, and crustaceans. Occasionally birds.

**Characteristics:** Remains just under the surface of the water in vegetation breathing through its long snout, which it uses like a straw. Females grow much larger than males. Males have thicker tails than the females.

# Mammals, Class Mammalia

## Common Otter, *Lontra canadensis* (Schreber, 1777)
### (Class Mammalia, Order Carnivora, Family Mustelidae)

**Etymology:** *Lontra* is Latin for otter, and *canadensis* is Latin, meaning of or from Canada.

**Size:** Body 3–4.3 feet (0.91–1.31 meters) in length.

**Description:** Long streamlined body with dark brown coloring. Webbed feet, long, thick tail, and a broad, flat head. The tail can be 12–20 inches (30.48–50.8 centimeters) in length.

**Range:** Fresh and marine wetlands throughout North America. Not found in the Florida Keys.

**Food sources:** Fish, aquatic crustaceans such as shrimp and crayfish, clams and mussels, amphibians.

**Characteristics:** Known for its playful antics, wrestling and chasing each other, and playing with prey. Do not try to touch an otter, while they prefer to flee humans, they will bite to defend themselves. Considered nocturnal but often seen during the day. Lives in dens near the water's edge.

# Raccoon, *Procyon lotor* (Linnaeus, 1758)
## (Class Mammalia, Order Carnivora, Family Procyonidae)

Also referred to as a coon.

**Etymology:** *Procyon* comes from Greek *pró*, meaning before, and *kúōn*, meaning dog. *Lotor* is Latin for one who washes.

The common name raccoon derives from several similar-sounding Algonquian words, *arocoun* meaning the scratcher. The words *arocoun* and similar *arougheun* were recorded in the early 1600s and gradually shifted by the mid-1700s to *raccoon*.

**Size:** Adults grow to 20–38 inches (50.8–96.52 centimeters) and weigh 8–15 pounds (3.63–6.8 kilograms).

**Description:** A medium-sized mammal with gray or grayish fur with a lighter underside and a distinctive mask-like black band across the eyes and face. Wide, erect, pointed ears, and a bushy tail ringed with broad black bands. Dexterous hands.

**Range:** Found throughout Florida. Native to North America, can now also be found in Europe and Japan. Adaptable to many kinds of environments, can be found in forests and neighborhoods, where they get the reputation of being "trash pandas" from their fondness of going through people's garbage in search of food.

**Food sources:** Omnivorous. Eats fruits, plants, eggs, crustaceans, fish, small animals such as frogs, and garbage.

**Characteristics:** Somewhat nocturnal, sleeping during the day, but will adjust its schedule to the best times for finding food.

Raccoons breed in early spring, and the young, called kits, are born two months later.

Raccoons can carry rabies, an infectious disease transmitted through saliva (typically from bites) that affects the nervous system and is preventable via vaccination. Rabies is almost always fatal.

# American Beaver, *Castor canadensis* (Kuhl, 1820)
## (Class Mammalia, Order Rodentia, Family Castoridae)

**Etymology:** *Castor* is Latin for beaver. *Castor* also refers to the secretions of the beaver, called castoreum, and is historically used medicinally. *Canadensis* is Latin meaning of or from Canada.

**Size:** Up to 2 feet (0.61 meter) long and weighing up to 60 pounds (27.22 kilograms).

**Description:** Has a thick body with a glossy, brown fur overcoat, dense undercoat, prominent front teeth, webbed hind feet, and a broad, flat tail.

**Range:** Throughout North America.

**Food sources:** Herbivorous, preferring aquatic plants, tree bark, and occasionally berries.

**Characteristics:** Florida's largest native rodent. Nocturnal. It has very poor eyesight but better hearing and smell. If threatened, it is known for the habit of slapping the water with its tail, making a loud sound and warning other beavers of the intrusion. The Florida beaver is as likely to inhabit a den as to build a lodge. Located through evidence of its activities, leaving chewed trees and stumps in areas where it lives.

**Note:** Beavers have been seen in early morning at Peacock Springs State Park.

# *Capybara, *Hydrochoerus hydrochaeris* (Linnaeus, 1766)
## (Class Mammalia, Order Rodentia, Family Caviidae)

**Etymology:** Both the genus and specific name come from Greek, the root word *hydro* for water or wet and *choiros*, meaning pig.

**Size:** Average 2 feet (0.61 meter) tall and 4 feet (1.22 meters) long. Can weigh up to 150 pounds (68.04 kilograms).

**Description:** Large, square body covered in reddish brown hair. Big, block-like head. Tiny, round ears. Webbed feet.

**Range:** Coastal and permanent waterbodies throughout Florida.

**Food sources:** Herbivores. Prefer aquatic plants.

**Characteristics:** Semiaquatic, spend time standing in water munching on aquatic plants. Largest rodent in the world. Not native to Florida, was brought from South America by sportsmen for hunting.

Lifespan usually from six to ten years.

**Note:** Records indicate earliest sightings in the 1990s, but residents along the Gulf Coast south of Yankeetown are familiar with the animals, which were introduced for hunting as early as the 1980s.

## *Rhesus Macaque, *Macaca mulatta* (Zimmerman, 1780)
### (Class Mammalia, Order Primates, Family Cercopithecidae)

Also referred to as a rhesus monkey, Silver River rhesus macaque.

**Etymology:** *Macaca* is the feminine of the Portuguese word *macaco*, meaning monkey. *Mulatta* possibly originates from the Portuguese word *mula* (a mule being the hybrid of a horse and a donkey).

**Size:** Medium-sized monkey. Males average 1.7 feet (51.82 centimeters) tall and weighing 17 pounds (7.71 kilograms), females 1.5 feet (45.72 centimeters) tall and weighing 11.8 pounds (5.35 kilograms).

**Description:** Hair is short, coarse yellowish brown to gray on the back, arms and legs, and white on chest and belly. Hair is darker lower on the body. Hands and feet are hairless and have opposing thumbs. Face and ears pink and largely hairless. Mouth pouch allowing the monkeys to store food. Short tail, nearly 9 inches (22.86 centimeters) in length, not prehensile (they do not hang from their tails).

**Range:** Native to South, Central, and Southeast Asia. Introduced by humans to additional habitats and are now considered the most widespread nonhuman primate species. Feral colonies can be found in various places in Florida, primarily near water sources such as the Silver River, in Silver Springs State Park.

**Food sources:** Primarily herbivores who prefer fruit (frugivores), but known to eat also leaves and vegetation, seeds, nuts, and roots. Will eat small insects and animals. Macaques are considered opportunistic feeders taking advantage of the food available in their habitat. There is concern that as the macaque population in an area grows, there will be an impact on the local bird population as the macaques eat eggs they find in nests.

**Characteristics:** Intelligent and social. Can live to between twenty-five and thirty years in the wild. Young are weaned at approximately nine months old and reach maturity at approximately four years for females and five years for males. Live and travel both in trees (arboreal) and on land (terrestrial) in groups of several males and females. Macaques will separate to form their own group if population pressure causes food to become scarce.

The rhesus is diurnal (meaning they sleep at night and are active during the day, like humans). Macaques can swim. Macaques adapt readily to human-influenced behavior. Feeding by curious humans and raiding refuse are some of the ways the macaque colonies survive near human populations.

**Note:** Because of their similarities to humans in physiology, metabolism, and genetics, these monkeys are commonly used in medical and psychological research. The original name rhesus can be abbreviated Rh. The use of Rh to human blood comes from the discovery in 1940 by Karl Landsteiner and Alexander S. Weiner of a test to determine a protein found on the surface of human red blood cells. People without this antigen (antigen D) are Rh negative, while people with antigen D are Rh positive. The Rh antigen is also called the Rh factor. Knowing the Rh can help determining incompatibility in blood types, such as between a baby and mother, or when needing a blood transfusion.

The Silver River macaques carry the herpes B virus. Herpesvirus 1 (aka herpes B) does not produce illness in the monkeys but can cause fatal encephalitis in humans if not treated. This disease can remain latent in the macaques, resurfacing without symptoms when the monkeys are under stress. There is no evidence of human infection or death from the monkeys at the park, despite apparently frequent casual interaction. Transmission of the herpes B virus happens through bodily fluid exchanges, such as scratches and bites, and recent studies reveal that the virus is also shed in the animal's urine and excrement. To be on the safe side, it would be prudent to observe these animals from a distance.

# Round-Tailed Muskrat, *Neofiber alleni* True, 1884
## (Class Mammalia, Order Rodentia, Family Cricetidae)

Also known as a Florida water rat or water rat.

**Etymology:** *Neo* means new, *fiber* is one Latin word for beaver (another is *castor*), and *alleni* after noted American zoologist Joel Asaph Allen (1838-1921).

**Size:** Grows to 14 inches (35.56 centimeters).

**Description:** A large rodent with darker brown or gray fur overcoat of longer hairs, and a shorter, lighter undercoat. Underside has lighter fur. Long, round, hairless tail. Short snout with lots of whiskers. Tiny, round ears. Prominent sharp nails on feet.

**Range:** Marshy wetlands in peninsular Florida and southeast Georgia. Not found in the Florida Keys.

**Food sources:** Herbivorous, prefers aquatic plants.

**Characteristics:** Nocturnal. Constructs dens by weaving grasses and other vegetative matter into huts, leaving underwater openings known as plunge holes. Teeth grow continuously and, like the beaver, the muskrat must constantly chew to maintain its teeth.

**Note:** One of these nearly scared the life out of me. One night, I was sitting in a johnboat in the darkness (to conserve flashlight batteries) while my husband and a friend dove a submerged cave. The sudden explosive sound of very loud breathing right next to my hand on the gunwale woke me right up. I sat very still as the breathing made its way across the little spring basin, finally realizing it was a water critter and not a drunk local messing with me!

**Note:** FNAI ranking G3/S3 (Globally: Rare/Statewide: Rare).

# Eastern Woodrat, *Neotoma floridana* (Ord, 1818)
## (Class Mammalia, Order Rodentia, Family Cricetidae)

Also known as the Florida woodrat, wood rat, pack rat, bush rat.

**Etymology:** *Neotoma* from Greek *neo* meaning new and *tomos* meaning cutting. *Floridana* refers to the type specimen being found in Florida.

**Size:** Grows to 12–17.72 inches (30.48–45.01 centimeters) in length.

**Description:** Medium-sized rodent with dark gray-brown hair along spine, fading to lighter brown along sides, and a white underbelly. White feet. A long tail covered in hair. Very round ears and protruding eyes. Some seasonal shading can occur, with the woodrat becoming lighter in winter.

**Range:** Southern United States from Kansas south and east into central Florida.

**Food sources:** Plant material such as fruits, nuts and seeds, foliage, and fungi.

**Characteristics:** Enjoys a variety of habitats, such as marshes, scrublands, and human structures. Builds nests in which the family lives for generations. Builds structures that protect and hide the actual nest. Nocturnal. Territorial and solitary, very aggressive toward other woodrats. Known for caching, or storing, their food and materials for building houses and nests. Does not hibernate.

## Cotton Mouse, *Peromyscus gossypinus* (Le Conte, 1853)

### (Class Mammalia, Order Rodentia, Family Cricetidae)

**Etymology:** From the Greek *pero* for pointed, *myskos* for little mouse, and *gossypinus*, meaning of the cotton.

**Size:** Body length typically 2 inches (5.08 centimeters).

**Description:** Small, light tan to brown mouse with white underside.

**Range:** Throughout the southeastern United States. Seen at the entrances to Florida caves.

**Food sources:** Herbivorous.

**Characteristics:** Follows cavers throughout Warren Cave. Observed descending the rope at the front fissure and running into a small hole in the floor. This mouse does not appear particularly afraid of cavers.

## Florida Manatee, *Trichechus manatus latirostris* (Harlan, 1824)

### (Class Mammalia, Order Sirenia, Family Trichechidae)

Also known as American manatee, West Indian manatee, and sea cow. Sometimes jokingly referred to as a "river slug."

**Etymology:** From the Greek *tricho*, a prefix meaning hair, and *manatus* from an old Caribbean language word *manati*, meaning breast or udder, but also possibly from the Latin word *manus* for hand. The subspecies name *latirostris* comes from the Latin *latus* for wide and *rostrum* for snout or beak.

**Size:** May grow to 15 feet (4.57 meters) long and weigh up to 3,649 pounds (1,655.16 kilograms).

**Description:** Large, gray, rotund, aquatic mammal having front flippers but no hind limbs, a walrus-like mouth covered in whiskers and a large, wide, paddle-shaped tail. Vibrissae are the hairs covering the manatees' bodies. The whiskers on a manatee's face are a denser growth of these vibrissae.

**Range:** Manatees are a euryhaline species, meaning they can live in a wide range of salinity. Manatees can live in fresh water or salt water and travel between the two, living in the marine water along the Florida coast during warm weather and migrating into freshwater rivers for the warmth of spring water during colder months. King Spring and Three Sisters Springs in Kings Bay in Crystal River, Blue Springs State Park on the St. Johns River, and Manatee Springs near Chiefland are well-known places to see manatees.

**Food source:** Herbivores, feed on aquatic plants in both fresh water and salt water. Can also eat submerged grass and leaves. The ones I watched in feedings at Homosassa Springs State Park appeared to love lettuce and would climb up staff almost out of the water to reach a handful.

**Characteristics:** Curious and friendly, manatees will approach swimmers and boats. Federal and state laws protecting the manatee recommend that people not interact with manatees. This way the manatees will stay out of the way of boats and people who might harm them.

**Note:** Listed by FWC as FT (Federally designated Threatened). Federally protected under the Marine Mammal Protection Act. FNAI ranking for *Trichechus manatus* (not the specific subspecies) G2/S2 (Globally: Imperiled/Statewide: Imperiled).

# Stygophiles and Troglophiles

*Stygo* from Latin *Stygius* and Greek *Stygios* and referring to the river Styx, the river leading to the underworld. *Troglo* from Greek *troglos* meaning cave. And *-philes* referring to the Latin word *phila* meaning to like or love.

Stygophiles and troglophiles enjoy caves. Some individuals spend much of their lives within the cool serenity of caverns and caves but occasionally must return to the sunlit world for food or for love. Some use subterranean passages to travel between karst windows, sunlit openings where food may be present.

Underwater, from the basin into the twilight zone of a cave there is little to low light and fewer food sources, but still, there is plenty of oxygen-rich water.

Annulate Millipede
Marianna Cave Sheetweaver Spider
Elephant Spurred Sheetweaver
Daddy Longlegs
Rosy Wolfsnail
American Cockroach
Ringlegged Earwig
Camel Cricket
American Eel
Redeye Chub
Blackbanded Darter
Atlantic Croaker
White Catfish
Yellow Bullhead

Brown Bullhead
Madtoms
Flathead Catfish
*Vermiculated Sailfin Catfish
*Orinoco Sailfin Catfish
*Suckermouth Catfish
Three-lined Salamander
Florida Slimy Salamander
Big Brown Bat
Southeastern Myotis
Gray Bat
Tricolored Bat
Southeastern Big-eared Bat

# Cave Millipedes, Class Diplopoda

## Annulate Millipede, *Cambala annulata* (Say, 1821)
### (Class Diplopoda, Order Spirostreptida, Family Cambalidae)

The class name Diplopoda comes from Latin *diplous* meaning double and *podos* meaning feet. *Annulata* comes from Latin *annulus*, meaning ring or ringed. The word millipede comes from Latin *mille*, meaning thousand, and *ped* from *podos* for foot.

**Range:** Found in northern Florida along the border with Alabama and Georgia.

**Description:** Slender and cylindrical body. Light beige or yellowish-brown with a lateral row of dark brown spots.

**Food sources:** Carnivorous scavengers.

# Spiders, Class Arachnida

Many spiders live in and around Florida's caves. The two mentioned here are known only to caves in Jackson County. More study is needed to verify the diversity and habits of spiders found in the twilight of caverns and the darkness of the true cave zone.

## Marianna Cave Sheetweaver Spider, *Islandiana sp.*
### (Class Arachnida, Order Araneae, Family Linyphiidae)

The genus name *Islandiana* established by Braendegaard in 1932. The specific species is undetermined.

Referred to as sheetweavers because of the shape of their web.

**Note:** FNAI ranking G1/S1 (Globally: Critically Imperiled/Statewide: Critically Imperiled) because this spider is known from only one cave.

## Elephant Spurred Sheetweaver, *Centromerus latidens* (Emerton, 1882)
### (Class Arachnida, Order Araneae, Family Linyphiidae)

**Etymology:** *Centromerus* from Greek *centro*, meaning center, and *méros*, meaning part. *Latidens* from Latin *latus*, meaning wide, and *dens*, meaning tooth or tusk.

**Size:** Very small, 0.08–0.12 inch (0.2–0.3 centimeter).

**Description:** Body darker brown to black with long, thin, lighter brown legs. Eyes are small and close together.

**Range:** Found throughout eastern North America. These spiders can be found in leaf litter on forest floors. Referred to as sheetweavers because of the shape of their webs.

## Daddy Longlegs, *Bishopella marianna* C. J. Goodnight and M. L. Goodnight, 1942
### (Class Arachnida, Order Opiliones, Family Phalangodidae)

**Size:** Body length 0.2–0.3 inch (0.51–0.76 centimeter).

**Description:** Tiny. Typically, orange. Has a round body with long, thin legs, but the legs are not as exaggerated as those of the family Sclerosomatidae. While the body looks like one circle, it is actually made up of a head and a body.

**Range:** Found in detritus on the ground and in caves, such as Florida Caverns State Park.

**Food sources:** Omnivores, small insects, plants, detritus.

**Characteristics:** Not actually spiders. These also do not have venom and are therefore no danger to humans.

# Daddy Longlegs, *Leiobunum* C.L. Koch, 1839
## (Class Arachnida, Order Opiliones, Family Sclerosomatidae)

Also called harvestmen spiders.

**Size:** Body length 0.2–0.3 inch (0.51–0.76 centimeter).

**Description:** Small, round body with eight extremely long, thin legs. Although the body looks like one circle, it is a head and a body together in one section.

**Range:** Gardens and caves throughout Florida.

**Food sources:** Omnivores, small insects, plants, detritus.

**Characteristics:** Not actually spiders. Their body is not segmented, and they have only two eyes instead of eight. They do not have venom and are no danger to humans.

**Note:** My sister and I delighted in picking up daddy longlegs, carefully holding them in the palm of our hands to watch them bounce, although this seemed more a habit of the ones in Alabama than the ones here in central Florida. Bouncing is a defense strategy to confuse predators. Another defense is for the daddy longlegs to drop part of its leg. The leg will remain moving, fascinating potential predators, while the daddy longlegs escapes. Sadly, the leg does not grow back.

# Snails, Class Gastropoda

## Rosy Wolfsnail, *Euglandina rosea* (Ferussac, 1821)
### (Class Mollusca, Order Stylommatophora, Family Spiraxidae)

Also known as the rosey wolfsnail and cannibal snail.

**Etymology:** *Euglandina* begins with *eu-*, used as an adverb meaning well. The name, originally *glandina*, refers to the shape of the shell, *glans*, meaning acorn, and the suffix *ina*, meaning in the nature of or like. *Rosea* is Latin, meaning pink.

**Size:** The shell can grow to 3 inches (7.62 centimeters) long and 1.08 inches (2.74 centimeters) wide.

**Description:** Large pink-hued tan to brown shell with striations (growth lines). The shell is an elongated spiral. The snail's soft body is light brown to gray.

**Range:** Common throughout Florida.

**Food sources:** Other snails.

**Characteristics:** Predatory snail. Eats other snails. Pursues other snails by following their slime trails. Chemoreceptors in the tentacles allow it to differentiate between prey. Can go as fast as 19 miles per hour (30.57 kilometers per hour) to catch its prey. Lays eggs in a depression in the dirt. The eggs hatch in thirty to forty days, and the babies are off for the hunt.

# Insects, Class Insecta

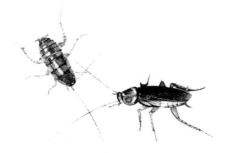

## American Cockroach, *Periplaneta americana* (Linnaeus, 1758)

### (Class Insecta, Order Blattodea, Family Blattinae)

**Etymology:** *Periplaneta* comes from Greek and means wanderer or wander about. The specific name *americana* means "of America." Order name Blattodea comes from Greek *blatta*, meaning cockroach. Common name cockroach comes from Spanish *cucaracha*, which means cockroach.

**Size:** Averages 1 inch (2.54 centimeters) in length.

**Description:** Flat, long, oval-shaped body. Shades of brown to black with darker markings. Long antennae. Exoskeleton covers head and thorax.

**Range:** Tropical environments worldwide.

**Food sources:** Omnivorous scavengers and detritivores.

**Characteristics:** Cockroaches exhibit sexual dimorphism. The males possess two styli between their cerci (the projections on their rear ends), the females lack styli. The ootheca, a hard shell, protects the cockroach eggs. Juvenile cockroaches are nymphs (they are not called naiads because they don't live in water).

Cockroaches prefer to live outside but will find their way into buildings to avoid extreme environmental conditions. Yes, your friendly household cockroaches also love the dark, damp cavern zone.

# Ringlegged Earwig, *Euborellia annulipes* (Lucas, 1847)

## (Class Insecta, Order Dermaptera, Family Carcinophoridae)

Also known as pincher bugs.

**Etymology:** The order name *Dermaptera* is from Greek *derma*, meaning skin, and *pteron*, meaning wings. *Annulipes* from Latin *anulus*, meaning ring, or *annulatus*, meaning decorated with, and *per* for foot. The common name is from the shape of the rarely used wings (when unfolded resembles a human ear). Some sources report the *wig* part of the word derives from an old Saxon word *wicga* meaning beetle, others have *wicga* meaning wiggle.

**Size:** From 0.20–1.97 inches (0.51–5 centimeters) including cerci.

**Description:** Shades of brown to solid black insect with a long narrow body. Two medium antennae and two long cerci at the other end. The cerci (paired appendages on the end of the earwig), which look like pinchers, are more curved on a male.

**Range:** Prefer humid, tropical areas.

**Food sources:** Omnivorous. Known to eat plants but also preys on small invertebrates.

**Characteristics:** There are many species of earwig in Florida. The ringlegged earwig is the most common. Not all earwigs have wings. Nocturnal. Female earwigs protect their eggs and watch over their young. Exhibit sexual dimorphism, male's cerci are more fierce-looking. Earwigs can be found crawling among the detritus in cave entrances.

Earwigs do not climb into people's ears, but they will use their cerci (pinchers) for defense.

# Camel Cricket, *Ceuthophilus* Scudder, 1863
## (Class Insecta, Order Orthoptera, Family Rhaphidophoridae)

Also called spider crickets or cave crickets.

**Etymology:** From the Greek *ceutho*, meaning hidden, and *philous*, meaning to have a strong affinity for or to love.

**Size:** Up to 1 inch (2.54 centimeters) long.

**Description:** Hump-backed, wingless cricket. Very long legs and antennae. Light tan to brown in color.

**Range:** Dark, wet places throughout the United States. Commonly found in caves, attics, and basements.

**Food sources:** Omnivorous. Decaying vegetative and animal matter.

**Characteristics:** Lays eggs in the soil. Unlike other crickets, does not make sounds.

# Fish, Class Teleostei

## American Eel, *Anguilla rostrata* (Lesueur, 1817)
### (Class Teleostei, Order Anguilliformes, Family Anguillidae)

**Etymology:** *Anguilla* is Latin for eel, and *rostrata* is from Latin *rostrum* for snout or beak. *Rostrata* means beaked or hooked.

**Size:** Adults average 3 feet (0.91 meter) in length.

**Description:** Snake-like body with a long dorsal fin. Most often recognized in its silver stage, with a black back and a silvery or sand-colored underside.

**Range:** Atlantic and Gulf drainages throughout the eastern United States. A common resident of Florida springs, inhabiting spring caves statewide.

Although the eel has a very large range, the population appears to be decreasing.

**Food sources:** Feeds on fish, crayfish, and insects. Larval insects make up most of its diet.

**Characteristics:** Catadromous; spends most of its life in fresh water, then returns to the sea to spawn. While all eels mature in fresh water, it is the female American eel most often found in underwater caves. Rarely seen during the day, it lives in the freshwater caves, coming out at night to feed in the basin and river. The female eel may stay in a cave from seven to twenty years before migrating to the Atlantic Ocean to spawn. The eel is born as a leaf-shaped larva and drifts along until it encounters a freshwater stream. It then metamorphoses into a "glass eel" phase, hiding in a transparent state in the sand of the riverbed until metamorphosing into a pencil eel. Then it changes into a yellow eel, and finally to the familiar silver eel, with a black back and a silver underside.

**Note:** Often seen in the ceiling nooks and crannies in the cavern at Peacock Springs just before the Peanut Tunnel. Although eels are enjoyed as a food source in other countries, they are not as popular a meal in America (although I have heard they are quite tasty). The North American eel is a different species than those found in other parts of the world.

**Note:** In addition, an unidentified light tan eel approximately a quarter-inch in diameter and less than a foot long is occasionally seen by cave divers in Florida's underwater caves. It would be scientifically important for one to be legally collected for identification.

## Unusual Cave Encounters, by Thomas R. Sawicki

Probably the only story I have that might be of interest to readers is regarding two encounters with the American eel, *Anguilla rostrata*, in Florida's caves. One was during a solo dive in Devil's Eye at Ginnie Springs, which occurred in the early 2000s. It was very brief. I was around the Maple Leaf on the main line, around 900 feet in the system, heading out of the cave. Suddenly something that appeared very snake-like and very large darted in front of me, just inches from my mask, swimming from my right to left. It was there and gone in an instant. A quick glance to my left and my light picked up an American eel swimming quickly away from me—and then I started to breathe again!

The second time I saw one of these animals was a couple of years ago in Jackson Blue Cave near the "Stoplight," around 2,000 feet or so back in the system. I was diving with Mike Stine. The animal did not quickly swim off, but instead meandered around us as we gawked at it. It must have been at least 4 feet long. I was amazed at how calm the animal was, especially considering it suddenly found itself in a brightly lit chamber with two large bubble-blowing aliens watching it.

The American eel is a fascinating animal, and although they are known to enter Florida's caves, they are a rare sight. Very little research has been done on the American eel in Florida's caves, and there is a lot that is not known about their cave habits. If you are lucky enough to encounter one of these enigmatic animals while cave diving in Florida, enjoy the experience. You may even make observations that increase our understanding of their biology in Florida's caves!

# Redeye Chub, *Pteronotropis harperi* Fowler, 1941
## (Class Teleostei, Order Cypriniformes, Family Cyprinidae)

Also known as redeye shiner and spring chub.

**Etymology:** *Pteronotropis* comes from *ptero*, Greek for wing, and *noton*, referring to the backside of an animal. *Notropis* refers to species with an enlarged dorsal fin on breeding males. *Harperi* refers to Francis Harper (1886–1972) who collected the type specimen.

**Size:** Average 1.5–2.5 inches (3.81–6.35 centimeters) in length.

**Description:** Small fish with a distinctive red eye (sometimes faint) and a dark band running the length of the body. Small barbels at the corners of mouth. Black at base of caudal fin.

**Range:** Found in springs and spring runs in north Florida, southern Alabama, and southern Georgia.

**Food sources:** Small crustaceans, small insects, and even smaller fish.

**Characteristics:** This is the little guy that hangs out with you during your deco stop at Friedman Sink. Encountered in cave systems by divers as far back as miles from the nearest streams. It is possible this small fish follows divers, using the divers' lights to find tasty and unsuspecting cave critters. Possibly the most common fish in Florida caves.

# Blackbanded Darter, *Percina nigrofasciata* (Agassiz, 1854)
## (Class Teleostei, Order Perciformes, Family Percidae)

**Etymology:** *Percina* from the Greek for little perch. *Nigrofasciata* means black-banded.

**Size:** Grows to 4.33 inches (11 centimeters).

**Description:** Small, cylindrical, light-colored fish with dark brown to black vertical bands that extend from a horizontal line. Color varies according to habitat, for instance, if living in a sandy stream with clear water the fish will be a lighter color.

**Range:** Southeastern United States Atlantic and Gulf Slope drainages from the Edisto River in South Carolina south to just above Lake Okeechobee.

**Food sources:** Prefers small invertebrates and crustaceans in the bottom sediment.

**Characteristics:** Lives in a variety of habitats, from headwaters to medium-sized rivers, and from silty, vegetated areas to rocky, sandy streams. Has been observed in caves.

# Atlantic Croaker, *Micropogonias undulatus* (Linnaeus, 1766)
### (Class Teleostei, Order Perciformes, Family Sciaenidae)

Also called king billies and hardheads.

**Etymology:** *Micropogonias* comes from the Greek *mikros* for small and *pogon* for beard. *Undulatus* from the Latin for wavy or undulating, refers to the markings on the fish.

The common name croaker refers to the thrumming or drumming noises croakers make by vibrating their swim bladder to attract females.

**Size:** Average 11.8 inches (30 centimeters). Can get as large as 20 inches (50.8 centimeters).

**Description:** Silvery body with wavy bronze lines on upper half. Serrated cheek bone (pre-opercle). Three to five pairs of small barbels on lower jaw.

**Range:** On the west coast of Florida north of Tampa and on the east coast north of West Palm Beach.

**Food sources:** Bottom feeders. Use their barbels to find small fish, mollusks, and crustaceans.

**Characteristics:** Croakers are a schooling, euryhaline fish, meaning they can tolerate a wide range of salinity. Young croakers live in estuaries. They are catadromous, meaning they live in fresh water but move downstream to marine water to spawn. Older fish live in deeper marine waters during the winter but move into estuaries and bays during the rest of the year. Have been observed in caverns, such as Croaker Hole in the St. Johns River.

# White Catfish, *Ameiurus catus* (Linnaeus, 1758)
## (Class Teleostei, Order Siluriformes, Family Ictaluridae)

Also called a fork-tail cat.

**Etymology:** *Ameiurus* is Greek and refers to the caudal (tail) fin not having a notch, as most species of catfish do not have a forked tail, *catus* is Latin and means intelligent, sagacious.

**Size:** Adults average 13 inches (33.02 centimeters) but can reach more than 24 inches (60.96 centimeters) in length.

**Description:** White catfish have a wider, flatter head than the bullhead catfish. Mostly shiny dark gray to silver on the back with a shiny white underbelly but can also be mottled. Most notably, the white catfish has a forked tail, and the anal fin is rounder than that of other catfish seen in and around Florida's caves.

**Range:** Prefers slightly deeper, warm rivers and streams throughout Florida. Occasionally found in slightly brackish waters.

**Food sources:** Small fish, aquatic insects, fish eggs, and occasionally aquatic vegetation.

**Characteristics:** The white catfish is a nocturnal hunter, emerging after sunset to scavenge the bottom sediments for food. It is also a nest builder, with both parents building the nest and guarding the fry.

**Note:** White catfish can be found far back in aquatic caves, although they are not as common as the bullhead catfishes. Mike and I observed a school of white catfish "moon gazing" at Cow Spring on a bright moonlit night. Over a period of about an hour, a large number of white catfish positioned themselves just inside the downstream cavern and hovered facing the full moon.

# Yellow Bullhead, *Ameiurus natalis* (Lesueur, 1819)
## (Class Teleostei, Order Siluriformes, Family Ictaluridae)

Also known as butter cat, yellow cat, creek cat, white-whiskered bullhead, greaser, polliwog, chucklehead.

**Etymology:** *Ameiurus* is Greek and refers to the caudal fin not having a notch, *natalis* is Latin and means birthday.

**Size:** Grow to a little over 1 foot (30.48 centimeters).

**Description:** The yellow bullhead looks very much like the brown bullhead, with the same dark mottled sides fading to a light belly and a square tail. The anal fin has twenty-four to twenty-seven rays. The difference between the yellow bullhead and the brown bullhead is that the chin barbels of the yellow bullhead are white to lightly colored.

**Range:** Throughout eastern United States. Prefers slow, warm water with a soft floor of mud or sand.

**Food sources:** Nocturnal scavenger of detritus; also eats small fish and invertebrates.

**Characteristics:** The yellow bullhead is the most common catfish found in Florida caves. Both parents build the nest and tend the eggs. The male guards the eggs and fry.

# Brown Bullhead, *Ameiurus nebulosus* (Lesueur, 1819)
## (Class Teleostei, Order Siluriformes, Family Ictaluridae)

Also known as creek cat, mud cat, horned pout, red cat, speckled cat.

**Etymology:** *Ameiurus* is Greek and refers to the caudal fin not having a notch, *nebulosus* is Latin for cloudy or foggy, in reference to the dark mottled coloration of the fish.

**Size:** Adults typically 8–14 inches (20.32–35.56 centimeters) long and 1–2.5 pounds (0.45–1.13 kilograms).

**Description:** The chin barbels on the brown bullhead catfish are colored brown to black (as opposed to light-colored barbels on the yellow bullhead). The body of the brown bullhead is tan to yellow with darker brown to black mottling fading to a white belly. Flat head. Has a square tail and long anal fin with nineteen to twenty-three rays.

**Range:** Throughout eastern United States. Prefers slow, warm water with a soft floor of mud or sand.

**Food sources:** Primarily a nocturnal bottom feeder, using the sensitive barbels to find a wide variety of food such as invertebrates, detritus, and small fish. Brown bullhead catfish have taste buds in their barbels and mouths as well as all over their bodies, helping them find food in low visibility.

**Characteristics:** Can tolerate low oxygen and muddy water. Commonly found in caves such as Peacock Springs. Creates nests near underwater snags or rocks. Both parents care for the eggs and fry. The brown bullhead is the second most common catfish found in Florida caves. Considered a delicious fish (I prefer them fried).

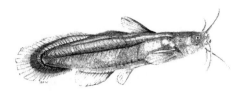

# Madtoms, *Noturus* Rafinesque, 1818

### Black Madtom, *Noturus funebris* Gilbert and Swain, 1891

Western Florida panhandle.

### Tadpole Madtom, *Noturus gyrinus* (Mitchill, 1817)

Throughout Florida. Shown in illustration.

### Speckled Madtom, *Noturus leptacanthus* Jordan, 1877

Florida peninsula.

### (Class Teleostei, Order Siluriformes, Family Ictaluridae)

There are thirty species of madtom catfish, but only three live in Florida.

Also known as madtom catfish and stone cats.

**Etymology:** From the Greek *noton* for back and *oura* for tail, "back tail," referring to the connection between the adipose fin and the caudal (tail) fin. *Funebris* refers to the uniform black coloration of this species. *Gyrinus* is Greek for tadpole. *Leptacanthus* from *leptos* meaning slender and *canthos* meaning spine.

**Size:** Very small catfish, generally only about 4.5 inches (11.43 centimeters) long.

**Description:** Range in color from yellowish to dark gray. Various madtoms are similar in appearance, telling them apart is difficult. Like other catfishes, the madtom has eight whiskers, four barbels on top and four on the bottom of the face, scaleless skin, and a rounded tail. Unlike other catfishes, the adipose fin (behind the dorsal fin) is attached to the tail fin.

**Range:** Throughout the eastern United States in a wide variety of water bodies with flowing water, including springs, rivers, and lakes.

**Food sources:** Carnivorous. Prefers small, aquatic insects and crustaceans.

**Characteristics:** Mostly nocturnal. Delivers a nasty sting through the spines on its pectoral fins if stepped on or carelessly handled. The pectoral fin has a poison sac at the base, the sting is painful but not dangerous. Common in caverns. Often mistaken for "baby" catfish.

**Note:** Madtoms are small enough to get into beverage cans discarded in the water. When picking up cans, it's a good idea to check them for madtom catfish or small crayfish before tossing the can in the recycling bin.

# Flathead Catfish, *Pylodictis olivaris*
# (Rafinesque, 1818)

## (Class Teleostei, Order Siluriformes, Family Ictaluridae)

Also known as yellow cat, mud cat, shovelhead, johnny cat, Opelousas.

**Etymology:** Rafinesque apparently coined the name *Pylodictis* (also spelled *pilodictis*) after the common name for the fish "mud cat." *Olivaris* is Latin, meaning olive-colored.

**Size:** Can get very large, up to 5 feet (1.52 meters) in length, although the ones in Florida are usually smaller.

**Description:** A large catfish with the head flattened between tiny eyes and a distinctive, jutting lower jaw. Mottled appearance of darker olive and brown colors on the fins and back fading to yellow and cream on the belly.

**Range:** Large, deep, slow-moving rivers and major tributaries in the southeast United States. Often seen in Madachuck Spring in the Chipola River.

**Food sources:** Primarily predatory, preferring live prey. Feed mostly at night. Juveniles feed on aquatic insect larvae, small microcrustaceans, and small fish. Adults feed on crayfish and fish.

**Characteristics:** Males build a nest and guard the fry. Solitary but will congregate near food sources. Reported to hybridize with channel catfish.

# *Armored Catfish, Genus *Pterygoplichthys*
# Gill, 1858

## *Vermiculated Sailfin Catfish, *Pterygoplichthys disjunctivus* (Weber, 1991)

*Pterygoplichthys disjunctivus* has a light belly with dark vermiculation (wiggly lines).

# *Orinoco Sailfin Catfish, *Pterygoplichthys multiradiatus* (Hancock, 1828)

*Pterygoplichthys multiradiatus* has a light belly with darker splotches that do not form vermiculation. Shown in illustration.

## (Class Teleostei, Order Siluriformes, Family Loricariidae)

Also known as armored catfish, walking catfish, sailfin catfish, vermiculated sailfin catfish.

**Etymology:** *Pterygoplichthys* from Greek words *pteron* or *pterux*, meaning wing, *hoplon*, referring to a large shield of the Greek infantry, and *ichthys*, meaning fish.

There are many described species of armored catfish, none are native to Florida. *Disjunctivus*, from the Latin *disjunctus*, may refer to the pattern of vermiculation. *Multiradiatus* from Latin *multi*, meaning many, and *radiatus*, meaning with rays.

**Size:** Reaches 11.8–21.65 inches (30–55 centimeters) in length.

**Description:** Triangular, torpedo-shaped catfish covered with large, bony plates. Has a sucker mouth with barbels located underneath the head. Dark background with light to white spots or patterns forming vermiculation and chevrons across body. Long, large, spined dorsal fin. Bottom tail lobe larger than top lobe.

**Range:** Warm streams and rivers throughout Florida. Also found in other states. Native to Central and South America.

**Food sources:** Benthic feeders, using sucker mouth and specialized teeth to eat decomposing organic matter (detritivores) but will eat small invertebrates and algae. Reported to eat wood.

**Characteristics:** Nonnative. Displaces native species through disturbance and destruction. Males dig tunnels along riverbanks, creating erosion. The female lays eggs in the tunnels. Adult sailfin guard the entrance to the nest burrow.

These fish can also displace native species through sheer numbers, having high numbers of offspring. They demonstrate care toward the young.

Intolerant of low temperatures, but able to withstand low water quality and can breathe air. Reported to walk over land using pectoral fins to pull themselves along to other water bodies. Can survive out of water for thirty hours.

They are also able to tolerate salty water and may be able to travel along the coast.

# *Armored Catfish, Genus *Hypostomus* Lacepede, 1803

**\*Suckermouth Catfish, *Hypostomus plecostomus* (Linnaeus, 1758)**

**(Class Teleostei, Order Siluriformes, Family Loricariidae)**

**Etymology:** *Hypostomus* from Greek *hypo*, meaning under and *stoma*, meaning mouth. *Plecostomus* is from Greek *pleco*, meaning pleated, and *stoma*, meaning mouth.

The main difference between these genera of armored catfish is that Pterygoplichthys has between nine and fourteen dorsal fin rays and Hypostomus has seven to eight dorsal fin rays.

# Salamanders, Class Amphibia

# Three-Lined Salamander, *Eurycea guttolineata* (Holbrook, 1838)

**(Class Amphibia, Order Caudata, Family Plethodontidae)**

**Etymology:** *Eurycea* possibly refers to Eurydice, daughter of Apollo and wife of Orpheus in Greek mythology. *Guttolineata* from Latin *gutta*, meaning spot, and *lineata*, meaning lined.

**Size:** Ranges in size from 4–6.25 inches (10.16–15.88 centimeters).

**Description:** Slender, tan to light brown salamander with three distinct dark brown to black stripes running the length of the body. Underside is yellowish with dark spots.

**Range:** Near water in the southeast United States, south into the Florida panhandle.

**Food sources:** Small invertebrates and insect larvae.

**Characteristics:** Nocturnal. Larvae are aquatic. Can be found in caverns and near cave openings.

# Florida Slimy Salamander, *Plethodon grobmani* (Allen and Neill, 1949)

## (Class Amphibia, Order Caudata, Family Plethodontidae)

Also known as the southeastern slimy salamander.

**Etymology:** *Plethodon* from Greek *plēthos*, meaning fullness or magnitude, and *odon*, meaning teeth. *Grobmani* is after Arnold B. Grobman (1918–2012), an American herpetologist and director of the Florida Museum of Natural History from 1952 to 1959.

**Size:** Large salamanders growing to 6.75 inches (17.15 centimeters) in length.

**Description:** Beautiful. Black with white, silver, or gold spots.

**Range:** Southern Alabama and Georgia south to central Florida.

**Food sources:** Insects and other small invertebrates.

**Characteristics:** Nocturnal. Typically buried under soil or debris, such as rotting wood or leaf litter. Eggs are laid in rotting wood, in rocks or underground. Can be found in caverns. Defend themselves by secreting a slimy, smelly, glue-like substance.

# Mammals, Class Mammalia

## Bats, Order Chiroptera
### (Class Mammalia, Family Vespertilionidae)

The scientific name of the order Chiroptera is from the Latin *chiro* for hand and the Greek *pteron* for wing. The wings of a bat are formed from elongated fingers.

Three species of bats are commonly found in Florida caves, which they use as daytime shelter, roosts for hibernation during winter, or as maternity roosts. Bats are usually crepuscular (most active in the late afternoon or early morning hours) or nocturnal (most active through the night), or both. Bats do a wonderful job eating insects we consider pests.

A note about White-nose syndrome: Bats are susceptible to a disease called White-nose syndrome (WNS). This is a sickness associated with the fungus *Pseudogymnoascus destructans*. The fungus is believed to have originated in Europe; bats there have adapted to the fungus. The fungus was discovered in North America in 2006. Thousands of bats have died after showing signs of the fungus, a white fuzz showing up on the muzzle, head, back, and wings. The fungus grows while the bats are hibernating. Once the white fuzz shows up, the bat has already been battling the infection and is weak from energy-expenditure and dehydration. White-nose syndrome is more prevalent during lower temperatures, the fungus is psychrophilic (cold-loving). The fungus can spread between caves through bats or other animals. People who visit caves where bats are present are asked to decontaminate their clothing to avoid spreading the fungus.

### Big Brown Bat, *Eptesicus fuscus* (Palisot de Beauvois, 1796)

**Etymology:** *Eptesicus* from Greek *epten*, meaning able to fly, and *oikos*, meaning house. *Fuscus* from Latin, meaning dark or dusky.

**Size:** Body length 4.33–5.12 inches (11–13 centimeters). Wingspan 13 inches (33.02 centimeters).

**Description:** Buff beige to dark brown, sometimes seems to have an oily sheen. The hairless face, ears, wings, and tail are black. Broad snout. Rarely, brown bats with white markings or even albino bats are known.

**Range:** In caves, forests, and man-made structures throughout the state.

**Food source:** Insects, mostly beetles.

**Characteristics:** Females are larger than males. Roost in colonies while raising their young. Mothers and young recognize each other, even in large colonies. Frequently live in and on human structures such as houses and bridges.

**Note:** FNAI ranking G5/S3 (Globally: Demonstrably Secure/Statewide: Rare).

## Southeastern Myotis, *Myotis austroriparius* (Rhoads, 1897)

Also called the southeastern bat.

**Etymology:** From Latin *myotis* for mouse ear, *austro* for southern, and *riparius*, meaning of or belonging to the bank of a stream.

**Size:** Body length 3.3–3.4 inches (8.38–8.64 centimeters). Wingspan 9–10.5 inches (22.86–26.67 centimeters).

**Description:** Gray to bright orange-brown fur. Females are slightly larger than males.

**Range:** Southeastern United States and north along the Mississippi and Ohio river valleys to Indiana. Florida has the highest concentration of southeastern myotis in the world.

**Food sources:** Begins feeding later in the evening and flies within 2 feet (60.96 centimeters) of the surface of water to catch insects.

**Characteristics:** Usually found in the northern half of the state. Tends to live near streams, ponds, and reservoirs. Roosts in large maternity colonies that are frequently located above water within caves. Southeastern myotis is rarely found roosting in manmade structures and hollow trees in areas where caves are not abundant.

**Note:** FNAI ranking G4/S3 (Globally: Apparently Secure/Statewide: Rare).

**Gray Bat, *Myotis grisescens* Howell, 1909**

Also known as gray myotis.

**Etymology:** From Latin *myotis* for mouse ear, *griseus* for gray.

**Size:** Body length 3.1–3.8 inches (7.87–9.65 centimeters). Wingspan 7.88–11.82 inches (20–30 centimeters).

**Description:** Grayish to brown uniform-colored fur. Wings attach at the ankles rather than the toes of the hind feet.

**Range:** Most of Florida's gray bat population is found in Jackson County west of Tallahassee. Known to inhabit Florida Caverns State Park.

**Food sources:** Insects.

**Characteristics:** Small, insectivorous bat often found occupying large colonial roosts in a few north Florida caves. One of a few species that live in caves year-round. The foraging habitat of gray bats is over riparian areas (riverbanks) and often over water.

**Note:** Listed by the FWC as FE (Federally designated Endangered). Gray bat numbers are critically low, and this species may already be absent from Florida. Disturbance of roosting bats and destruction of cave environments caused a decline in the gray bat population. White-nose syndrome is not believed to be a factor in the declining numbers.

FNAI ranking G4/S1 (Globally: Apparently Secure/Statewide: Critically Imperiled).

## Tricolored Bat, *Perimyotis subflavus* (F. Cuvier, 1832)

Formerly known as eastern pipistrelle, *Pipistrellus subflavus* (F. Cuvier, 1832). The genus *Pipistrellus* reclassified as *Perimyotis* by Henri Menu in 1984.

**Etymology:** From Latin *peri*, meaning near or about, and *myotis* for mouse ear. This bat is closely related to bats assigned to the genus *Myotis*. *Subflavus* comes from Latin, *sub*, meaning almost or below, and *flavus*, meaning yellow. Both together indicate that the bat has a light blonde color.

**Size:** Body length 3.2–3.5 inches (8.13–8.89 centimeters). Wingspan 9 inches (22.86 centimeters).

**Description:** Florida's smallest bat. Reddish yellow to light brown. Hairs are tricolor, darker at the base, pale in the middle, and dusky at the tip.

**Range:** Throughout most of Florida.

**Food sources:** Insects.

**Characteristics:** This small bat is primarily solitary but will form small maternity colonies. It swarms at cave entrances during mating season. It can be found sheltering in hollow trees, the underside of tree bark, manmade structures, and in Spanish moss in summer. In winter, the bat stays in caves and hollows in the sides of fissures and solution holes, as well as other places sheltered from the wind. It flies out in the early evening. Being so small and with such an erratic flight pattern, the tricolored bat is sometimes mistaken for a moth.

## Southeastern Big-Eared Bat, *Corynorhinus rafinesquii* (Lesson, 1827)

Also known as the southeastern long-eared bat, Rafinesque big-eared bat.

**Etymology:** *Corynorhinus* from Greek *coryn*, meaning club, and *rhinos*, meaning nose. Specific name *rafinesquii* refers to Constantine Samuel Rafinesque (1783–1840), a self-educated French polymath who studied natural history and Hebrew, created a unique system of classification, wrote books, and taught, among many other pursuits.

**Size:** Body length 3.6–4.1 inches (9.14–10.41 centimeters). Wingspan averages 10 inches (25.4 centimeters).

**Description:** Dark gray-brown hair on back, lighter on underside. Hairs on the underside are dark at the base and lighter at the tip. Very long hairless ears and large, protruding glands on the snout.

**Range:** Southeastern United States. In cave entrances with good airflow, forests, and man-made structures throughout Florida north of Collier County, but rarely seen. Known to live in the Ocala National Forest.

**Food source:** Insects, mostly moths.

**Characteristics:** Nocturnal, rather than crepuscular. Females are slightly larger than males. Live in and on human structures such as abandoned buildings and bridges, but sensitive to disturbance by human activities.

**Note:** NatureServe status G3/S1 (Globally: Rare/Statewide: Critically Imperiled). IUCN Least Concern.

# Stygobites and Troglobites

*Stygo* from Latin *Stygius* and Greek *Stygios* and referring to the river Styx, the river leading to the underworld, and *-bites* referring to the Greek word *bios,* meaning life. These are the aquatic cave inhabitants.

*Troglo* comes from the Greek word *troglos,* meaning cave. Troglobites are the true cave inhabitants, spending their entire lives in caves.

Restricted to living in caves, these animals exist in darkness. Without natural light, there is no need to see, and no reason to be seen. Colorless and eyeless, stygobites and troglobites develop other senses to travel and find food and love. They have antennae with chemoreceptors to detect nearby life forms and food sources. They have longer, more sensitive limbs. Lower food intake and a slower metabolism make these critters the leaders in energy conservation. As a result, the life spans of the cave-adapted can surpass their light-dwelling cousins.

The small size and mobility of stygobites contributes to the widespread distribution of individuals. Some cave crayfish are found in isolated cave systems across a large geographic area. The dispersal of the species does not prevent extinction however, because isolated populations can face threats from which they are unable to escape. The loss of an isolated population of a species is referred to as extirpation.

Further study and identification of cave fauna, while difficult, is necessary for a thorough understanding of the life in this ecosystem. Our drinking water comes from this subterranean world. Keeping it clean is good for us and for every organism depending on this water.

Protection of aquatic cave environments will allow stygobites and troglobites to flourish and maintain a place that is sacred in many ways for many of us.

In the darkness beyond the reach of sunlight, there is low oxygen and very little food.

Peck's Cave Springtail

Shaggy Ghostsnail

Amphipods

Cave Crayfish

Squirrel Chimney Cave Shrimp

Isopods

Georgia Blind Salamander

# Springtails, Class Collembola

## Peck's Cave Springtail, *Pseudosinella pecki* Christiansen and Bellinger, 1980
### (Class Collembola, Order Collembola, Family Entomobryidae)

Also called the Marianna cave springtail.

**Etymology:** *Pseudosinella* comes from Greek *pseudes*, meaning false or deceptive; the genus name *Sinella* was established by George Brook in 1882 and named after J. Sinel, who collected specimens for Brook.

Named for Stewart Peck, the original discoverer of this springtail in Florida Caverns State Park in 1965.

**Size:** Typically, smaller than 0.25 inch (0.64 centimeter).

**Description:** Terrestrial, cave-dwelling springtail. White, wingless critters with six legs and long antennae.

**Range:** Known from caves in Jackson County, Florida, and southern Alabama and Georgia.

**Food Sources:** Bacteria, fungi, minerals, and detritus.

**Characteristics:** Prefer damp environments. An arthropod with three sets of legs, not a crustacean.

**Note:** Florida Caverns State Park is located in Marianna, Florida, and offers camping and cave tours.

FNAI ranking G2G3/S1 (Globally: Imperiled or Rare/Statewide: Critically Imperiled).

# Snails, Class Gastropoda

## Shaggy Ghostsnail, *Dasyscias franzi*
## Thompson and Hershler, 1991
### (Class Gastropoda, Order Neotaenioglossa, Family Hydrobiidae)

**Etymology:** *Dasyscias* derives from Greek *dasus*, meaning hairy or shaggy, and *skias*, a shadow, in reference to the colorless shell. Named for Richard Franz, a herpetologist with the Florida Museum of Natural History renowned for his contributions to the biology of cave systems in Florida and adjacent regions of the southeastern United States.

**Size:** Average 0.08 inch (0.2 centimeter).

**Description:** Tiny, conical white snail with hairy spiral growths on the whorls of the shell develop immediately after the larval stage (the mature shell is called the teleoconch). Lacks eyes and the body has no pigmentation.

**Range:** Limited to the Blue Springs Cave System on Econfina Creek.

**Food sources:** Feeds on microbial mats.

**Characteristics:** Extremely rare. Their inclusion in this guide is to raise awareness of their presence.

**Note:** FNAI ranking G1/S1 (Globally: Critically Imperiled/Statewide: Critically Imperiled).

# Crustaceans, Class Malacostraca

## Amphipods, Family Crangonyctidea
### (Class Malacostraca, Order Amphipoda, Family Crangonyctidae)

Also called scuds, burrowing scuds, sand fleas, lawn shrimp, and gammarids.

**Etymology:** From *amphi* (both sides, around) and *poda* (foot, leg). Crangonyctidae are a family of cave-dwelling freshwater amphipods.

**Size:** 0.19–0.25 inch (0.48–0.64 centimeter).

**Description:** Terrestrial amphipods can be brown, green, or black. Some aquatic and cave-adapted amphipods are white. Laterally compressed, the thin body makes them appear flat when seen from the side. Some of their eight pairs of legs point forward and some point backward. The first two sets of legs (gnathopods) are for grasping and eating, the next three (pereopods) are for walking, and the last three (pleopods) for swimming. First antennae are longer than second antennae.

**Range:** Prefers cracks and crevices in marine, brackish, and freshwater habitats. Subterranean amphipods can be found in freshwater cave systems throughout the United States.

**Food sources:** Typically scavengers and detritivores, eating algae, and dead and decaying plant and animal matter. Cave amphipods eat protozoans, bacteria, and other organic matter on cave floors and suspended in the water column. Some are predatory, such as *Crangonyx grandimanus*.

Amphipods are reported to be voracious eaters. In a submerged cave in Mexico, I observed an amphipod attached to and apparently feeding on a piece of crayfish suspended in the water. When I pulled the debris from the amphipod, the tiny crustacean immediately attached itself to the flesh at the edge of my thumbnail, apparently continuing to feast!

Amphipods walk, jump, swim, scull on their side, and scoot through the water column. In caves, amphipods can be found crawling along surfaces, often on goethite, moving through bottom sediment and swimming in the water column. Amphipods usually appear as isolated individuals except in certain goethite environments where they are more easily seen as quick-moving white specks against the dark brown and black deposits. They are believed to quickly colonize new areas.

### Florida Crangonyctid, *Crangonyx floridanus* Bousfield, 1963

**Etymology:** *Crangonyx* derives from *Crangon*, the Greek word for shrimp. *Floridanus* refers to the state in which this species was discovered. The word "crangonyctid" in the common name refers to amphipods in the family Crangonyctidae.

Largest females 0.67 inch (1.7 centimeters) and the largest males 0.12 inch (1.3 centimeters).

Throughout the eastern United States.

FNAI ranking G5 (Globally: Apparently secure/Statewide: No ranking).

### Florida Cave Amphipod, *Crangonyx grandimanus* (Bousfield, 1963)

Also called the Florida cave crangonyctid.

**Etymology:** *Crangonyx* derives from *Crangon*, the Greek word for shrimp. *Grandimanus* refers to the large "hands" of this amphipod. The word "crangonyctid" in the alternate common name refers to amphipods in the family Crangonyctidae.

Largest females 0.67 inch (1.7 centimeters) and the largest males 0.12 inch (1.3 centimeters).

FNAI ranking G2G3/S2S3 (Globally: Imperiled to Rare/Statewide: Imperiled to Rare).

### Hobb's Cave Amphipod, *Crangonyx hobbsi* (Shoemaker, 1941)

**Etymology:** *Crangonyx* derives from *Crangon*, the Greek word for shrimp. *Hobbsi* named for Horton H. Hobbs, Jr., a world-renowned zoologist.

Found only in Florida.

FNAI ranking G2G3/S2S3 (Globally: Imperiled to Rare/Statewide: Imperiled to Rare).

## Jackson County Cave Amphipod, *Crangonyx manubrium* (Cannizzaro and Sawicki, 2019)

**Etymology:** *Crangonyx* derives from *Crangon*, the Greek word for shrimp. *Manubrium* comes from Latin for handle, referring to the species being found only in Jackson County in the Florida panhandle, although it likely occurs in surrounding areas. It is also the first stygobitic species of *Crangonyx* described west of the Apalachicola River basin in Florida.

FNAI ranking G1/S1 (Globally: Critically Imperiled/Statewide: Critically Imperiled).

## Sulphurous Cave Amphipod, *Crangonyx sulphurium* Sawicki and Holsinger, 2017

**Etymology:** *Crangonyx* derives from *Crangon*, the Greek word for shrimp. *Sulphurium* refers to the microbial mats found within caves where the species was collected. The mats are described as sulfur oxidizing, meaning microorganisms living in the mats get their energy by the oxidation of hydrogen sulfide (they eat by converting chemicals into energy).

Found in DeLeon Springs, Wekiwa Springs, and Blue Springs state parks. These amphipods appear to share areas with mats of *Thiothrix* and *Beggiatoa* bacteria. If you find growths or deposits during your subterranean dives, it might be worth a closer look.

FNAI ranking G1/S1 (Globally: Critically Imperiled/Statewide: Critically Imperiled).

## Dougherty Plain Cave Amphipod, *Stygobromus doughertyensis* Cannizzaro and Sawicki, 2019

**Etymology:** *Stygobromus* coined by Edward Drinker Cope (1840-1897) in 1872. *Stygo* refers to caves, and *bromus* is Greek for oat. *Doughertyensis* refers to the distribution of the species within the Dougherty Karst Plain in Dougherty County, Georgia, and Jackson County, Florida. Found in the same caves with *S. floridanus* but differs in physical attributes, such as having shorter, less segmented antennae.

**Size:** Around 0.33-0.36 inch (0.84-0.91 centimeter).

FNAI ranking G1/S1 (Globally: Critically Imperiled/Statewide: Critically Imperiled).

## Florida Panhandle Cave Amphipod, *Stygobromus floridanus* Holsinger and Sawicki, 2016

**Etymology:** *Stygobromus* coined by Edward Drinker Cope (1840-1897) in 1872. *Stygo* refers to caves, and *bromus* is Greek for oat. *Floridanus* is from this being the first hypogean (from Greek meaning found in caves) *Stygobromus* described in the state of Florida.

Found only in Washington and Jackson counties.

**Size:** Around 0.24-0.62 inch (0.61-1.57 centimeters).

Found in the same area of Florida as *S. doughertyensis* but differs in physical attributes, such as longer, more segmented antennae.

FNAI ranking G1/S1 (Globally: Critically Imperiled/Statewide: Critically Imperiled).

# Crayfish, Order Decapoda
## (Class Malacostraca, Order Decapoda, Family Cambaridae)

Also known as crawdads, crawfish, mudbugs, and freshwater lobsters.

Although cave divers encounter them throughout submerged caves, cave crayfish are considered rare among the cave critters. This is due to their isolation within relatively confined cave systems, meaning they are restricted to certain systems although sometimes they are able to travel between them. Even so, Florida has more species of stygobitic cave crayfish than any other state or similarly sized area in the world. Many are found in only one cave and have a range of only a few miles.

Cave crayfish are ancient, having colonized the state almost as soon as the peninsula was established, and long-lived, however they are vulnerable to changes in water quality.

Crayfish species are similar, many are only identified by the mature males' gonopods (a set of swimming appendages that are also used in reproduction), primarily by a specialist, an astacologist, using a microscope. Astacology is the study of crayfish and an astacologist is someone who studies crayfish (*astacus* is Latin and from Greek *astakos* meaning crayfish or lobster).

Male crayfish have slightly larger claws and narrower tails than females. Female crayfish retain their eggs and hatched young underneath their abdomen, curling it under to protect their young. Juvenile cave crayfish have been observed leaving the safety of the mother's abdomen and returning when a threat is perceived.

Cave crayfish have a little of the wanderer in them, intergrade species resulting from breeding with their basin cousins have been found among cave populations (Walsh, 2001). New species are occasionally discovered. The list below contains some of the species of cave crayfish encountered in caves. The genus names *Cambarus* and *Procambarus* differentiate between the shape of the tip of the first pleopod (on the abdominal segment, the first of the five pairs of limbs used for propulsion.)

**Food sources:** Crayfish are omnivores and will eat pretty much anything living or dead. They scavenge organic debris on the cave floors, graze on bacterial growth, and eat worms, snails, small fish, and other troglobites. Juvenile crayfish feed on very small plankton and are voracious cannibals. Many cave crayfish forage near cave openings, where debris falls into the cave habitat. This feeding activity contributes to their vulnerability from outside pressures.

### Dougherty Plain Cave Crayfish, *Cambarus cryptodytes* Hobbs, 1941

Also called the Apalachicola cave crayfish.

**Etymology:** *Cambarus* from the Greek word *kammaros* for lobster Latinized as *cammarus* or *gammarus*. *Cryptodytes* is Latin from *crypto*, meaning hidden, and Greek *dutēs*, meaning diver.

**Range:** Limited to Jackson, Calhoun, and Washington counties. Found in the same locations as the Georgia blind salamander *Eurycea wallacei*.

**Characteristics:** Also known to live outside the state of Florida, having been found in the Apalachicola River drainage system in Georgia.

**Note:** Shown in illustration. FNAI ranking G2G3/S2 (Globally: Imperiled to Rare/Statewide: Imperiled).

### Orlando Cave Crayfish, *Procambarus acherontis* (Lonnberg, 1894)

Also known as the Orange-Seminole cave crayfish and Palm Springs cave crayfish.

**Etymology:** *Procambarus* from Latin prefix *pro*, meaning before or in front of, and *cambarus* from the Greek word *kammaros* for lobster, Latinized as *cammarus* or *gammarus*. *Acherontis* refers to Greek mythology; Acheron is a river in the underworld.

**Range:** Limited to northern Orange and southern Seminole counties.

**Note:** The first troglobitic crayfish species found in Florida. FNAI ranking G1/S1 (Globally: Critically Imperiled/Statewide: Critically Imperiled).

### Silver Glen Springs Cave Crayfish, *Procambarus attiguus* Hobbs and Franz, 1992

**Etymology:** *Procambarus* from Latin prefix *pro*, meaning before or in front of, and *cambarus* from the Greek word *kammaros* for lobster, Latinized as *cammarus* or *gammarus*. *Attiguus* is from Latin, meaning neighboring and alluding to the similarities between this crayfish and *Procambarus delicatus*.

**Range:** Found only in Silver Glen Spring in the Ocala National Forest.

**Note:** FNAI ranking G1/S1 (Globally: Critically Imperiled/Statewide: Critically Imperiled).

### Big-Cheeked Cave Crayfish, *Procambarus delicatus* Hobbs and Franz, 1986

**Etymology:** *Procambarus* from Latin prefix *pro*, meaning before or in front of, and *cambarus* from the Greek word *kammaros* for lobster, Latinized as *cammarus* or *gammarus*. *Delicatus* can mean dainty, delicate, or fastidious.

**Range:** Found only in Alexander Springs in Lake County.

**Note:** FNAI ranking G1/S1 (Globally: Critically Imperiled/Statewide: Critically Imperiled).

### Santa Fe Cave Crayfish, *Procambarus erythrops* Relyea and Sutton, 1975

Also known as the red-eyed cave crayfish.

**Etymology:** *Procambarus* from Latin prefix *pro*, meaning before or in front of, and *cambarus* from the Greek word *kammaros* for lobster, Latinized as *cammarus* or *gammarus*. *Erythrops* derived from Greek *erythros*, meaning red, and *ops*, meaning eye.

**Range:** Limited to the Santa Fe River watershed in Suwannee and Columbia counties.

**Description:** Can grow to 3.5 inches (8.9 centimeters) long. White to light tan. The eyes of this subterranean crayfish have a red pigment spot.

**Note:** Listed by the FWC as ST (State-designated Threatened). FNAI ranking G1/S1 (Globally: Critically Imperiled/Statewide: Critically Imperiled).

### Orange Lake Cave Crayfish, *Procambarus franzi* Hobbs and Lee, 1976

**Etymology:** *Procambarus* from Latin prefix *pro*, meaning before or in front of, and *cambarus* from the Greek word *kammaros* for lobster, Latinized as *cammarus* or *gammarus*. Named for Richard Franz, a renowned herpetologist with the Florida Museum of Natural History.

**Range:** Limited to an area south of Orange Lake, in Marion County.

**Note:** FNAI ranking G1/S1 (Globally: Critically Imperiled/Statewide: Critically Imperiled).

### Big Blue Springs Cave Crayfish, *Procambarus horsti* Hobbs and Means, 1972

Also known as Big Blue Springs crayfish and Horst's cave crayfish.

**Etymology:** *Procambarus* from Latin prefix *pro*, meaning before or in front of, and *cambarus* from the Greek word *kammaros* for lobster, Latinized as *cammarus* or *gammarus*. *Horsti* after Michael N. Horst, who provided the type specimen.

**Range:** Limited to a few springs on the Wacissa River and Shepard Spring in St. Marks National Wildlife Refuge.

**Note:** FNAI ranking G1/S1 (Globally: Critically Imperiled/Statewide: Critically Imperiled).

## Coastal Lowland Cave Crayfish, *Procambarus leitheuseri* Franz and Hobbs, 1983

Also known as Leitheuser's cave crayfish.

**Etymology:** *Procambarus* from Latin prefix *pro*, meaning before or in front of, and *cambarus* from the Greek word *kammaros* for lobster, Latinized as *cammarus* or *gammarus*. Named for Arthur Terrence Leitheuser, who collected the type specimens.

**Range:** Limited to Hernando and Pasco counties.

**Note:** FNAI ranking G1G2/S1S2 (Globally: Critically Imperiled to Rare/Statewide: Critically Imperiled to Rare). Needing further study.

## Alachua Light Fleeing Cave Crayfish, *Procambarus lucifugus alachua* (Hobbs, 1940)

**Etymology:** *Procambarus* from Latin prefix *pro*, meaning before or in front of, and *cambarus* from the Greek word *kammaros* for lobster, Latinized as *cammarus* or *gammarus*. *Lucifugus* means light-fleeing or nocturnal. *Alachua* indicates the location of the holotype (the specimen that determines the species description).

**Range:** Limited to caves in Alachua and Gilchrist counties.

*Procambarus lucifugus* FNAI ranking G2G3/S2S3 (Globally: Imperiled to Rare/Statewide: Imperiled to Rare). In some locations rarer than in others.

## Withlacoochee Light-Fleeing Cave Crayfish, *Procambarus lucifugus lucifugus* (Hobbs, 1940)

**Etymology:** *Procambarus* from Latin prefix *pro*, meaning before or in front of, and *cambarus* from the Greek word *kammaros* for lobster, Latinized as *cammarus* or *gammarus*. *Lucifugus* means light-fleeing or nocturnal. The specific name is written twice to indicate that this species is the type for the species.

**Range:** Limited to Citrus, Hernando, Lake, and Marion counties.

*Procambarus lucifugus* FNAI ranking G2G3/S2S3 (Globally: Imperiled to Rare/Statewide: Imperiled to Rare). In some locations rarer than in others.

## Putnam County Cave Crayfish, *Procambarus morrisi* Hobbs and Franz, 1991

Also known as the Devil's Sink cave crayfish.

**Etymology:** *Procambarus* from Latin prefix *pro*, meaning before or in front of, and *cambarus* from the Greek word *kammaros* for lobster, Latinized as *cammarus* or *gammarus*. Named after Florida biologist, cave explorer, and all-around nice guy Tom Morris.

**Range:** Found only in Devil's Sink Cave in Putnam County.

**Note:** FNAI ranking G1/S1 (Globally: Critically Imperiled/Statewide: Critically Imperiled).

## Woodville Karst Cave Crayfish, *Procambarus orcinus* Hobbs and Means, 1972

Also known as the Woodville cave crayfish.

**Etymology:** *Procambarus* from Latin prefix *pro*, meaning before or in front of, and *cambarus* from the Greek word *kammaros* for lobster, Latinized as *cammarus* or *gammarus*. *Orcinus* is Latin and refers to the realm of the dead.

**Range:** Limited to the Woodville Karst Plain in Leon and Wakulla counties.

**Note:** FNAI ranking G1/S1 (Globally: Critically Imperiled/Statewide: Critically Imperiled).

## Pallid Cave Crayfish, *Procambarus pallidus* (Hobbs, 1940)

**Etymology:** *Procambarus* from Latin prefix *pro*, meaning before or in front of, and *cambarus* from the Greek word *kammaros* for lobster, Latinized as *cammarus* or *gammarus*. *Pallidus* translates from Latin, meaning pale.

**Range:** Limited to northern peninsular Florida, found in the Suwannee River and tributaries and system-connected sinkholes.

**Characteristics:** Also known to live outside the state of Florida, having been found in the Withlacoochee River system in Georgia.

**Note:** FNAI ranking G2G3/S2S3 (Globally: Imperiled to Rare/Statewide: Imperiled to Rare). Known from many caves but needing further study.

## North Florida Spider Cave Crayfish, *Troglocambarus maclanei* Hobbs, 1942

Also known as spider cave crayfish, northern spider cave crayfish, and McLane's cave crayfish.

**Etymology:** *Troglocambarus* derives from *troglo*, meaning caves or cave dweller, and *cambarus* derived from the Greek word *kammaros* for lobster, Latinized as *cammarus* or *gammarus*. Named after William M. McLane, who first collected a specimen while out and about in Florida with Horton Hobbs, Jr., and Harley Bakwel Sherman from the University of Florida.

**Range:** The most widespread cave crayfish, found throughout central Florida in Alachua, Citrus, Gilchrist, Hernando, Levy, Marion, Pasco, and Suwannee counties. While considered common for cave crayfishes, the population is globally small.

**Size:** 0.39–1.97 inches (1–5 centimeters).

**Characteristics:** Found hanging from cave ceiling, divers' exhalations can cause the crayfish to drop through the water column.

**Note:** FNAI ranking G2/S2 (Globally: Imperiled/Statewide: Imperiled).

**Orlando Spider Cave Crayfish, *Troglocambarus sp.***

**Note:** It has not been described and has no specific name.

**Etymology:** *Troglocambarus* derives from *troglo*, meaning caves or cave dweller, and *cambarus* derived from the Greek word *kammaros* for lobster, Latinized as *cammarus* or *gammarus*.

**Range:** Known only from Apopka Blue Sink in Orange County.

**Note:** FNAI ranking G1/S1 (Globally: Critically Imperiled/Statewide: Critically Imperiled).

# Squirrel Chimney Cave Shrimp,
## *Palaemonetes cummingi* Chase, 1954
### (Class Malacostraca, Order Decapoda, Family Palaemonidae)

Also called the Florida cave shrimp.

**Etymology:** The genus derives from the Greek *paleo*, meaning ancient or primitive, *monetes* for dwell, dweller, or one who dwells. *Cummingi* from the name of the collector, Robert B. Cumming of the University of Florida Department of Biology.

**Size:** 1.2 inches (3.05 centimeters).

**Description:** Small shrimp with a faintly white or translucent body and six dorsal spines on its rostrum (a forward projection on the top of the head).

**Range:** Known only from a single sinkhole, Squirrel Chimney Cave, in Alachua County.

**Food sources:** Primarily microscopic plankton and microbes found in silt.

**Characteristics:** The only cave shrimp known to live in Florida. Possibly already extinct. Although few individuals have been found, it is possible more exist in deeper portions of the cave. This cave-adapted shrimp is closely related to the surface shrimp *Palaemonetes paludosus*, known as grass shrimp or glass shrimp.

**Note:** Listed by the FWC as FT (Federally designated Threatened). Owners maintain and protect the site, which is very susceptible to erosion and pollution. The site was proposed for designation as a National Natural Landmark for the density and variety of aquatic cave creatures living there, including North Florida spider cave crayfish (*Troglocambarus maclanei*), the light-fleeing cave crayfish (*Procambarus lucifugus alachua*), the pallid cave crayfish (*Procambarus pallidus*) and Hobb's cave amphipod (*Crangonyx hobbsi*).

FNAI ranking GH/SH (Of historical occurrence, possibly extirpated [locally extinct], may be rediscovered).

# Isopods, Order Isopoda
## (Class Malacostraca, Order Isopoda, Family Asellidae)

From Greek *isos*, meaning equal or uniform, and *pod*, meaning foot.

Also called isopods, aquatic sow bugs. Related to roly-polys (pill bugs, sow bugs) and wood lice.

**Size:** Usually less than 0.25 inch (0.64 centimeter) in length.

**Description:** Vertically compressed, appearing flat from above with legs sticking out on both sides.

**Range:** Throughout Florida

**Food sources:** Scavenge organic matter suspended in the water column and on cave floors.

**Characteristics:** There are four known species of freshwater stygobiotic isopods found in central Florida north through the panhandle and into southern Georgia.

Isopods can be found on the ceilings and floors of inundated caves as well as hanging suspended in the water column in the middle of passages. Isopods appear in colonies in certain passages in densities of one to five per square foot (929 sq. centimeters). Isopods swim in a straight direction, frequently spiraling vertically up or down through the water column.

They appear to have breeding seasons, mass numbers of isopods appearing in the spring over mounds of fairly fine sand and silt in undisturbed areas of cave passage, such as in the Crossunder Tunnel of Madison Blue. Sheck Exley referred to these areas as "isopod party rooms."

**Florida Cave Isopod, *Caecidotea hobbsi* (Maloney, 1939)**

Also called the Hobb's cave isopod.

**Etymology:** *Caecidotea* comes from "*Idotea* but blind." *Idotea* was the genus name assigned by Fabricius in 1798, and *caeci* is Latin, meaning blind. Named for Horton H. Hobbs, Jr., a world-renowned zoologist.

Only known to caves in Alachua, Citrus, and Marion counties.

Shown in illustration. FNAI ranking G1G2/S1 (Globally: Critically Imperiled to Imperiled/ Statewide: Critically Imperiled).

**Econfina Cave Isopod, *Caecidotea putea* Lewis, 2009**

Also called the Econfina Springs cave isopod.

**Etymology:** *Caecidotea* comes from "*Idotea* but blind." *Putea* is Latin referring to a well or pit.

Known only from three locations in southern Georgia and Florida panhandle.

FNAI ranking G1G2/S1 (Globally: Critically Imperiled to Imperiled/Statewide: Critically Imperiled).

**Marianna Cave Isopod, *Mexistenasellus floridensis* Lewis and Sawicki, 2016**

Also known as Florida cave isopod.

**Etymology:** *Mexistenasellus* refers to this family of isopod (Stenasellidae) being known from Mexico. *Floridensis* to acknowledge that this is the first of its genus found east of the Mississippi.

Known only to one aquatic cave system, Hole in the Wall, in Jackson County.

FNAI ranking G1/S1 (Globally: Imperiled/Statewide: Imperiled).

**Swimming Little Florida Cave Isopod, *Remasellus parvus* (Steeves, 1964)**

**Etymology:** *Remasellus* from Latin *remus*, meaning oar, and *asellus* refers to the shape and use of pereopods (the walking limbs attached to the body). *Asellus* means a little ass. *Parvus* is Latin for small.

These isopods do not have gills and also lack a carapace, they breathe through special pleopods, limbs on the back of their body. Known only to caves in northern Florida.

**Note:** This is the only species in the genus *Remasellus*.

FNAI ranking G1G2/S1S2 (Globally: Critically Imperiled to Imperiled/Statewide: Critically Imperiled to Imperiled).

# Salamanders, Class Amphibia

## Georgia Blind Salamander, *Eurycea wallacei* (Carr, 1939)
### (Class Amphibia, Order Caudata, Family Plethodontidae)

Also known as the blind cave salamander, cave salamander, Southeastern blind cave salamander.

**Etymology:** *Eurycea* may derive from the name *Eurydice* of Greek mythology. *Wallacei* honors Howard K. Wallace of the Department of Zoology at the University of Florida. The earlier genus name *Haideotriton*, synonymized with *Eurycea*, comes from Greek *Hades*, the abode of the dead, and *triton* meaning salamander.

**Size:** Reaches a maximum 3 inches (7.62 centimeters) in length.

**Description:** An almost completely white salamander with a broad, flat head, rounded snout, and finned tail. Possesses no eyes and no lungs. Respiration is through feathery pink or red external gills and through the skin.

**Range:** In clear water caves and deep wells across southwestern Georgia and the Florida panhandle between Apalachicola and Choctawhatchee rivers. Often found in caves near where bats are present.

**Food sources:** Troglobitic crustaceans such as amphipods and other microcrustaceans.

**Characteristics:** The only aquatic, cave-adapted vertebrate in Florida. Crawls along the walls and ceilings of inundated passages and swims through caves with clear water. A perfect example of neoteny, the cave salamander retains many juvenile characteristics.

The blind salamander occurs in Florida only in the caves west of the Apalachicola River.

Diving in Hole in the Wall Cave near Marianna, we observed salamanders far back in the system.

**Note:** Listed by the FWC as ST (State-designated Threatened) and the Georgia Department of Natural Resources Commission as a threatened species. FNAI ranking G2/S2 (Globally: Imperiled/Statewide: Imperiled).

## Dr. Archie Carr Reconnects with an Old Acquaintance, by Richard Franz, Herpetologist, Florida Museum of Natural History, University of Florida, retired

Sitting at the entrance gate to Florida Caverns State Park, I was waiting for the arrival of Dr. Archie Carr, who was driving in from New Orleans. I had promised to meet him here this Sunday morning in spring 1971 to show him his first live Georgia blind salamander, *Haideotriton wallacei*, which he named in 1939 but had not seen since. I had driven up from Gainesville early that morning to Marianna with great anticipation. . . . What a thrill! I would have Dr. Archie Carr, my famed hero, all to myself, and lead him into a cave with this amazing population of white salamanders.

Dave Lee and I originally located this cave salamander population in the late 1960s on one of our many trips with our high school students from Baltimore. We had found them in other local caves in the Marianna area, but nothing compared to the incredible population here.

Dr. Carr met me at 10 a.m., and we drove to a park picnic area, abandoned our cars, and hiked to the cave. The cave was located on a low hill in a cleared area near the Chipola River. The opening was a small slot in Eocene-aged limestone; entry required negotiating a tight squeeze before we dropped into a low chamber, maybe 30 feet long, 4–5 feet high, containing a substantial pool of crystal clear water. Carr and I stood at the water edge, stooped-over in our cramped quarters, scanning the pool at our feet with our caving lights. Water dripped continuously from multitudes of soda-straw formations attached to the ceiling, causing concentric rings to spill out across on the pool surface. Our caving lights scanned the first 5–6 feet of the pool. First, one salamander came into focus, then another, and another. . . . Right there, just beyond our boots, Archie witnessed at least eight 3–4-inch, ghost-like individuals of this rare amphibian . . . his first encounter with it in thirty-two years.

Well, I chanced a look over at Dr. Carr . . . he was grinning and pointing his fingers; his light was shaking in his hand, and he was muttering to himself . . . his body vibrated with excitement, almost bouncing. My first thought was, "He is going to puncture the top of his skull with one or more of those sharp soda-straws just directly above his head. . . ." My second thought was, "Oh crap, what if I kill the famed Archie Carr." Obviously that didn't happen, but his enthusiastic response and my first personal interaction with Dr. Carr will remain one of the highlights of my career.

**Final Notes:** Carr's original specimen, on which he based the description of this new salamander, was obtained from groundwater pumped from a 200-foot well within the city of Albany, Dougherty County, Georgia. Carr named this new species in honor of his friend and colleague, Dr. H. K. Wallace. Wallace, also a faculty member in the Department of Biology at the University of Florida, was a spider expert, who had passions for wolf spiders and other native arachnids.

The scientific name of Georgia blind salamander was recently changed to *Eurycea wallacei*. It is currently listed as state threatened in both Florida and Georgia; the USFWS has been petitioned in 2010 to federally list it. Concerns include its very limited geographic distribution and its confinement to groundwater habitats that are currently subject to extensive groundwater withdraws and potential pollution.

# Oddities

What exactly are these? Although these organisms are found throughout Florida's aquatic world, we'll try to help you figure out whether you are seeing some of our lesser-known critter friends or, if you are a diver, you've been too deep too long and are narced out of your gourd.

Since these special life forms can be found nearly everywhere, I've added a separate section.

Many are open-water creatures, flushed into cave systems by reverse flows. Saltwater intrusion due to both tidal action and over-withdrawal in some of our southerly and coastal cave systems can contribute food sources to the ecosystems, leading to unusual and unexpected life forms. Others become stranded in the cavern or cave environment after a flood event. Some life forms have even been trapped by a closure of their cavern, forcing them to adapt to the available food sources in the dark zone of their new home. Some of these adaptations take many years and lead to very specialized ways of eating, moving, reproducing, and communicating. All of this life happens on a very tiny scale. Presence of these creatures is usually unnoticed by humans, but occasionally it will dawn on us that even in the deepest, darkest caves, we are not alone.

## Freshwater Jellyfish

### (Class Hydrozoa, Order Limnomedusae, Family Olindiidae)

Also referred to as a medusa.

Occasionally a cave diver encounters something that defies explanation. In this case, and lacking a sample for study, we must use the closest approximate creature to describe the characteristics of what we saw, or thought we saw.

What may look like a jellyfish in calm, cool, fresh water is most likely a Hydra, probably from the genus *Craspedacusta*. These translucent bell- or parachute-shaped creatures grow to about 0.8-1 inch (2-2.5 centimeters) in diameter. Originating as tiny polyps on lake and reservoir beds, if environmental factors are just right, the imperceptible polyps grow into little mobile creatures that move by opening and closing like an umbrella. They do not sting like marine jellyfish but do use tentacles to capture food and are even reported to be light-sensitive. They eat tiny zooplankton.

*Craspedacusta* derives from Greek *craspeda*, meaning wardrobe, and refers to the otocysts (organs used by the jellyfish for stabilizing itself) being completely contained within velum or membrane. *Sowerbii* is after James De Carle Sowerby (1787-1871), secretary of the Botanical Society of London, who discovered these species in a water-lily tank in Regent's Park, London, and provided them to Sir Edwin Ray Lankester (1847-1929), who described them in 1880.

Very tiny hydra are observed in the Wayne's World cave system (aka School Sink) in Hudson, Florida. Saltwater intrusion may be a contributor to the existence of these marine creatures in this tidally influenced cave system.

A friend and I, while waiting on some buddies on a dive in the Rose Creek Cave System, witnessed something resembling a jellyfish hydra descending the water column. It clearly moved of its own accord, independently of the water flow; however, since it was quite far back in the cave, well beyond the cavern zone, we can't be certain what we saw was a hydra or some other organism we are unfamiliar with.

# Freshwater Bryozoan

## (Class Phylactolaemata, Order Plumatellida)

Sometimes referred to as Ectoprocta (a synonym of the phylum name Bryozoa).

**Etymology:** *Bryozoa* from the Greek word *bryon*, meaning moss, and *zoon*, meaning animals. Bryozoa are referred to as "moss animals."

Bryozoa are communities of tiny aquatic invertebrate animals, the individuals of which are referred to as zooids. They are approximately 0.02 inch (0.5 millimeter) in length, with the average size of a colony being less than 4 inches (10 centimeters) across. Freshwater colonies resemble a dense, clear, gelatinous substance (strongly resembling a blob of clear jelly).

Bryozoa are filter-feeders, eating microorganisms such as diatoms. Fish, insects, and filter-feeding creatures such as snails eat bryozoa.

Bryozoa form a variety of colonies made of individuals with many different roles and can be found as a coating on all kinds of surfaces and sediments. Some even live on algae and kelp. Colony sizes can be from less than 1 inch (1 centimeter) to more than 3 feet (1 meter) across.

Bryozoa can reproduce by budding. If a piece of the colony is broken off, it can resettle and create a new colony. Freshwater bryozoa are able to reproduce sexually and asexually, as hermaphrodites. They may also form groups of cells called statoblasts that can germinate to create a new individual. The statoblasts are protected by a chitin shell and can survive being frozen and being dried out (as in a severe water drop due to drought or being accidentally picked up on a piece of dive equipment and taken to the diver's home).

Found throughout the world, only the class Phylactolaemata inhabits freshwater environments. The colonies of Phylactolaemata are made entirely of clones of the founding zooid.

While most bryozoa remain static, some are actually capable of movement. Bryozoa live in networks that may be hard or gelatinous depending on the species.

# Tube Worm

## (Class Clitellata, Order Tubificida, Family Naididae)

Also referred to as aquatic oligochaete worm and sludge worm.

**Etymology:** Order name Tubificida comes from the Latin words *tubus*, meaning tube, and *facere*, meaning to make. The family name Naididae, described by C. G. Ehrenberg in 1828, appears to be derived from the word Naiad.

My favorite accidental cave critters.

From sheer basin walls of Troy Spring to the silt-blanketed bedding plane at the threshold of Bonnet Spring and throughout entire cave systems after flood events, these little guys dance the days away. The hair-sized worms are difficult to see but can be observed by shining a light beam at an angle to the floor. They are typically 0.8 inch (2.03 centimeters) in length by 0.04 inch (0.1 centimeter) in width. Two sizes have been most widely reported by Florida cave divers, a small hair-sized variety and a larger pinkish variety. The hair-sized ones are most prevalent. The larger pinkish ones may actually belong to the family Lumbriculidae, described by Czech zoologist František Vejdovský in 1884.

To accurately identify which tubificid species you encounter, mature adults must be examined microscopically.

Tubificids are open-water oligochaetes that get flushed into the cave system as eggs during flood events and other seasonal water fluctuations. This is why they are called an accidental inhabitant. They live in burrows in the silt (another reason to practice good fin technique) with their heads down and derrieres sticking out. They are filter feeders, constantly undulating their bodies to move food upward to their mouths, working their way down into the sediment in pursuit of food, such as bacteria.

Tubificids colonize silty areas out of direct flow and appear more prevalent in cave systems after floods. They are most abundant in eutrophic (excessive nutrient) environments where there is an abundance of their foods and a general depletion of dissolved oxygen in the water. The pockmarks found in cave floors are believed to be the result of catfish gulping mouthfuls of silt in hope of filtering out delicious tubificid worms.

Tubificid worms are potential indicators of water quality. The lower the oxygen level in the water, the fewer the predators and more prominent the tubificids.

Remnant tubes with rounded or square cross-sections from old tubificid colonies can be observed on ledges in many aquatic caves and sinkhole walls. Round tubes may also be the result of activity by the aquatic nymphs of Plecoptera (stoneflies) or Ephemeroptera (mayflies). Tubes with a square cross-section may have small rods on each upper corner supporting a web that snares food from the water. This would be the tubes of larval Chironomidae (aquatic midges). These aquatic creatures are also considered accidental, being primarily open-water animals that may get washed or chased into a subterranean environment.

Tubificids sway like dancers independently of water flow patterns. They pause and retract into their burrows upon detection of potential threats. I've observed tubificids leaning over to each other's burrows.

# Biofilms and Aufwuchs

We may not see the individuals without using a microscope—but collectively these are the slimes, molds, fuzzies, and crusts we notice on rocks and caverns and cave walls. These interesting and odd textures are often made up of and are the result of the activities of communities of living organisms. Other noticeable evidence of microbial activity includes unusual colors. Many cave divers notice the white fuzz surrounding deceased crayfish on a silty cave floor, or a distinct black coloration on an otherwise tannin-stained gold limestone wall. Many of these growths are a collection of microbial cells.

Aufwuchs is a German word meaning surface-growth, overgrowth, or "to grow upon." Because the word Aufwuchs is a noun from the German language, it is capitalized in biological writing. Aufwuchs are the communities of plants, small animals, and detritus on rock surfaces that depend on a light source. Previously, the term periphyton was used to describe organic aquatic colonies. Because the word periphyton was insufficient for the great variety of environments and complexities of microbial life forms involved, biofilm and Aufwuchs are the preferred words.

Biofilms and Aufwuchs are complex biological communities of microorganisms, microscopic bacteria, plants, fungi, and animals such as protozoans attached to surfaces such as plants, rocks, logs, and organisms in aquatic environments. While appearing as a variety of forms and colors, they are made up of distinct layers and exist wherever there is water. Some microbial activities lead to actual structural changes due to biochemical exchanges between the biofilm and the rock itself.

Biofilms are a host to microorganisms. A few biofilms create complex communal structures that will even fossilize over time.

Biofilms are often found near an energy source, such as downstream from a cave opening. Something falls or is washed into the cave and becomes part of a grand buffet. Subterranean biofilms are often a primary food source for snails, crayfish, and some fish. Many biofilms easily become dislodged and float through the water, wreaking havoc with visibility, so it's a good idea not to mess with them. These features are an important part of the cave environment and deserve the same interest and respect as the macroscopic creatures we can easily see. The science of subterranean biofilms is relatively new and fascinating. Noting the presence of a new growth in your favorite passage just might lead to the discovery of a new species!

# Algae

Algae (singular alga) are photosynthetic eukaryotic organisms. Eukaryotic refers to algae having a membrane-bound cell nucleus (compared to prokaryotes, which have no cell nuclei, such as bacteria). The nuclei store genetic resources. Algae are photosynthetic but lack the structures of plants such as leaves and roots. Some algae are unicellular (made up of only one cell, such as diatoms); others are multicellular (such as seaweed). Some multicellular algae groups develop specialized cells for specific functions.

Algae are being reclassified and redefined as new information is discovered, they are turning out to be sophisticated, complicated organisms! Unicellular algae are in the kingdom Protista (from *protozoa*, *proto* for first and *zoa* for animals). Some algae are under the kingdom Plantae (plants), others the kingdom Chromista (a special group of organisms with cells for photosynthesis that, unlike plants, contain chlorophyll c and do not store energy as starch). Because they have a membrane-bound cell nucleus, algae are classified under the domain Eukarya.

While we are unable to see the individual members without a microscope, algal colonies are noticeable as greenish, yellowish, brownish, and reddish-tinted masses in the water. Algal colonies provide a basic food source for life in the springs. There are many types of algae, and different springs support different kinds of algal communities. Commonly found in basins, algae are washed into caves during reverse-flow events. Most algae require light, and because of this, almost no algae grow in the dark zone of caves (although there are heterotrophic microalgae, which use organic compounds as food sources!). While algae are beneficial, warm temperatures and nutrient loading from various sources can lead to explosive growth of algae, called algal blooms. These blooms have unpleasant effects on spring life by growing densely, blocking sunlight, and lowering oxygen levels in the water. While algae are photosynthetic, creating oxygen as a by-product during the day, at night they consume oxygen. When the algal bloom dies, the depleted oxygen in the water makes breathing difficult for the remaining inhabitants. Overgrowth of algae can also smother and kill aquatic plants.

## Chlorophyta
### (Domain Eukaryota, Kingdom Plantae, Division Chlorophyta)

Chlorophytes, or green algae, such as water net (*Hydrodictyon reticulatum* (Linnaeus) Bory), and diatoms (such as *Aulacoseria*) are the predominant members of the Aufwuchs community (communities of plants and very small organisms that adhere to underwater surfaces). The word plankton refers to the tiny plants (phytoplankton) and tiny animals (zooplankton) floating along in the current. Plankton derives from the Greek word *planktos* meaning wandering.

Algae may be part of the Aufwuchs community when attached to a surface (periphyton) or the phytoplankton community when free-floating or suspended in the water column. Algae are primary producers, and the foundation of many food chains. Invertebrates, such as snails, and fish, such as mosquito fish and sunfish, eat algae. You can watch large schools of mullet grazing on algae in the basin at Peacock Springs. Another part of the Aufwuchs, fungi, decompose organic matter, also contributing to the nutrient content of the aquatic environment. Small invertebrates eat the fungi. Some species of algae consume nutrients released by fungi in the water.

Interestingly, when cold from long dives, divers can stick their hands into the masses of bright green algae growing in springs basins to feel an increase in the water temperature. I've done this in the basin at Peacock III, where the fuzzy masses of green algae are comfortably warm.

# Bacteria

## (Domain Bacteria, Phylum Cyanobacteria, Class Cyanophyceae)

Also called blue-green algae and cyanophyta.

Cave divers encounter many odd growths and deposits. Orange and brown, black and white, fuzzy and slimy, these are often colonies of a variety of bacteria living off minerals in the water and on cave walls. Bacteria almost always create mineral deposits. Even gold veins are the result of bacterial activity, but don't expect to find gold veins in Florida's limestone (different bacteria live here).

One of the three domains of life on earth: Archaea, Bacteria, and Eukarya. We cannot see individual bacterium, they are microscopic, but we can see biofilms. Bacteria live in every part of the springs ecosystem and affect or are affected by every aspect of the environment. Bacteria are believed to contribute to the formation of caves. Some bacteria, such as fecal coliform, can be an indicator of the human impact on and health of the aquatic ecosystem.

Bacteria colonize an area as a biofilm when they attach to a surface and gradually develop specialized behaviors leading to complex communities. The bacteria communicate using chemical and physical signals. Some develop the ability to channel food sources. Bacteria contribute a lot to the biofilm habitat through their presence and activities.

Cyanobacteria are prokaryotes (bacteria have no nucleus) that use photosynthesis.

Some cyanobacteria live suspended in the water column, such as *Merismopedia*. *Aphanizomenon* and *Microcystis* are familiar as the scums and strings we find on the water surface. *Scytonema* are the fuzzy green clumps along the shoreline. While a common part of algal assemblages, some cyanobacteria, such as lyngbia, can be toxic.

## *Beggiatoa gigantea* Klas, 1937
### (Class Gammaproteobacteria, Order Thiotrichales, Family Thiotrichaceae)

**Etymology:** *Beggiatoa* after the Italian botanist and medic Francesco Secondo Beggiato (1806–1883). *Gigantea* means gigantic.

Leucothiobacteria, sulfur-oxidizing filament bacteria that grow unattached to a substrate, but can be settled in clouds on sediment surfaces. A chemoorganotroph (freshwater), able to obtain energy from inorganic compounds (sulfur and sulfur compounds, such as hydrogen sulfide). *Beggiatoa* is capable of oxidizing sulfide to elemental sulfur, which is then stored internally. When the environmental sulfide is depleted, the bacterium further oxidizes the stored sulfur to sulfate. The sulfate is then released into the environment. Referred to as colorless sulfur bacteria to differentiate *Beggiatoa* from pigmented sulfur-oxidizing bacteria that accomplish photosynthesis. Prefers to grow in water rich in hydrogen sulfide. Found in sulfur springs and water polluted by effluent. Because these bacteria colonize contaminated water, their presence can be an indicator of poor water quality.

## Lyngbia, *Microseira wollei* (Farlow ex Gomont) McGregor and Sendall ex Kenins, 2017
### (Class Cyanophyceae, Order Nostocales, Family Oscillatoriaceae)

Formerly known as *Lyngbia wollei* and commonly called lyngbia.

**Etymology:** *Microseira* from Latin *micrós* for small and *seira* like a woven basket.

**Description:** An aquatic, single-cell, blue-green cyanobacterium that forms dense filamentous colonies covering the bottom (benthos) and surface of freshwater ecosystems. Possibly several species. Prefers spring-fed water. Various shades of olive green to black. Appears as dense mats of green fuzz. Presence can be related to increased nutrient levels in the water, such as nitrogen, phosphorous, iron, and dissolved organic matter.

Nitrogen fixers, able to take atmospheric and aquatic nitrogen and convert it to a form used by the lyngbia for food. Spreads by contact with boats and wind dispersal in water drops spread by storms.

Cyanobacteria are responsible for creating a breathable atmosphere on Earth. We know from the fossil record, cyanobacteria have existed for more than three billion years, their presence is associated with the massive increase in free oxygen in the atmosphere during the Proterozoic Era (2.5 billion years ago). They are also most likely the first organism to develop oxygenic photosynthesis.

## *Thiothrix* Winogradsky, 1888 emend. Howarth et al., 1999 emend. Aruga et al., 2002

### (Class Gammaproteobacteria, Order Thiotrichales, Family Thiotrichaceae)

**Etymology:** *Thiothrix* from Greek *theion*, meaning brimstone (sulfur), and *thrix*, meaning hair. The word "emend" in the attribution is Latin for altered and is followed by the name of the person responsible for the change.

Filamentous sulfur-oxidizing bacteria that can grow in colonies large enough to be noticeable as white mats or filaments in underwater caves. Found growing attached to a variety of substances, such as the crusty dark iron oxyhydroxide found in underwater caves, on detritus on the floor of systems, and on clay layers. *Thiothrix* has also been found venting from seeps within underwater systems. A mixotroph, meaning they can use a mix of sources for energy. *Thiothrix* obtains energy from the oxidation of sulfur, from organic and inorganic carbon (released by the decay of plants, for example), and can use oxygen or nitrogen. While this process creates an acidic product, it is believed the dissolution of limestone counterbalances the acidity.

*Thiothrix* may be a food source for cave crayfish.

# Bibliography

Abrams, S. 2019. *Rhesus Macaque Macaca mulatta*. New England Primate Conservancy. [Accessed June 10, 2021]. https://www.neprimateconservancy.org/rhesus-macaque.html.

Altschul, D. M., Terrace, H. S., Weiss, A. 2016. Serial Cognition and Personality in Macaques. *Animal Behavior and Cognition, 3*(1), 46–64. doi:10.12966/abc.02.04.2016.

AmphibiaWeb: *Amphiuma means*. 2019. Berkeley: University of California. [Accessed June 22, 2019]. https://amphibiaweb.org/species/3853.

Anderson, C. J., Heard, D. J., Andreu, M. A., Hostetler, M. E., Johnson, S. A. 2017. Winter Home Range and Habitat Selection of a Rhesus Macaque Group (*Macaca Mulatta*) at Silver Springs State Park. *Florida Scientist, 80*(4), 159–64.

Aresco, M. J. 2003. The Florida Softshell: A Unique Florida Turtle. Master Wildlife Conservationists (MWC) Bulletin. 6:4. [Accessed July 14, 2021]. https://www.lakejacksonturtles.org/softshell.pdf.

Art and Medicine. *Il dottor Beggiato*. Commemorazione. [Accessed August 12, 2019]. http://www.artandmedicine.com/biblio/authors/italia/Lioy1885.html.

Auffenberg, K., Stange, L. A. 2011. Featured Creatures: Common Name: Snail-Eating Snails of Florida, Scientific Name: Gastropoda. University of Florida, Institute of Food and Agricultural Sciences. EENY-251.

Bailey, R. M., Hubbs, C. L. 1949. The Black Basses (Micropterus) of Florida, with Description of a New Species. *Occasional Papers of the Museum of Zoology, 516*, 1–40.

Barton, H. A. 2006. Introduction to Cave Microbiology: A Review for the Non-Specialist. *Journal of Cave and Karst Studies, 68*(2), 43–54.

Barton, H. A., Northup, D. E. 2007. Geomicrobiology in Cave Environments: Past, Current and Future Perspectives. *Journal of Cave and Karst Studies, 69*(1), 163–78.

Bauer, R. T., Delahoussaye, J. 2008. Life History Migrations of the Amphidromous River Shrimp *Macrobrachium Ohione* from a Continental Large River System. *Journal of Crustacean Biology, 28*(4), 622–32. doi:10.1651/08-2977.1.

Beltz, E. 2007. Scientific and Common Names of the Reptiles and Amphibians of North America—Explained: Snakes. [Accessed June 11, 2019]. http://ebeltz.net/herps/etymain.html#Snakes.

Berenbaum, M. 2007. Lend Me Your Earwigs. *American Entomologist, 53*(4), 196–97. doi:10.1093/ae/53.4.196.

Berkeley University of California Museum of Paleontology. Introduction to the Chromista, From Microbes to Giants. [Accessed June 19, 2021]. https://ucmp.berkeley.edu/chromista/chromista.html.

Birkenholz, D. E. 1972. *Neofiber alleni*. *Mammalian Species, 15*, 1–4. doi:10.2307/3503816.

Biss, J. 2015. Non-Native Freshwater Jellyfish in Florida? University of Florida, Institute of Food and Agricultural Sciences Extension, Curiosities, Invasives. [Accessed May 15, 2019]. https://nwdistrict .ifas.ufl.edu/nat/2015/03/27/nonnative-freshwater-jellyfish-in-florida/.

Brandon, R. A. 1967. *Haideotriton* and *H. wallacei. Catalogue of American Amphibians and Reptiles, 39*, 1–2. doi:10.15781/T2X05XH7M.

Brewster, D. 1830. Entomology. *The Edinburgh Encyclopaedia in Eighteen Volumes.* Vol. 9. W. Blackwood. pp. 57–172. https://archive.org/details/edinburghencyclo09edinuoft/page/123. [Accessed July 14, 2021]. https://babel.hathitrust.org/cgi/pt?id=chi.12007137&view=page&seq =181&skin=2021&q1=entomology.

Brigmon, R. L., Martin, H. W., Morris, T. L., Bitton, G., Zam, S. G. 1994. Biogeochemical Ecol- ogy of *Thiothrix* spp. in Underwater Limestone Caves. *Geomicrobiology Journal, 12*, 141–59. doi:10.1080/01490459409377982.

Brook, G. 1882. On a New Genus of Collembola (*Sinella*) Allied to *Degeeria*, Nicolet. *London: Journal of the Linnean Society Zoology, 16*, 541–45. doi:10.1111/j.1096-3642.1882.tb02398.x.

Buchsbaum, R., Buchsbaum, M., Pearse, J., Pearse, V. 1987. *Animals Without Backbones.* 3rd ed. Uni- versity of Chicago Press.

Burns, J. E. Lake Maxinkuckee: Its Intrigue History and Genealogy: Josiah T. Scovell, M.D. Accessed November 23, 2021. http://www.maxinkuckee.history.pasttracker.com/biographies/josiah_t_ scovell.htm

Butler, R. S. 1998. Endangered and Threatened Wildlife and Plants: Determination of Endangered Sta- tus for Five Freshwater Mussels and Threatened Status for Two Freshwater Mussels from the Eastern Gulf Slope Drainages of Alabama, Florida, and Georgia. *Federal Register, 63*(50), 12664–686.

Caldwell, A. B. 1909. *Makers of America: An Historical and Biographical Work by an Able Corps of Writers.* Vol. 3. Florida Historical Society.

Cannizzaro, A. G., Balding, D., Stine, M., Sawicki, T. R. 2019. A New Syntopic Species of *Stygobromus* Cope, 1872 (Amphipoda: Crangonyctidae) from Groundwaters in Georgia and Florida, USA, with notes on *S. floridanus* Holsinger and Sawicki, 2016. *Journal of Crustacean Biology, 39*(4), 407–18. doi:10.1093/jcbiol/ruz034.

Cannizzaro, A. G., Balding, D., Lazo-Wasem, E. A., Sawicki, T. R. 2019. Morphological and Molecular Analysis Reveal a New Species of Stygobitic Amphipod in the Genus *Crangonyx* (Crustacea: Cran- gonyctidae) from Jackson County, Florida, with a redescription of *Crangonyx floridanus* and notes on its taxonomy and biogeography. *Journal of Natural History, 53*(7–8), 1–49. doi:10.1080/00222933 .2019.1584341.

Cannizzaro, A. G., Balding, D., Lazo-Wasem, E. A., Sawicki, T. R. 2018. A Redescription of the Stygo- bitic Amphipod *Crangonyx grandimanus* (Amphipoda: Crangonyctidae), including phylogenetically significant sequence data for mitochondrial and nuclear genes. *Bulletin of the Peabody Museum of Natural History, 59*(2), 109–25. doi:10.3374/014.059.0202.

Capinera, J. L. 2021. Featured Creatures: Common Name: Ringlegged Earwig, Scientific Name: *Euborellia annulipes* (Lucas) (Insecta: Dermaptera: Anisolabididae). University of Florida, Institute of Food and Agricultural Sciences. EENY-88. [Accessed July 30, 2021]. https://entnemdept.ufl.edu/ creatures/veg/ringlegged_earwig.htm.

Centers for Disease Control and Prevention. 2019. Cause and Frequency. B Virus (Herpes B, Mon- key B Virus, Herpesvirus Simiae, and Herpesvirus B). [Accessed June 11, 2021]. https://www.cdc .gov/herpesbvirus/cause.html#:~:text=B%20virus%20infections%20in%20people%20are%20 rare.,infections%3B%2021%20of%20them%20died.

Chace, F. A., Jr. 1954. Two New Subterranean Shrimps (Decapoda: Caridea) from Florida and the West Indies, with a revised key to the American species. *Journal of the Washington Academy of Sciences, 44*(10), 318–24. https://decapoda.nhm.org/pdfs/25132/25132.pdf.

*Chambers's Encyclopaedia: A Dictionary of Useful Knowledge.* Vol. IV. 1901. Earwig. (Dionysius-Friction). J. B. Lippincott Company. https://books.google.com/books?id=plUMAAAAYAAJ&pg=PA171&dq=Earwig+etymology&hl=en&sa=X&ved=0ahUKEwiwsNnblv7iAhVHeKwKHWCrAJMQ6AEIVzAI#v=onepage&q=Earwig%20etymology&f=false.

Childers, M. *Noturus gyrinus* (Mitchill, 1817). [Accessed May 8, 2019]. http://www.scotcat.com/factsheets/noturus_gyrinus.htm.

Cochran, G. 2004. *Florida's Fabulous Fishes.* World Publications.

Conant, R., Collins, J. T. 1998. *A Field Guide to Reptiles and Amphibians: Eastern and Central North America, Peterson Field Guides.* Houghton Mifflin Company.

Cook, A. 1985. Functional Aspects of Trail Following by the Carnivorous Snail *Euglandina Rosea. Malacologia, International Journal of Malacology, 26,* 173–81. Also available at https://archive.org/details/malacologia261985inst/page/173.

Cook, A. 1985. The Organisation of Feeding in the Carnivorous Snail *Euglandina Rosea. Malacologia, International Journal of Malacology, 26,* 183–90. Also available at https://archive.org/details/malacologia261985inst/page/182.

Cope, E. D. 1867. Synopsis of the Cyprinidae of Pennsylvania with a Supplement on Some New Species of American and African Fishes. *Transactions of the American Philosophical Society, 13*(3), 351–410.

Cope, E. D. 1872. On the Wyandotte Cave and Its Fauna. *Nature, 158,* 11–14. (Reprint from *Am. Nat., 6,* 406–22). doi:10.1038/007011a0.

Cowley, M. Florida Wildlife: Lungless Salamanders. NSIS. [Accessed May 8, 2019]. https://www.nsis.org/wildlife/amph/sal-lungless.html#blind.

Cowley, M. Florida Wildlife: Raccoons. NSIS. [Accessed June 10, 2019]. https://www.nsis.org/wildlife/mamm/raccoon.html.

Culver, D. C., Hobbs, H. H. III, Christman, M. C., Master, L. L. 1999. Distribution Map of Caves and Cave Animals in the United States. *Journal of Cave and Karst Studies, 61*(3), 139–40.

Culver, D. C., Holsinger, J. R., Christman, M. C., Pipan, T. 2010. Morphological Differences Among Eyeless Amphipods in the Genus *Stygobromus* Dwelling in Different Subterranean Habitats. *Journal of Crustacean Biology, 30*(1), 68–74.

Dall, W. H. 1885. Notes on Some Floridian Land and Fresh-Water Shells with a Revision of the Auriculea of the Eastern United States. Proceedings of United States National Museum, *8*(519), 255–94. [Accessed November 23, 2021.] doi:10.5479/si.00963801.8-519.255.

Daniel, W. M., Benson, A. J., Neilson, M. E. 2019. *Melanoides tuberculata* (Muller, 1774). USGS Nonindigenous Aquatic Species Database. [Accessed May 15, 2019]. https://nas.er.usgs.gov/queries/FactSheet.aspx?SpeciesID=1037.

Deyrup, M., Franz, R. 1994. *Rare and Endangered Biota of Florida.* Vol. IV. Invertebrates. University Press of Florida.

Ding, S., Li, W., Wang, Y., Cameron, S. L. 2019. The Phylogeny and Evolutionary Timescale of Stoneflies (Insecta: Plecoptera) Inferred from Mitochondrial Genomes. *Molecular Phylogenetics and Evolution, 135.* doi:10.1016/j.ympev.2019.03.005.

Dodd, C. K., Jr. 2013. *Frogs of the United States and Canada.* Vols. 1–2. Johns Hopkins University Press.

Drumm, D. T., Knight-Gray, J. 2019. A New Species of the *Hyalella "azteca"* Complex (Crustacea: Amphipoda: Hylellidae) from Florida. *Zootaxa, 4545*(1), 93–104. doi:10.11646/zootaxa4545.1.5.

Duke, S. 2010. *Nerodia erythrogaster*, Plainbelly Water Snake. Animal Diversity Web. [Accessed July 29, 2019]. https://animaldiversity.org/accounts/Nerodia_erythrogaster/.

Etymologia: *Eptesicus Fuscus*. 2005. *Emerging Infectious Diseases, 11*(12), 1954. doi:10.3201/eid1112.ET1112.

Evans, E., Doonan, T., Ober, H. 2018. Florida's Bats: Tricolored Bat. University of Florida, Institute of Food and Agricultural Sciences Extension. [Accessed June 25, 2019]. http://edis.ifas.ufl.edu/uw434#FOOTNOTE_1.

Fasulo, T. R. Featured Creatures: Common Name: Applesnails of Florida, Scientific Name: *Pomacea* spp. (Gastropoda: Ampullariidae). University of Florida, Institute of Food and Agricultural Sciences. EENY-323. [Accessed May 14, 2019]. http://entnemdept.ufl.edu/creatures/misc/gastro/apple_snails.htm.

Fasulo, T. R. Featured Creatures: Common Name: Terrestrial Amphipods or Lawn Shrimp, Scientific Name: (Crustacea: Amphipoda: Talitridae). University of Florida, Institute of Food and Agricultural Sciences. EENY-220. [Accessed May 14, 2019]. http://entnemdept.ufl.edu/creatures/misc/amphipods.htm.

Fenner, B. The Conscientious Marine Aquarist: American Soles, Flatfishes of the Family Achiridae. [Accessed May 8, 2019]. http://www.wetwebmedia.com/achiridae.htm.

Fish Base. *Alosa sapidissima* (Wilson, 1811), American Shad. [Accessed June 4, 2019]. https://www.fishbase.se/summary/1584.

Fish Base. *Aphredoderus sayanus* (Gilliams, 1824), Pirate perch. [Accessed May 8, 2019]. https://www.fishbase.de/summary/Aphredoderus-sayanus.html.

Fish Base. *Heterandria formosa* (Girard, 1859), Least killifish. [Accessed June 5, 2019]. https://www.fishbase.in/summary/Heterandria-formosa.html.

Fish Base. *Menidia beryllina* (Cope, 1867), Inland silverside. [Accessed July 22, 2021]. https://www.fishbase.in/summary/Menidia-beryllina.html.

Fish Base. *Noturus gyrinus* (Mitchill, 1817), Tadpole madtom. [Accessed May 8, 2019]. https://www.fishbase.de/summary/Noturus-gyrinus.html.

Fish Base. *Oreochromis aureus* (Steindachner, 1864) Blue tilapia. [Accessed July 19, 2021]. https://www.fishbase.in/summary/1387.

Florida Bat Conservancy. [Accessed May 8, 2019]. https://www.floridabats.org/bats-of-florida.html.

Florida Department of Environmental Protection Division of Recreation and Parks. Silver River State Park Unit Management Plan. Approved April 25, 2002.

Florida Department of Environmental Protection Division of Recreation and Parks. Peacock Springs State Park Unit Management Plan. Approved June 6, 2002.

Florida Fish and Wildlife Conservation Commission. Barbour's Map Turtle, *Graptemys barbouri*. [Accessed July 5, 2019]. https://myfwc.com/wildlifehabitats/profiles/reptiles/freshwater-turtles/barbours-map-turtle/.

Florida Fish and Wildlife Conservation Commission. Bluenose shiner, *Pteronotropis welaka*. [Accessed July 26, 2021]. https://myfwc.com/wildlifehabitats/profiles/freshwater/bluenose-shiner/.

Florida Fish and Wildlife Conservation Commission. 2019. Endangered and Threatened Species Management and Conservation Plan, Progress Report Fiscal Year 2017–18. Also available at https://myfwc.com/media/18721/fy2017-18-eandt-legislative-report-final.pdf.

Florida Fish and Wildlife Conservation Commission. Flathead Catfish, *Pylodictis olivaris*. [Accessed May 8, 2019]. https://myfwc.com/wildlifehabitats/profiles/freshwater/flathead-catfish/.

Florida Fish and Wildlife Conservation Commission. Florida Gar, *Lepisosteus platyrhincus.* [Accessed May 8, 2019]. https://myfwc.com/wildlifehabitats/profiles/freshwater/florida-gar/.

Florida Fish and Wildlife Conservation Commission. Gulf Sturgeon, *Acipenser oxyrinchus desotoi.* [Accessed May 22, 2019]. https://myfwc.com/wildlifehabitats/profiles/saltwater/gulf-sturgeon/.

Florida Fish and Wildlife Conservation Commission. Largemouth Bass, *Micropterus salmoides.* [Accessed May 8, 2019]. https://myfwc.com/wildlifehabitats/profiles/freshwater/largemouth-bass/.

Florida Fish and Wildlife Conservation Commission. Blue Tilapia. [Accessed July 19, 2021]. https://myfwc.com/wildlifehabitats/profiles/freshwater/blue-tilapia/.

Florida Fish and Wildlife Conservation Commission, Fish and Wildlife Research Institute. 2008. Florida's Freshwater Mussels and Clams. [Accessed July 25, 2021]. https://www.fws.gov/panama city/resources/Mussel%20harvest%20pamphlet%20March%202008.pdf.

Florida Fish and Wildlife Conservation Commission Freshwater Mussel Conservation Program. 2021. [Accessed November 23, 2021.] https://myfwc.com/media/27005/mussel-brochure.pdf.

Florida Geological Survey. 1994. Florida's Geological History and Geological Resources. Special Publication No. 35. Ed Lane, editor. Florida Geological Survey. Also available at http://pub licfiles.dep.state.fl.us/FGS/FGS_Publications/SP/SP35LaneHistoryResources.pdf.

Florida Museum of Natural History. Discover Fishes: *Atractosteus spatula*, Alligator Gar. University of Florida. [Accessed June 5, 2019]. https://www.floridamuseum.ufl.edu/discover-fish/species-pro files/atractosteus-spatula/.

Florida Museum of Natural History. Discover Fishes: *Dasyatis sabina*, Atlantic Stingray. University of Florida. [Accessed July 26, 2019]. https://www.floridamuseum.ufl.edu/discover-fish/species-pro files/dasyatis-sabina/.

Florida Museum of Natural History. 2018. Discover Fishes: *Lepisosteus osseus*, Longnose Gar. Prepared by Nathaniel Goddard. University of Florida. [Accessed July 26, 2019]. https://www.florida museum.ufl.edu/discover-fish/species-profiles/lepisosteus-osseus/.

Florida Museum of Natural History. Discover Fishes: *Mugil cephalus*, Striped Mullet. University of Florida. [Accessed May 8, 2019]. https://www.floridamuseum.ufl.edu/discover-fish/species-profiles /mugil-cephalus.

Florida Museum of Natural History: Division of Herpetology. *Drymarchon couperi*, Eastern Indigo Snake, Indigo Snake, Racer. University of Florida. [Accessed June 10, 2019]. https://www.florida museum.ufl.edu/herpetology/fl-snakes/list/drymarchon-couperi/.

Florida Museum of Natural History: Division of Herpetology. *Nerodia erythrogaster erythrogaster*, Red-belly Water Snake. University of Florida. [Accessed July 29, 2019]. https://www.floridamuseum.ufl .edu/herpetology/fl-snakes/list/nerodia-e-erythrogaster/.

Florida Museum of Natural History: Division of Herpetology. *Nerodia erythrogaster flavigaster*, Yellow-belly Water Snake. University of Florida. [Accessed July 29, 2019]. https://www.floridamuseum.ufl .edu/herpetology/fl-snakes/list/nerodia-erythrogaster-flavigaster/.

Florida Museum of Natural History: Division of Herpetology. *Nerodia fasciata fasciata*, Banded Water Snake. University of Florida. [Accessed June 11, 2019]. https://www.floridamuseum.ufl.edu/herpe tology/fl-snakes/list/nerodia-fasciata-fasciata/.

Florida Natural Areas Inventory. [Accessed May 8, 2019]. http://www.fnai.org.

Florida Natural Areas Inventory. 2001. Oval Pigtoe, *Pleurobema pyriforme.* [Accessed June 25, 2019]. https://www.fnai.org/FieldGuide/pdf/Pleurobema_pyriforme.pdf.

Florida Natural Areas Inventory. 2018. Bluenose Shiner *Pteronotropis welaka.* [Accessed July 26, 2021]. https://www.fnai.org/FieldGuide/pdf/Pteronotropis_welaka.pdf.

Fofonoff, P. W., Ruiz, G. M., Steves, B., Simkanin, C., Carlton, J. T. 2018. *Melanoides turricula*. National Exotic Marine and Estuarine Species Information System. Smithsonian Environmental Research Center. [Accessed June 24, 2019]. https://invasions.si.edu/nemesis/browseDB/SpeciesSummary .jsp?TSN=71535.

Fofonoff, P. W., Ruiz, G. M., Steves, B., Simkanin, C., Carlton, J. T. 2018. *Tarebia granifera*. National Exotic Marine and Estuarine Species Information System. Smithsonian Environmental Research Center. [Accessed June 6, 2019]. https://invasions.si.edu/nemesis/browseDB/SpeciesSummary .jsp?TSN=71539.

Foster, A. M., Fuller, P., Benson, A., Constant, S., Raikow, D., Larson, J., Fusaro, A. 2019. *Corbicula fluminea* (O. F. Müller, 1774). USGS Nonindigenous Aquatic Species Database. [Accessed May 8, 2019]. https://nas.er.usgs.gov/queries/factsheet.aspx?SpeciesID=92.

Fowler, H. W. 1945. Study of the Fishes of the Southern Piedmont and Coastal Plain. The Academy of Natural Sciences of Philadelphia: Monographs No. 7. Wickersham Printing Co.

Fox, A. G., Stowe, E. S., Dunton, K. J., Peterson, D. L. 2018. Seasonal Occurrence of Atlantic Sturgeon (*Acipenser oxyrinchus oxyrinchus*) in the St. Johns River, Florida. *Fish B-NOAA*, *116*(3–4), 219–27. doi:10.7755/FB.116.3.1.

Franz, R., Bauer, J., Morris, T. 1994. Review of Biologically Significant Caves and Their Faunas in Florida and South Georgia. *Brimleyana*, *20*, 1–109.

Franz, R., Lee, D. S. 1982. Distribution and Evolution of Florida's Troglobitic Crayfishes. *Bulletin of the Florida State Museum*, *28*(3), 53–78.

Franz, R., Hobbs, H. H., Jr. 1983. Procambarus (Ortmannicus) Leitheuseri, New Species, Another Troglobitic Crayfish (Decapoda: Cambaridae) from Peninsular Florida. *Proceedings of the Biological Society of Washington*, *96*(2), 323–32.

Freshwater Mollusk Conservation Society Freshwater Gastropod Identification Workshop. 2004. Showing Your Shells, A Primer to Freshwater Gastropod Identification. K. E. Perez, S. A. Clark, C. Lydeard, eds. University of Alabama. [Accessed July 14, 2021]. https://www.researchgate.net/publi cation/40663591_Freshwater_gastropod_identification_workshop_showing_your_shells.

Froese, R., Torres, A. G. *Pteronotropis welaka* (Evermann and Kendall, 1898), Bluenose shiner. [Accessed July 26, 2021]. https://www.fishbase.de/summary/2914.

Fuller, P. 2021. *Morone chrysops × saxatilis*. USGS Nonindigenous Aquatic Species Database [Accessed June 21, 2021]. https://nas.er.usgs.gov/queries/factsheet.aspx?SpeciesID=784.

Fuller, P., Neilson, M. E., Hopper, K. 2021. *Dorosoma cepedianum* (Lesueur, 1818). USGS Nonindigenous Aquatic Species Database. [Accessed July 22, 2021]. https://nas.er.usgs.gov/queries/fact sheet.aspx?SpeciesID=492.

Gill, N. K. 2017. *Sternotherus oderatus (sic)*: The Common Musk Turtle. Tortoise Trust. [Accessed May 8, 2019]. http://www.tortoisetrust.org/articles/oderatus.html.

Gillilland, M. 2000. *Lithobates clamitans*, Green Frog. Animal Diversity Web. University of Michigan. [Accessed July 29, 2019]. https://animaldiversity.org/accounts/Lithobates_clamitans/.

Godwin, J. Eastern Indigo Snake Fact Sheet. U.S. Fish and Wildlife Service. [Accessed June 10, 2019]. https://www.fws.gov/panamacity/resources/EasternIndigoSnakeFactSheet.pdf.

Graham, S., Steen, D. A. 2018. Song of the Siren—The Story Behind How We Found and Described a Two-Foot Long Amphibian New to Science. Living Alongside Wildlife. [Accessed June 22, 2019]. http://livingalongsidewildlife.com/?p=230.

Grainer, B. G. 2005. The Bluenose Shiner, the Jewel of the Southeast. North American Native Fishes Association reprinted from American Currents, Spring 1988. [Accessed July 26, 2021]. http://www.nanfa.org/articles/acbluenose.shtml.

Guiry, M. D. 2021. *Hydrodictyon reticulatum* (Linnaeus) Bory 1824. AlgaeBase. [Accessed 2021 June 18]. https://www.algaebase.org/search/species/detail/?tc=accept&species_id=Ub955 66d9c6f50829.

Harrison, L. 2018. The Rosy Wolf Snail Is Fast for a Snail. Institute of Food and Agricultural Sciences. Blogs. University of Florida. [Accessed July 29, 2019]. http://blogs.ifas.ufl.edu/wakullaco/2018 /07/13/the-rosy-wolf-snail-is-fast-for-a-snail/.

Harvey, M. J., Altenbach, J. S., Best, T. L. 1999. Bats of the United States. Arkansas Game and Fish Commission, Asheville Field Office U.S. Fish and Wildlife Service.

Heard, W. H. 1979. Identification Manual of the Freshwater Clams of Florida. Florida Department of Environmental Regulation. *Technical Series, 4*(2), 83. Also available at https://www.researchgate .net/publication/27394339_Identification_manual_of_the_freshwater_clams_of_Florida.

Herrig, J., Shute, P. AQUA-5: Aquatic Animals and Their Habitats. Southern Forest Resource Assessment Draft Report. Also available at http://www.srs.fs.usda.gov/sustain/draft/aqua5/aqua5.pdf.

Herrington, Z. 2011. *Pteronotropis welaka* Bluenose Shiner. Animal Diversity Web. University of Michigan. [Accessed July 26, 2021]. https://animaldiversity.org/accounts/Pteronotropis_welaka/.

Higgens, P. 2020. Mollusking in the Fakahatchee—Part 1. Friends of the Fakahatchee Armchair Interpretive Walks. [Accessed July 25, 2021]. https://orchidswamp.org/mollusking-in-the-fakahatchee -part-1/.

Hill, J. 2000. *Lithobates heckscheri*, River Frog. Animal Diversity Web. University of Michigan. [Accessed July 26, 2019]. https://animaldiversity.org/site/accounts/information/Rana_heckscheri .html.

Hill, S., Connelly, R. 2013. Featured Creatures Entomology and Nematology: Common Name: Southern House Mosquito, Scientific Name: *Culex quinquefasciatus* Say (Insecta: Diptera: Culicidae). University of Florida, Institute of Food and Agricultural Sciences. EENY-457. [Accessed July 23, 2021]. https://entnemdept.ufl.edu/creatures/aquatic/southern_house_mosquito.htm.

Hobbs, H. H., Jr. 1971. A New Troglobitic Crayfish from Florida. *Quarterly Journal of the Florida Academy of Sciences, 34*(2), 114–24. Also available at http://www.jstor.org/stable/24318041.

Hobbs, H. H., Jr., Franz, R. 1992. *Procambarus (Ortmannicus) attiguus*, A New Troglobitic Crayfish (Decapoda: Cambaridae) from the Saint Johns River Basin, Florida. *Proceedings of the Biological Society of Washington, 105*(2), 359–65. Also available at https://biodiversitylibrary.org/page /35607532.

Hobbs, H. H., Jr., Means, D. B. 1972. Two New Troglobitic Crayfishes (Decapoda, Astacidae) from Florida. *Proceedings of the Biological Society of Washington, 84*(46), 393–41. Also available at https://www.biodiversitylibrary.org/page/34563471#page/451/mode/1up.

Hodson, R. G. 1989. Hybrid Striped Bass: Biology and Life History. North Carolina State University and University of North Carolina Sea Grant Program. Southern Regional Aquaculture Center. 300. [Accessed June 21, 2021]. https://appliedecology.cals.ncsu.edu/wp-content/uploads /300.pdf.

Hoehn, T. 1998. Rare and Imperiled Fish Species of Florida: A Watershed Perspective. Office of Environmental Services, Florida Game and Fresh Water Fish Commission. Also available at http://ufdc .ufl.edu/UF00000118/00001/1j.

Holcomb, J. M., Shea, C. P., Johnson, N. A. 2018. Cumulative Spring Discharge and Survey Effort Influence Occupancy and Detection of a Threatened Freshwater Mussel, the Suwannee Moccasinshell. *Journal of Fish and Wildlife Management, 9*(1), 95–105. doi:10.3996/052017-JFWM-042.

Holzwart, K. R., Deak, K., Miller, J., Johnson, E., Simonton, L., Dluzniewski, T., Stanfil, A., Taylor, A. 2020. Springs Coast Long-Term Fish Community Assessment: The Rainbow River System. *Florida*

Scientist, *83*(3–4), 83–97. Also available at https://www.swfwmd.state.fl.us/sites/default/files /Springs%20Coast%20Assessment_0.pdf.

Hormiga, G., Scharff, N., Coddington, J. A. 2000. The Phylogenetic Basis of Sexual Size Dimorphism in Orb-Weaving Spiders (Araneae, Orbicularie). *Systematic Biology, 49*(3), 435–62. doi:10.1080/10635159950127330.

Houston, S. 2019. Bug Guide. The Most Misunderstood Spiders. Iowa State University Department of Entomology. [Accessed July 7, 2019]. https://bugguide.net/node/view/240451.

Howard, T. Odum Florida Springs Institute. Florida's Springs, Protecting Nature's Gems: Fish. [Accessed November 23, 2021.] https://floridaspringsinstitute.org/fish/.

Indian River County Main Library, Archive Center. 2016. George Nelson (1876–1962): The George Nelson Collection. Vero Beach (FL). [Accessed June 11, 2019]. http://www.irclibrary.org/geneal ogy/pdf/nelsongeorge.pdf.

Integrated Taxonomic Information System. 2021. [Accessed July 27, 2021]. https://www.itis.gov.

International Commission on Stratigraphy, Subcommission on Cambrian Stratigraphy. Welcome to the Cambrian. [Accessed May 8, 2019]. http://www.palaeontology.geo.uu.se/ISCS/ISCS_home.html.

International Commission on Stratigraphy. International Stratigraphic Chart. v2018/08. [Accessed May 8, 2019]. http://www.stratigraphy.org/ICSchart/ChronostratChart2018-08.pdf.

Isnaningsh, N. R., Basukriadi, A., Marwoto, R. M. 2017. The Morphology and Ontogenetic of *Tarebia granifera* (Lamarck, 1822) From Indonesia (Gastropoda: Cerithioidea: Thiaridae). *Treubia, 44*, 1–14. doi:10.14203/treubia.v44i0.2914.

Ittner, L. D., Junghans, M., Werner, I. 2018. Aquatic Fungi: A Disregarded Trophic Level in Ecological Risk Assessment of Organic Fungicides. *Frontiers in Environmental Science*. doi:10.3389/fenvs .2018.00105.

Jackson, D. R. 2008. Database on the Status, Distribution, and Biology of Florida's Rare Invertebrates. A Florida's Wildlife Legacy Initiative Project. Final Report. Project No. 05034. Florida Natural Areas Inventory. Also available at https://public.myfwc.com/crossdoi/fundedprojects/Dale_Jack son_final_report.pdf.

Jobling, J. A. 2010. *The Helm Dictionary of Scientific Bird Names: From Aalge to Zusii.* Christopher Helm. Also available at: https://citeseerx.ist.psu.edu/viewdoc/download?doi=10.1.1.695.7104 &rep=rep1&type=pdf.

Johnson, N. A., McLeod, J. M., Holcomb, J., Rows, M., Williams, J. D. 2016. Early Life History and Spatiotemporal Changes in Distribution of the Rediscovered Suwannee Moccasinshell *Medionidus walkeri* (Bivalvia: Unionidae). *Endangered Species Research, 31*, 163–75. doi:10.3354/esr00752.

Jordan, D. S. 1921. Franz Steindachner. *Science, 53*(1360), 68. doi:10.1126/science.53.1360.68.

Jüttner, F., Stiesch, M., Ternes, W. 2013. Biliverdin: The Blue-green Pigment in the Bones of the Garfish (*Belone belone*) and Eelpout (*Zoarces viviparus*). *European Food Research and Technology, 236*(6), 943–53. doi:10.1007/s00217-013-1932-y.

Kaiser, G. 2021. The Prokaryotic Cell—Bacteria. [Accessed November 23, 2021.] https://bio.lib retexts.org/Bookshelves/Microbiology/Book%3A_Microbiology_(Kaiser)/Unit_1%3A_Intro duction_to_Microbiology_and_Prokaryotic_Cell_Anatomy/2%3A_The_Prokaryotic_Cell_- _Bacteria

Kara, M. H., Quignard, J. P. 2019. *Fishes in Lagoons and Estuaries in the Mediterranean 3A: Migratory Fish.* John Wiley and Sons, Inc.

Karwautz, C., Kus, G., Stockl, M., Neu, T. R., Lueders, T. 2018. Microbial Megacities Fueled by Methane Oxidation in a Mineral Cave. *ISME Journal, 12*, 87–100.

Katz, B. G., Griffin, D. W., Swarzenski, P. W., Walsh, S. J., Jelks, H. L. 2003. Florida Springs Interdisciplinary Science Study. USGS. FS-008-03. doi:10.3133/fs00803.

Kema, M., Rosario, K., Sawaya, N. A., Szekely, A. J., Tisza, M. J., Breitbart, M. 2020. Prokaryotic and Viral Community Composition of Freshwater Springs in Florida, USA. *mBio, 1*(2). doi:10.1128 /mBio.00436-20.

Koutrakis, E., Machino, Y., Mylona, D., Perdikaris, C. 2008. Crayfish Terminology in Ancient Greek, Latin, and Other European Languages. *Crustaceana, 82*(12), 1535-546. doi:10.1163/001121609 X12475745628586.

Krysko, K. L., Granatosky, M. C., Nunez, L. P., Smith, D. J. 2016. A Cryptic New Species of Indigo Snake (Genus *Drymarchon*) from the Florida Platform of the United States. *Zootaxa, 4138*(3), 549-69. doi:10.11646/zootaxa.4138.3.9.

Kulzer, L. 2005. Bug of the Month: Water Striders: Family Gerridae. [Accessed May 8, 2019]. https:// crawford.tardigrade.net/bugs/BugofMonth04.html.

Laber-Warren, E. 2020. Can an "Invasive Species" Earn the Right to Stay? Sapiens Anthropology Magazine. [Accessed June 11, 2021]. https://www.sapiens.org/culture/multispecies-macaques/.

Lamoreux, J. 2004. Stygobites Are More Wide-Ranging Than Troglobites. *Journal of Cave and Karst Studies, 66*(1), 18-19.

Landy, J. A., Travis, J. 2015. Shape Variation in the Least Killifish: Ecological Associations of Phenotypic Variation and the Effects of a Common Garden. *Ecology and Evolution, 5*(23): 5616-631. doi: 10 .1002/ece3.1780.

Lankester, E. R. 1880. On a New Jelly-Fish of the Order Trachomedusae, Living in Fresh Water. *Nature, 22*, 147-48.

Lazur, A. M., Chapman, F. A. Golden Shiner Culture: A Reference Profile. University of Florida Cooperative Extension Service, Institute of Food and Agricultural Sciences. [Accessed May 8, 2019]. https://agrilifecdn.tamu.edu/fisheries/files/2013/09/Golden-Shiner-Culture-A-Reference-Profile .pdf.

Lea, I. 1840. Proceedings of the American Philosophical Society held at Philadelphia for Promoting Useful Knowledge, v.1 1838-1840. Also available at https://biodiversitylibrary.org/page/34512774.

Lee, H. G. What's in a Name or Two? [Accessed May 30, 2019]. https://www.jaxshells.org/heckscher .htm.

Lewis, A. D., Prongay, K. 2015. Basic Physiology of *Macaca mulatta*. The Nonhuman Primate in Nonclinical Drug Development and Safety Assessment. J. Bluemel, S. Korte, E. Schenck, and G. Weinbauer, eds. ScienceDirect. [Accessed June 10, 2021]. https://www.sciencedirect.com/topics /agricultural-and-biological-sciences/macaca-mulatta.

Lewis, J. J., Sawicki, T. R. 2016. *Mexistenasellus floridensis* sp.n., the First Stenasellid Isopod Discovered from the Floridan Aquifer (Crustacea, Isopoda, Asellota). *Subterranean Biology, 17*, 121-32. doi:10.3897/subtbiol.17.7703.

Long, K. 1999. *Frogs: A Wildlife Handbook*. Johnson Books.

Lord, C. L. 2021. Ticks in Florida. University of Florida, Institute of Food and Agricultural Sciences. [Accessed June 25, 2021]. https://fmel.ifas.ufl.edu/publication/buzz-words/buzz-words-archive /ticks-in-florida/.

Louisiana State University. 1993. *History of Carcinology*. F. Truesdale, ed. A. A. Balkema Publishers.

Mayden, R. L., Allen, J. S. 2015. Molecular Systematics of the Phoxinin Genus Pteronotropis (Otophysi: Cypriniformes). BioMed Res. Int. 2015, 298658. doi10.1155/2015/298658.

McBride, R. S., Matheson, R. E. 2011. Florida's Diadromous Fishes: Biology, Ecology, Conservation, and Management. *Florida Scientist, 74*, 187-213.

McCulloch, G. A., Wallis, G. P., Waters, J. M. 2015. A Time-Calibrated Phylogeny of Southern Hemisphere Stoneflies: Testing for Gondwanan Origins. *Molecular Phylogenetics and Evolution*, 96, 150–60. doi:10.1016/j.ympev.2015.10.028.

McKercher, E. O., Connell, D., Fuller, P., Liebig, J., Larson, J., Makled, T. H., Fusaro, A., Daniel, W. M. 2019. *Craspedacusta sowerbyi* (Lankester, 1880). USGS Nonindigenous Aquatic Species Database. [Accessed May 9, 2019]. https://nas.er.usgs.gov/queries/factsheet.aspx?SpeciesID=1068.

Mecham, J. S. 1967. *Notophthalmus viridescens. Catalogue of American Amphibians and Reptiles.* J. D. Anderson, ed. *American Society of Ichthyologists and Herpetologists, 53*(1–4). doi:10.15781 /T2Q814X4D.

Melville, R. V., Smith, J. D. D. 1987. *Official Lists and Indexes of Names and Works in Zoology.* International Trust for Zoological Nomenclature. Also available at https://pdfs.semanticscholar.org/41b5/ b4d56057ef6bddbbb6e0d45db994a808d773.pdf.

Menu, H. 1984. Revision du statut de *Pipistrellus subflavus* (F. Cuvier, 1832). Proposition d'un taxon generique noveau : *Perimyotis* nov. gen. *Mammalia* 48(3). doi:10.1515/mamm.1984.48.3.409.

Meyer, J. R. 2016. Dermaptera. NC State University General Entomology. [Accessed June 22, 2019]. https://projects.ncsu.edu/cals/course/ent425/library/compendium/dermaptera.html.

Micrographia. 2000. Crustaceans, Freshwater Ostracods, and Shrimps. Micrographia. [Accessed May 8, 2019]. http://www.micrographia.com/specbiol/crustac/ostraco/ostr0100.htm.

Miller, R. R. 1960. Systematics and Biology of the Gizzard Shad (*Dorosoma cepedianum*) and Related Fishes. U.S. Fish and Wildlife Service. Fishery Bulletin 173. Vol. 60. [Accessed July 22, 2021]. http:// www.nativefishlab.net/library/textpdf/15335.pdf.

Milligan, M. R. 1997. *Identification Manual for the Aquatic Oligochaeta of Florida.* Vol. I: Freshwater Oligochaetes. State of Florida Department of Environmental Protection.

Mirocha, A. A Snail's Tale: The Itsy-Bitsy, Teeny-Weenie Ichetucknee Siltsnail. Save the Weirdos. Center for Biological Diversity. [Accessed July 24, 2021]. https://medium.com/center-for-biological -diversity/who-isnt-a-little-weird-7b3332a06dc3.

Moler, P. E. 1999. Checklist of Florida's Amphibians and Reptiles. Florida Fish and Wildlife Commission.

Monty, A-M., Feldhamer, G. A. 2002. Conservation Assessment for the Eastern Woodrat (*Neotoma floridana*) and the Allegheny Woodrat (*Neotoma magister*). USDA Forest Service, Eastern Region, May 2002. Available online at: https://www.fs.usda.gov/Internet/FSE_DOCUMENTS/fsm91 _054316.pdf.

Morris, C. 2001. *Dorosoma cepedianum,* Eastern Gizzard Shad. Animal Diversity Web. University of Michigan. [Accessed July 22, 2021]. https://animaldiversity.org/accounts/Dorosoma_cepedia num/.

Mulheisen, M., Berry, K. 2000. *Eptesicus fuscus,* Big Brown Bat. Animal Diversity Web. Ann Arbor: University of Michigan. [Accessed June 25, 2019]. https://animaldiversity.org/accounts/Eptesi cus_fuscus/.

National Park Service. 2017. What Is White-Nose Syndrome? National Park Service. [Accessed June 25, 2019]. https://www.nps.gov/articles/what-is-white-nose-syndrome.htm.

National Speleological Society. 1946. Society Loses Valuable Member. D. Bloch, ed. *Bulletin of the National Speleological Society, 8,* 134. Also available at https://caves.org/pub/journal/NSS%20 Bulletin/Vol_8.pdf.

Naturalists' Agency. 1872. The Mammoth Cave and Its Inhabitants, or Descriptions of the Fishes, Insects and Crustaceans Found in the Cave. A. S. Packard and F. W. Putnam, eds. Salem. doi:10.5962/bhl.title.20632.

NatureServe Explorer. An Online Encyclopedia of Life. *Lepisosteus osseus*–(Linnaeus, 1758). Version 7.1. NatureServe. [Accessed November 23, 2021.] https://explorer.natureserve.org/Taxon/ELE MENT_GLOBAL.2.106443/Lepisosteus_osseus

NatureServe Explorer. An Online Encyclopedia of Life. *Medionidus walker*–(Wright, 1897). Version 7.1. NatureServe. [Accessed July 26, 2019]. http://explorer.natureserve.org/servlet/NatureServe ?searchName=Medionidus+walkeri+.

NatureServe and National Geographic. 2019. Landscope Florida: Species List from Florida. [Accessed June 21, 2019]. http://www.landscope.org/florida/.

NCFishes.com Team. 2020. "Minnow" Species (Families Cyprinidae, Xenocyprididae, and Leuciscidae) Diversity in North Carolina. [Accessed July 27, 2021]. https://ncfishes.com/minnow-species -diversity-in-north-carolina/.

Nico, L. G., Fuller, P., and Neilson, M. E. 2021. *Oreochromis aureus* (Steindachner, 1864). U.S. Geological Survey, Nonindigenous Aquatic Species Database. [Accessed July 18, 2021]. https://nas.er .usgs.gov/queries/FactSheet.aspx?speciesID=463.

Nico, L. G., Jelks, H. L., Tuten, T. 2009. Nonnative Suckermouth Armored Catfishes in Florida: Description of Nest Burrows and Burrow Colonies with Assessment of Shoreline Conditions. *Aquatic Nuisance Species Research Program Bulletin, 9*(1), 1–30.

Nico, L., Cannister, M., Neilson, M. 2019. *Pterygoplichthys pardalis* (Castelnau, 1855). USGS Nonindigenous Aquatic Species Database. [Accessed June 13, 2019]. https://nas.er.usgs.gov/queries /FactSheet.aspx?SpeciesID=769.

Nico, L., Fuller, P., Neilson, M. 2019. *Heterandria formosa* (Girard, 1859). USGS Nonindigenous Aquatic Species Database. [Accessed June 5, 2019]. https://nas.er.usgs.gov/queries/FactSheet .aspx?SpeciesID=852.

Norment, C. J. 2000. Francis Harper (1886–1972). *Arctic, 53*(1), 72–75. doi:10.14430/arctic837.

Nuttall, G. H. F., Robinson, L. E., Warburton, C. 1926. *Ticks, a Monograph of the Ixodoidea: The Genus Amblyomma*, Part 4 (First Part of Volume 2). London: Cambridge at the University Press. doi:10.5962/bhl.title.33956.

Ohs, C. L., Miller, C. L., Creswell, R. L. 2019. Candidate Species for Florida Aquaculture: Hybrid Striped Bass, *Morone saxatilis x Morone chrysops*. University of Florida, Institute of Food and Agricultural Sciences. [Accessed June 21, 2021]. https://edis.ifas.ufl.edu/publication/FA155.

Orange County, Florida. BioView: A Biological Snapshot of Rock Springs at Kelly Park. University of South Florida Water Institute, School of Geosciences. [Accessed June 6, 2019]. http://www.semi nole.wateratlas.usf.edu/upload/documents/RockSprings-Bioview.pdf.

Orth, D. 2015. Virginia Tech Ichthyology Class: Atlantic Needlefish. [Accessed June 3, 2019]. http:// vtichthyology.blogspot.com/2015/12/atlantic-needlefish-by-don-orth.html.

Page, L. L., Robins, R. H. 2006. Identification of Sailfin Catfishes (Teleostei: Loricariidae) in Southeastern Asia. *Raffles Bulletin of Zoology, 54*(2), 455–57. Also available at https://www.researchgate.net /publication/279600769_Identification_of_sailfin_catfishes_Teleostei_Loricariidae_in_South eastern_Asia.

Palmer, A. S. *Folk-Etymology: A Dictionary*. Haskell House Publishers Ltd. 1969. Also available at https://books.google.com/books?id=fXrlvr_kPXwC&pg=PA412&lpg=PA412&dq=%22wig%22 +beetle+etymology&source=bl&ots=uxiQn5_bZZ&sig=ACfU3U29YkV1RF78nNAkIY2BGiazu -UsYg&hl=en&sa=X&ved=2ahUKEwiz_fPynP7iAhUNiqwKHZbZBEsQ6AEwEHoECAcQAQ #v=snippet&q=earwig&f=false.

Partymiller, L. Savannah River Ecology Laboratory University of Georgia Herpetology Program: Barbour's Map Turtle (*Graptemys Barbouri*). [Accessed July 5, 2019]. https://srelherp.uga.edu/turtles /grabar.htm.

Patnaude, M. R. 2021. Featured Creatures: Entomology and Nematology: Common Name: Black-legged Tick or Deer Tick: Scientific name: *Ixodes scapularis* (Arachnida: Acari: Ixodidae). University of Florida, Institute of Food and Agricultural Sciences. EENY-143. [Accessed June 25, 2021]. https://entnemdept.ufl.edu/creatures/urban/medical/deer_tick.htm.

Pells, P., Pells, S. Hydrogeologists and Geotechnical Engineers—Lost Without Translation. Pells Consulting and University of New South Wales.

Penn State. 2006. Snottites, Other Biofilms Hasten Cave Formation. Science Daily. [Accessed May 9, 2019]. https://www.sciencedaily.com/releases/2006/12/061212091813.htm.

Pescador, M. L., Rasmussen, A. K., Richard, B. A. 2000. A Guide to the Stoneflies (Plecoptera) of Florida. State of Florida Department of Environmental Protection, Division of Water Resource Management. Also available at http://publicfiles.dep.state.fl.us/dear/labs/biology/biokeys/stonefly.pdf.

Phelps, G. G., Walsh, S. J., Gerwig, R. M., Tate, W. B. 2006. Characterization of the Hydrology, Water Chemistry, and Aquatic Communities of Selected Springs in the St. Johns River Water Management District, Florida, 2004. USGS Open-File Report 2006-1107. Also available at https://pubs.usgs.gov/of/2006/1107/pdf/ofr2006_1107_phelps.pdf.

Piermarini, P. 2000. Florida's Freshwater Stingrays. [Accessed July 26, 2019]. http://nersp.nerdc.ufl.edu/~pmpie/ecoray.htm (site discontinued).

Piermarini, P. The Atlantic Stingray (*Dasyatis sabina*). [Accessed July 26, 2019]. http://nersp.nerdc.ufl.edu/~pmpie/dsabina.html (site discontinued).

Poly, W. J., Wetzel, J. E. April 2003. Transbranchioral Spawning: Novel Reproductive Strategy Observed for the Pirate Perch *Aphredoderus sayanus* (Aphredoderidae). *Ichthyological Exploration of Freshwaters*, *14*(2), 151–58.

Rafinesque, C. S. 1819. Prodrome. De 70 Nouveaux Genres d'Animaux Découverts dans l'Intérieur des Etats-Unis d'Amérique, Durant l'Année 1818. *Journal de Physique, de Chimie, d'Histoire Naturelle*, *88*, 417–29. Also available at https://www.biodiversitylibrary.org/page/6172335#page/455/mode/1up.

Ragasa, E. V., Kaufman, P. E. 2018. Featured Creatures: Entomology and Nematology: Common Name: A Mosquito, Scientific Name: *Psorophora ciliata* (Fabricius) (Insecta: Diptera: Culicidae). University of Florida, Institute of Food and Agricultural Sciences. EENY-540. [Accessed July 23, 2021]. https://entnemdept.ufl.edu/creatures/AQUATIC/Ps_ciliata.htm.

Rauchenberger, M. 1989. Systematics and Biogeography of the Genus *Gambusia* (Cypriodontiformes: Poecilidae). *American Museum Novitates* (2951), 1–47. Also available at http://hdl.handle.net/2246/5107.

Rawlings, T. A., Hayes, K. A., Cowie, R. H., Collins, T. M. 2007. The Identity, Distribution, and Impacts of Nonnative Apple Snails in the Continental United States. *BMC Evolutionary Biology*, *7*, 97. doi:10.1186/1471-2148-7-97.

Riley, E. P., Wade, T. W. 2016. Adapting to Florida's Riverine Woodlands: The Population Status and Feeding Ecology of the Silver River Rhesus Macaques and Their Interface with Humans. *Primates*, *57*, 195–210. doi:10.1007/s10329-016-0517-3.

Rios, L., Maruniak, J. E. 2018. Featured Creatures: Entomology and Nematology: Common Name: Asian Tiger Mosquito, Scientific Name: *Aedes albopictus* (Skuse) (Insecta: Diptera: Culicidae). University of Florida, Institute of Food and Agricultural Sciences. EENY-319. [Accessed July 23, 2021]. https://entnemdept.ufl.edu/creatures/aquatic/asian_tiger.htm.

Robertson, T., Sargeant, B., Urgelles, R., Easton, J. A., Huselid, L., Abreu, A. 2012. Invertebrate Identification Guide. Florida International University Aquatic Ecology Lab. [accessed May 8, 2019]. http://faculty.fiu.edu/~trexlerj/lab_invert_guide.pdf.

Rogers, J., Katze, M., Bumgarner, R., Gibbs, R. A., Weinstock, G. M. White Paper for Complete Sequencing of the Rhesus Macaque (*Macaca mulatta*) Genome. [Accessed June 9, 2021]. https://www.genome.gov/Pages/Research/Sequencing/SeqProposals/RhesusMacaque SEQ021203.pdf.

Rogers, J., Gibbs, R. 2014. Comparative Primate Genomics: Emerging Patterns of Genome Content and Dynamics. *Nature Reviews Genetics, 15,* 347-359. doi:10.1038/nrg3707.

Romero, A. 2009. *Cave Biology: Life in Darkness (Ecology, Biodiversity and Conservation).* Cambridge University Press. Also available at https://epdf.pub/cave-biology-life-in-darkness.html.

Rookmaaker, K. 2017. The Zoological Contributions of Andrew Smith (1797-1872) with an Annotated Bibliography and a Numerical Analysis of Newly Described Animal Species. *Transactions of the Royal Society of South Africa, 72*(2), 105-73. doi:10.1080/0035919X.2016.1230078.

Rossman, D. A. 1963. The Colubrid Snake Genus *Thamnophis*: A Revision of the Sauritus Group. *Bulletin of the Florida State Museum: Biological Sciences, 7*(3), 165.

Rudy, B. 2003. *Lepisosteus osseus.* Animal Diversity Web. University of Michigan. [Accessed July 26, 2019]. https://animaldiversity.org/accounts/Lepisosteus_osseus/.

Salman, V. 2011. Diversity Studies and Molecular Analyses with Single Cells and Filaments of Large, Colorless Sulfur Bacteria. Dissertation. Max Planck Institute for Marine Microbiology. Also available at https://d-nb.info/107189787X/34.

Salter, M. Cladocerans. [Accessed May 9, 2019]. http://academics.smcvt.edu/dfacey/AquaticBiology /Freshwater%20Pages/Cladocerans.html.

Sanders, A. E. 1984. *Rana heckscheri.* Catalogue of American Amphibians and Reptiles. J. D. Anderson, ed. *Society for the Study of Amphibians and Reptiles, 348*(1-2). Also available at http://hdl.han dle.net/2152/45260.

Savannah River Ecology Laboratory. Greater Siren (*Siren lacertina*). University of Georgia Herpetology. [Accessed July 26, 2019]. https://srelherp.uga.edu/salamanders/sirlac.htm.

Sawicki, T. R., Holsinger, J. R., Lazo-Wasem, E. A., Long, R. A. 2017. A New Species of Subterranean Amphipod (Amphipoda: Gammaridae: Crangonyctidae) from Florida, with a Genetic Analysis of Assorted Microbial Mats. *Journal of Crustacean Biology, 37*(3), 285-95. doi:10.1093/jcbiol /rux031.

Scarborough, J. 1992. *Medical and Biological Terminologies: Classical Origins.* University of Oklahoma Press.

Scharpf, C. 2004. American Beauties: Flagfin Shiners (Pteronotropis) of the Southeastern U.S. *American Currents, 30*(2), 1-8. Also available at http://www.nanfa.org/ac/flagfin-shiners-pteronotropis -southeastern-us.pdf.

Scharpf, C. 2005. Annotated Checklist of North American Freshwater Fishes, Including Subspecies and Undescribed Forms. Part I: Petromyzontidae Through Cyprinidae. *American Currents, 31*(4), 29, 36. Also available at http://www.desertfishes.org/cuatroc/literature/pdf/Scharpf_2005 _Checklist_North_American_Fishes_Pt1.pdf.

Scharpf, C., Lazara, K. J. 2019. The ETYFish Project, Fish Name Etymology Database. Order MYLIO-BATIFORMES (Stingrays). v.23.0. [Accessed July 26, 2019]. https://www.etyfish.org/myliobati-formes/.

Scharping, R. J., Garey, J. R. 2020. Relationship Between Aquifer Biofilms and Unattached Microbial Indicators of Urban Groundwater Contamination. *Molecular Ecology, 30,* 324-42. dio:10.1111 /mec.15713.

Schmitz, E., Baker, C. 1969. Digestive Anatomy of the Gizzard Shad, *Dorosoma cepedianum* and the Threadfin Shad, *D. petenense. Transactions of the American Microscopical Society, 88*(4), 525-46. doi:10.2307/3224247.

Schneider, K., Culver, D. 2004. Estimating Subterranean Species Richness Using Intensive Sampling and Rarefaction Curves in a High Density Cave Region in West Virginia. *Journal of Cave and Karst Studies*, 66(2), 39–45.

Schroeder, S. 2017. "*Esox americanus.*" Animal Diversity Web. University of Michigan. [Accessed July 26, 2019]. https://animaldiversity.org/accounts/Esox_americanus/.

Scott, C. 2004. *Endangered and Threatened Animals of Florida and Their Habitats.* The Corrie Herring Hooks Series: Number Fifty-Eight. University of Texas Press.

Scott, T. M., Means, G. H., Meegan, R. P., Means, R. C., Upchurch, S., Copeland, R. E., Jones, J., Roberts, T., Willet, A. 2004. Springs of Florida. FGS Bulletin 66. Florida Geological Survey. Also available at https://www.nrc.gov/docs/ML1232/ML12325A141.pdf.

Scribner, K. T. 1993. Hybrid Zone Dynamics are Influenced by Genotype–Specific Variation in Life-History Traits: Experimental Evidence from Hybridizing Gambusian Species. *Evolution*, 47(2), 632–46. doi:10.2307/2410075.

Seinfeld, J. 2000. "*Macaca mulatta,* Rhesus Monkey." Animal Diversity Web. University of Michigan. [Accessed June 10, 2021]. https://animaldiversity.org/accounts/Macaca_mulatta/

Shelley, R. M. 1999. Centipedes and Millipedes with Emphasis on North America Fauna. *The Kansas School Naturalist*, 45(3). Also available at https://www.emporia.edu/ksn/v45n3-march1999/.

Simpson, D. P. 1968. *Cassell's Latin Dictionary*, fifth edition. Wiley Publishing, Inc.

Smith, A. 1849. *Illustrations of the Zoology of South Africa.* Smith, Elder and Co. doi: 10.5962/bhl .title.120508.

Smithsonian Institution Bureau of American Ethnology. 1910. Handbook of American Indians North of Mexico: in two parts; Part 2. FW Hodge, ed. Bulletin 30. Also available at https://books.google .com/books?id=mABSxpaHOO4C&pg=PA348&dq=arocoun&hl=en&sa=X&ved=Oah UKEwiplpvFkd_iAhVMOqOKHcVkBcU4ChDoAQhOMAg#v=onepage&q=arocoun&f=false.

Sorenson, K., Hostetler, M. E. Giant Salamanders of Florida. University of Florida, Institute of Food and Agricultural Sciences Extension. [Accessed May 9, 2019]. https://edis.ifas.ufl.edu/uw168.

South Florida Water Management District. Groundwater Modeling. [Accessed June 23, 2019]. https://www.sfwmd.gov/science-data/gw-modeling.

Southern Historical Association. 1895. *Memoirs of Georgia: Containing Historical Accounts of the State's Civil, Military, Industrial and Professional Interests, and Personal Sketches of Many of Its People.* Vol. II.

St. Johns River Water Management District. 2019. Florida's Aquifers. [Accessed June 23, 2019]. https://www.sjrwmd.com/water-supply/aquifer/.

Stamm, D. 2008. *The Springs of Florida.* Pineapple Press.

Streever, W. J. 1992. First Record of Corbicula Clams Within Flooded Cave Systems. *Florida Scientist*, 55(1), 35–37.

Streever, W. J. 1992. Report of a Cave Fauna Kill at Peacock Springs Cave System, Suwannee County, Florida. *Florida Scientist*, 55(2), 125–28.

Streever, W. J. June 1995. Recovery of the Cave Crayfish (Decapoda: Cambridae) Population in Peacock Springs, Florida. *Brimleyana*, 22, 61–65.

Strohl, W. R. 2015. Beggiatoa. In Whitman, W. B. Bergey's Manual of Systematics of Archaea and Bacteria. Wiley. doi:10.1002/9781118960608.gbm01223. Also available at https://onlinelibrary.wiley .com/doi/10.1002/9781118960608.gbm01223.

Strohl, W. R., Larkin, J. M. 1978 Enumeration, Isolation, and Characterization of *Beggiatoa* from Freshwater Sediments. *Applied and Environmental Microbiology*, 36(5), 755–70.

Suttkus, R. D., Mettee, M. F. 2001. Analysis of Four Species of *Notropis* Included in the Subgenus *Pteronotropis* Fowler, with Comments on Relationships, Origins, and Dispersion. *Geological Survey of Alabama*, *170*, 1-50.

Tarter, A. Slimy Salamander (*Plethodon glutinosus* complex). Revised by J. D. Wilson. Savannah River Ecology Laboratory. University of Georgia Herpetology. [Accessed July 26, 2019]. https://srelherp.uga.edu/salamanders/pleglu.htm.

Taticchi, M. I., Elia, A. C., Battoe, L., Havens, K. E. 2007. First Report about Freshwater Bryozoa in Florida (Lake Apopka). *Italian Journal of Zoology*, *76*(2), 194-200. doi:10.1080/11250000 802258024.

Taticchi, M. I., Battoe, L., Elia, A. C., Havens, K. E. 2011. Freshwater Bryozoa (Phylactolaemata) from Central Florida Lakes. *Florida Scientist*, *74*(4), 238-52.

Taylor, T. N., Taylor, E. L. *The Biology and Evolution of Fossil Plants*. Prentice Hall.

Texas A&M University System, Agrilife Research Extension. 2011. The TickApp for Texas and the Southern Region. [Accessed June 27, 2021]. https://tickapp.tamu.edu/tickbiology.html.

Texas A&M University System, AgriLife Extension. Aquaculture, Fisheries, and Pond Management. Hybrid Striped Bass (*Morone hybrid*). [Accessed June 14, 2021]. https://fisheries.tamu.edu/pond-management/species/hybrid-striped-bass/.

Texas Invasive Species Institute. 2014. Blue Tilapia *Oreochromis aureus*. [Accessed July 19, 2021]. http://www.tsusinvasives.org/home/database/oreochromis-aureus.

Thompson, F. G. An Identification Manual for the Freshwater Snails of Florida. 1999. *Walkerana*, *10*(23), 1-104. [Accessed July 25, 2021]. https://molluskconservation.org/PUBLICATIONS/WALKERANA/Vol10/walkerana%20vol10%20no23%201-96.PDF.

Thompson, F. G. Freshwater Snails of Florida ID Guide. Florida Museum of Natural History Invertebrate Zoology. [Accessed June 6, 2019]. https://www.floridamuseum.ufl.edu/iz/resources/florida-snails/.

Thompson, F. G., Hershler, R. 2002. Two Genera of North American Freshwater Snails: *Marstonia* Baker, 1926, Resurrected to Generic Status, and *Floridobia*, New Genus (Prosobranchia: Hydrobiidae: Nymphophilinae). *Veliger*, *45*(3), 269-71. Also available at http://hdl.handle.net/10088/11346.

Thompson, F. G., Hershler, R. 1991. Two New Hydrobiid Snails (Amnicolinae) from Florida and Georgia, with a Discussion of the Biogeography of Freshwater Gastropods of South Georgia Streams. *Malacological Review*, *24*, 55-72. Also available at https://pdfs.semanticscholar.org/5836/fe68 c654107df641ec50f0a0d8a58ffa307e.pdf.

Thorp, J. H., Rogers, D. C. 2011. *Freshwater Invertebrates of North America*. Academic Press.

Tian, Y., Lord, C. C., Kaufman, P. E. 2018. Featured Creatures. Entomology & Nematology: Common Name: Brown Dog Tick Scientific Name: *Rhipicephalus sanguineus* Latreille (Arachnida: Acari: Ixodidae). University of Florida Institute of Food and Agricultural Sciences. EENY-221. [Accessed June 30, 2021]. https://entnemdept.ufl.edu/creatures/urban/medical/brown_dog_tick.htm.

Umen, J. G. 2014. Green Algae and the Origins of Multicellularity in the Plant Kingdom. *Cold Spring Harbor Perspectives in Biology*, *6*, 11. doi:10.1101/cshperspect.a016170.

U.S. Department of Agriculture Forest Service. 2006 Final Environmental Impact Statement for the Access Designation on the Ocala National Forest. Volume 1 FEIS and Appendices. [Accessed July 24, 2021]. https://books.google.com/books?id=Op82AQAAMAAJ&pg=RA3-PA13&lpg=RA3-PA13&dq=alexander+siltsnail&source=bl&ots=_x-IA6jNHI&sig=ACfU3U0 JnrpxR3Qwcm9RuiEpX9xVrwDEOw&hl=en&sa=X&ved=2ahUKEwjNyMWb4fzxAhUFK 80KHTYCBnAQ6AEwIHoECEoQAw#v=onepage&q=alexander%20siltsnail&f=false.

U.S. Fish and Wildlife Service, Department of the Interior. 2018. American Bullfrog (*Lithobates catesbeianus*): Ecological Risk Screening Survey. Also available at https://www.fws.gov/fisheries/ans/erss/highrisk/ERSS-Lithobates-catesbeianus-final-February2018.pdf.

U.S. Fish and Wildlife Service, Department of the Interior. 2016. Endangered and Threatened Wildlife and Plants; 12-Month Findings on Petitions to list the Eagle Lake Rainbow Trout and the Ichetucknee Siltsnail as Endangered or Threatened Species. Unified Listing Team, Ecological Services Program. *Federal Register, 81*(129), 43972–3979.

U.S. Fish and Wildlife Service, Department of the Interior. 2019. Suwannee Moccasinshell *Medionidus walkeri*. [Accessed June 21, 2019]. https://www.fws.gov/southeast/wildlife/mussels/suwannee-moccasinshell/.

U.S. Fish and Wildlife Service, Department of the Interior. 2016. Endangered and Threatened Wildlife and Plants: Threatened Species Status for Suwannee Moccasinshell. [Accessed June 8, 2021]. https://www.federalregister.gov/documents/2016/10/06/2016-24138/endangered-and-threatened-wildlife-and-plants-threatened-species-status-for-suwannee-moccasinshell.

U.S. Fish and Wildlife Service, Department of the Interior. 2016. Inland Silverside (*Menidia beryllina*): Ecological Risk Screening Summary. [Accessed July 22, 2021]. https://www.fws.gov/fisheries/ANS/erss/highrisk/ERSS-Menidia-beryllina_Final.pdf.

U.S. Fish and Wildlife Service, Department of the Interior. 2018. Quilted Melania (*Tarebia granifera*): Ecological Risk Screening Summary. [Accessed June 6, 2019]. https://www.fws.gov/fisheries/ANS/erss/highrisk/ERSS-Tarebia-granifera-FINAL-March2018.pdf.

U.S. Fish and Wildlife Service, Department of the Interior. 2018. Red-Rim Melania (*Melanoides tuberculatus*): Ecological Risk Screening Summary. [Accessed June 24, 2019]. https://www.fws.gov/fisheries/ANS/erss/highrisk/ERSS-Melanoides-tuberculatus-FINAL-March2018.pdf.

U.S. Fish and Wildlife Service, Department of the Interior. 2019. West Indian Manatee, *Trichechus manatus*. [Accessed June 7, 2019]. https://www.fws.gov/southeast/wildlife/mammals/manatee/.

U.S. Fish and Wildlife Service: Environmental Conservation Online System (ECOS). 2019. Listed species believed to or known to occur in Florida. [Accessed May 9, 2019]. https://ecos.fws.gov/ecp0/reports/species-listed-by-state-report?state=FL&status=listed.

U.S. Fish and Wildlife Service, Fish and Aquatic Conservation. American Shad. [Accessed July 6, 2019]. https://www.fws.gov/fisheries/freshwater-fish-of-america/american_shad.html.

U.S. Fish and Wildlife Service, Fish and Aquatic Conservation. Striped bass. [Accessed June 23, 2019]. https://www.fws.gov/fisheries/freshwater-fish-of-america/striped_bass.html.

U.S. Fish and Wildlife Service, North Florida Ecological Services Office. 2018. Species Account/Biologue: Squirrel Chimney Cave Shrimp. [Accessed May 9, 2019]. https://www.fws.gov/northflorida/Species-Accounts/Squirrel-Chimney-Cave-Shrimp-2005.htm.

U.S. Geological Survey. Ground Water Atlas of the United States. Alabama, Florida, Georgia, South Carolina. HA-730-G. Floridan Aquifer System. [Accessed July 22, 2021]. https://pubs.usgs.gov/ha/ha730/ch_g/G-text6.html.

U.S. Geological Survey Nonindigenous Aquatic Species. *Pterygoplichthys multiradiatus*. [Accessed June 25, 2019]. https://nas.er.usgs.gov/queries/FactSheet.aspx?speciesID=768.

U.S. Geological Survey. Patuxent Wildlife Research Center. USGS Frog Quizzes, Frog Call Lookup. [Accessed May 30, 2019]. https://www.pwrc.usgs.gov/frogquiz/index.cfm?fuseaction=main.lookup.

UniProt Consortium. 2019. Taxonomy—*Pseudogymnoascus destructans* (strain ATCC MYA-4855 / 20631-21) (Bat white-nose syndrome fungus) (*Geomyces destructans*). [Accessed June 25, 2019]. https://www.uniprot.org/taxonomy/658429.

University of California Museum of Paleontology. 1993. Cyanobacteria: Fossil Record. In T. N. Taylor and E. L. Taylor, *The Biology and Evolution of Fossil Plants*. Prentice Hall. Also available at https://ucmp.berkeley.edu/bacteria/cyanofr.html.

University of California Museum of Paleontology. 1998. Fungi: Systematics. University of California. [Accessed June 25, 2019]. https://ucmp.berkeley.edu/fungi/fungisy.html.

University of California Museum of Paleontology. 2000. Introduction to the Odonata: Dragonflies and Damselflies. University of California. [Accessed June 22, 2019]. https://ucmp.berkeley.edu/arthropoda/uniramia/odonatoida.html.

University College of London. MIRACLE (Microfossil Image Recovery and Circulation for Learning and Education): Ostracods. [Accessed May 9, 2019]. https://www.ucl.ac.uk/GeolSci/micropal/ostracod.html.

University of Florida, Florida Wildlife Extension. Southern Leopard Frog, *Lithobates sphenocephalus*. Wildlife Ecology and Conservation. [Accessed June 13, 2019]. https://wec.ifas.ufl.edu/extension/wildlife_info/frogstoads/rana_utricularia.php.

University of Florida, Institute of Food and Agricultural Sciences, Center for Aquatic and Invasive Plants. 2018. Plant Management in Florida Waters—An Integrated Approach: Algae. University of Florida. [Accessed June 13, 2019]. https://plants.ifas.ufl.edu/manage/why-manage-plants/aquatic-and-wetland-plants-in-florida/algae/.

Vibbert, B. 2019. Fish Survey on Rainbow River. Dunnellon: Rainbow River River Conservation Inc. and High Springs: The Howard T. Odom Florida Springs Institute. Report. [Accessed July 15, 2021]. http://www.rainbowriverconservation.com/RRC%20Documents/Fish%20Survey%20on%20Rainbow%20River.pdf.

Virginia Herpetological Society. 2019. Plain-Bellied Watersnake *Nerodia erythrogaster*. [Accessed July 29, 2019]. https://www.virginiaherpetologicalsociety.com/reptiles/snakes/red-bellied-water-snake/red-bellied_watersnake.php.

Volk, T., Blehert, D., Gargas, A., Trest, M., Christensen, M. 2009. *Geomyces destructans*, a Fungus Associated with Bat White-Nose Syndrome (WNS). [Accessed June 25, 2019]. http://botit.botany.wisc.edu/toms_fungi/may2009.html.

Walsh, S. J. 2001. Freshwater Macrofauna of Florida Karst Habitats. E. L. Kuniansky, ed., U.S. Geological Survey Karst Interest Group Proceedings. Water-Resource Investigations. Report 01-4011: 78-88. Also available at https://water.usgs.gov/ogw/karst/kigconference/sjw_freshwater.htm.

Walters, D. M., Freeman, B., Schaefer, S. A. 2000. Distribution of Gambusia (Poeciliidae) in a Southeastern River System and the Use of Fin Ray Counts for Species Determination. *Copeia*, 2000(2), 555-59. doi:10.1643/0045-8511(2000)000[0555:DOGPIA]2.0.CO;2.

Warner, K. 2019. Are Earwigs Dangerous or Harmless? Institute of Food and Agricultural Sciences. Blogs. University of Florida. [Accessed June 22, 2019]. http://blogs.ifas.ufl.edu/nassauco/2017/06/26/q-earwigs-dangerous-harmless/.

Warren, G. L., Bernatis, J. L. 2015. Status of the Ichetucknee Siltsnail (*Floridobia mica*) in Coffee Spring, Ichetucknee Springs State Park, Suwannee County, Florida, November 2015. Project Report for Florida Department of Parks and Wildlife and U.S. Fish and Wildlife Services. Florida Fish and Wildlife Conservation Commission, Fish and Wildlife Research Institute. [Accessed July 22, 2021]. http://static1.squarespace.com/static/5645105de4b0ba0f65eaa14a/t/57508c1286db43fc15d43cf4/1464896531563/Status.

Water Quality Monitoring Program. 2011. The Hydrology and Water Quality of Select Springs in the Southwest Florida Water Management District. Southwest Florida Water Management District. Also available at https://www.swfwmd.state.fl.us/sites/default/files/medias/documents/Hydrology_Water_Quality_Select_Springs.pdf.

Wetland Solutions, Inc. 2014. Silver Springs Restoration Plan; prepared for the Howard T. Odum Florida Springs Institute, High Springs, Florida. [Accessed June 19, 2021]. https://floridaspringsinstitute.org/wpcontent/uploads/2018/07/Silver_Springs_Restoration_Plan.pdf.

Wheeler, W. M. *George Baur's Life and Writings. The American Naturalist* Reprint, 33(385). Jan 1899. Boston: Ginn and Company, Athenaeum Press. doi:10.1086/277098.

Whitney, E., Means, D. B. 2014. *Florida's Uplands: High Pine, Scrub, Prairies, Hardwood Forests and Dunes. Florida's Natural Ecosystems and Native Species.* Vol. 1. Pineapple Press.

Whitney, E., Means, D. B., Rudloe, A. 2004. *Priceless Florida: Natural Ecosystems and Native Species.* Pineapple Press.

Wikipedia contributors. Bryozoa. Wikipedia, The Free Encyclopedia. [Accessed May 9, 2019]. https://en.wikipedia.org/w/index.php?title=Bryozoa&oldid=889022602.

Wikipedia contributors. Phylactolaemata. Wikipedia, The Free Encyclopedia. [Accessed May 9, 2019]. https://en.wikipedia.org/w/index.php?title=Phylactolaemata&oldid=831596452.

Williams, J. D., Butler, R. S., Wisniewski, J. M. 2011. Annotated Synonymy of the Recent Freshwater Mussel Taxa of the Families Margaritiferidae and Unionidae Described from Florida Drainages Contiguous with Alabama and Georgia. University of Florida. *Florida Museum of Natural History Bulletin, 51*(1), 1–84.

Williams, R. 2021. Guest Blog: Why We Should Care About the Ichetucknee Siltsnail. Ichetucknee Alliance. [Accessed July 25, 2021]. https://ichetuckneealliance.org/guest-blog-why-should-we-care-about-the-ichetucknee-siltsnail/.

Wisely, S. M., Sayler, K. A., Anderson, C., et al. 2018. Macacine Herpesvirus 1 Antibody Prevalence and DNA Shedding among Invasive Rhesus Macaques, Silver Springs State Park, Florida, USA. *Emerging Infectious Diseases, 24*(2), 345–51. doi:10.3201/eid2402.171439.

Wisenbaker, M. Florida's Aquatic Troglobites. [Accessed November 12, 2017]. http://floridafisheries.com/nongame/mw3.html.

Woodward, D. 2015. Biology 110 Basic Concepts and Biodiversity. [Accessed June 18, 2021]. https://wikispaces.psu.edu/display/BIOL110F2013/Subcellular+Architecture+of+the+Eukaryotic+Cell.

# Index

Page numbers in *italics* refer to illustrations and maps.

dusky pipefish, 2, 53, *53*

dwarf siren: narrow-striped, 2, 79, *79*; northern, 2, 79, 80, *80*

earwig, ringlegged, 115, 121, *121*

eastern chicken turtle, 94, *94*

eastern grass shrimp, 1, 22, *22*, 152; as food, 37, 38

eastern indigo snake, 2, 84, *84*

eastern mosquitofish, xxi, 2, 6, 50, *50*, 51, 165

eastern mud turtle, 2, 102, 103, *103*

eastern musk turtle, 2, 104, *104*

eastern ribbonsnake, 2, 90, *90*

eastern shiner, 2, 48; coastal, 48, *48*; ironcolor, 48; taillight, 48

eastern woodrat, 2, 112, *112*

Econfina cave isopod, 154

eel, American, xix, 43, 79, 80, 115, *123*, 123, 124; as food, 85

eggs: as food, 78, 89, 91, 107, 108, 110, 127; of alligators, 89; of blue crab, 23; of cladocera, 25; of crayfish, 147; of fish, 36, 43, 44, 47, 51, 53, 54, 56, 59, 63–65, 67, 68, 70, 71, 128, 129, 132; of frogs, 71, 73, 75, 76; of insects, 15, 28, 30, 32–35, 120–22; of mussels, 5; of salamanders, 77, 79–81, 134; of shrimp, 22; of snails, 8–10, 119; of snakes, 91; of turtles, 97; of tubificid worms, 162

elephant spurred sheetweaver, 115, 117, *117*

*Elliptio jayensis* (Florida shiny spike), 1, 4, *4*

*Eptesicus fuscus* (big brown bat), 115, 135, *135*

*Erimyzon sucetta* (lake chubsucker), 2, 46, *46*

*Esox: americanus* (redfin pickerel), 2, 52, *52*, 53; *niger* (chain pickerel), 2, 52, *52*, 53

*Etheostoma: colorosum* (coastal darter), 68; *edwini* (brown darter), 68; *fusiforme* (swamp darter), 68, *68*, 69

*Euborellia annulipes* (ringlegged earwig), 115, 121, *121*

*Euglandina rosea* (rosy wolfsnail), 115, 119, *119*

*Eurycea: guttolineata* (three-lined salamander), 115, 133, *133*; *wallacei* (Georgia blind salamander), 141, 148, *155*, 155–57

euryhaline, xix, 13, 38, 43, 45, 66, 114, 126

*Farancia erytrogramma erytrogramma* (rainbow snake), 2, 85, *85*

fish, xvi, xix, xxi, xxii, 2, 5, 6, 36–71, 115, 123–33, 161–63, 165; as food, 19, 24, 39–44, 47, 50, 52, 53, 55–58, 61–64, 66, 67, 70, 77, 78, 81, 86–88, 90, 98, 100, 102, 104–7, 123, 122, 124–29, 131, 148. *See also* bass; catfish; darter; gar; shiners; sturgeon; sunfish

fishing spider, 1, 19, *19*

flagfin shiner, 2, 49, *49*, 50; Apalachee, 49; bluenose, 49, *49*; flagfin, 49; metallic, 49

flathead catfish, 115, 131, *131*

flat spike, *See* Florida shiny spike

flier, 2, 56, *56*

Florida apple snail, 1, 9, *9*, 10

Florida cave amphipod, 144, 145, *145*

Florida cave isopod, *153*, 154

Florida Caverns State Park, 118, 137, 142, 156

Florida chicken turtle, 94–95

Florida cottonmouth, 2, 87, 88, *91*, 91–93

Florida crangonyctid, *144*, 145

Florida gar, 2, 40, 41, *41*

Florida largemouth bass, 2, 63, *63*

Florida manatee, xix, 2, 113, *113*, 114

Florida mud turtle, 2, 102, *102*

Florida panhandle cave amphipod, 146

Florida redbellied cooter, 2, 97, *97*

Florida shiny spike, 1, 4, *4*

Florida slimy salamander, 115, 134, *134*

Florida softshell turtle, xv, 2, 10, 105, *105*

Florida Statute 810.13, xxii

Florida watersnake, 87

*Floridobia: alexander* (Alexander siltsnail), 11; *helicogyra* (crystal siltsnail), 11; *leptospira* (flatwood siltsnail), 11; *mica* (Coffee Spring siltsnail), 1, 10, *10*, 11; *monroensis* (Enterprise siltsnail), 11; *parva* (pygmy siltsnail), 11; *petrifons* (Rock Spring siltsnail), 11; *ponderosa* (Ponderous Spring siltsnail), 11; *porterae* (Green Cove Springsnail), 12; *vanhyningi* (Seminole Spring siltsnail), 12; *wekiwae* (Wekiwa siltsnail), 12

flounder, freshwater, xix, 2, 69, *69*

# About the Author

A native of Florida's Gulf Coast, **Sandra Poucher** enjoys being outdoors as much as she enjoys researching, reading, and writing. She has explored and helped survey caves in Florida as well as in Mexico and in the Caribbean. Her articles and photographs have been published in magazines such as *Underwater Speleology* and the *NSS News*. She is editor of Sheck Exley's *The Taming of the Slough: A Comprehensive History of Peacock Springs*, co-compiler with Dr. Rick Copeland of the Florida Geological Survey on the *Speleological and Karst Glossary of Florida and the Caribbean*, and writer and illustrator of *A Field Guide to the Critters of Florida's Springs*.